TEN PERSPECTIVES ON MILTON

TEN PERSPECTIVES
ON MILTON

by MERRITT Y. HUGHES

with a Foreword by Douglas Bush

NEW HAVEN AND LONDON

YALE UNIVERSITY PRESS

1965

Published with assistance from the foundation established in memory of Philip
Hamilton McMillan of the Class of 1894, Yale College.

For my Colleagues in English at the University of Wisconsin

Acknowledgments

The existence of this book is due to the initiative of my colleagues J. G. Nelson, R. K. Presson, and G. T. Tanselle, and to the kindness of David Horne and the staff of the Yale University Press, particularly to John O. C. McCrillis, who designed it. For its substance I am indebted to the Henry E. Huntington Library, the British Museum, the Folger Shakespeare Library, the Institute for Research in the Humanities of the University of Wisconsin, and to grants under the Fulbright Act, and by the Marie Kohler Foundation.

All but one ("The Filiations") of the studies in this volume have been published before, and several were originally written as lectures. The latter were revised before publication, and slight revisions have now been made in all the material included here. "Lydian Airs" was published in *MLN* in 1925; "Milton and the Sense of Glory" in *PQ*, the E. N. S. Thompson Memorial Volume, in 1949; "The Christ of *Paradise Regained* and the Renaissance Heroic Tradition" in *SP* in 1938; "Milton and the Symbol of Light" in *SEL* in 1964; "Myself Am Hell" in *MP* in 1956; "Satan and the 'Myth' of the Tyrant" in *Essays in English Literature from the Renaissance to the Victorian Age,* presented to A. S. P. Woodhouse in 1964; "Milton's Celestial Battle and the Theogonies" in *Studies in Honor of T. W. Baldwin* in 1958; "Milton's Treatment of Reformation History in *The Tenure of Kings and Magistrates*" in *The Seventeenth Cen-*

tury: Studies in the History of English Thought and Literature from Bacon to Pope, by Richard Foster Jones and others (Stanford, 1951); and "Milton as a Revolutionary" in *ELH* in 1943. The author is grateful to the original publishers for permission to use this material here.

M. Y. H.

Madison, Wisconsin
September 1964

Contents

Acknowledgments   vii
Foreword by Douglas Bush   xi
Abbreviations   xv
 1. Lydian Airs   1
 2. Milton and the Sense of Glory   12
 3. The Christ of *Paradise Regained* and the Renais-
    sance Heroic Tradition   35
 4. Milton and the Symbol of Light   63
 5. The Filiations of Milton's Celestial Dialogue   104
 6. "Myself Am Hell"   136
 7. Satan and the "Myth" of the Tyrant   165
 8. Milton's Celestial Battle and the Theogonies   196
 9. Milton's Treatment of Reformation History in
    The Tenure of Kings and Magistrates   220
10. Milton as a Revolutionary   240
Index   277

Foreword

Every department of every graduate school has its body of folklore, and in acting as prologue to this volume I must put into print one bit of oral tradition. Merritt Hughes received his Ph.D. degree at Harvard in 1921, several months before I arrived there, but someone told me this tale and I have often told it since by way of cheering apprehensive doctoral candidates. The tale is brief: on being asked at his oral examination to name the first editor of the *Edinburgh Review,* Merritt replied: "I can't remember his name, but I have an article on him coming out in the *Modern Language Review.*" Since his article duly appeared, I trust that its author will not disavow the anecdote as apocryphal; its inspirational value alone should protect it. No friend or acquaintance of Merritt Hughes, nor any hearer of his public utterances, would—remembering that jutting chin and downright vigor of delivery—suspect him of ever suffering from such a common human frailty as nervousness.

The tale is also a reminder that Merritt's productive career began early; and his early topics ranged from Jeffrey to W. H. Hudson. But his literary and scholarly interests were soon centered on the Renaissance, in particular on Spenser and Milton and the complex patterns of ideas that both authors embodied or touched. For the study of this period and these poets—which means of course study of the whole classical-Christian tradition in antiquity and in the Middle Ages—Hughes was admirably equipped with ancient and modern languages (not to mention the purely ornamental Gothic in which his and my generation were trained). His first elaborate publication was a monograph in comparative literature, *Virgil and Spenser* (1929), one of the early modern contributions to the precise and corrective defining of Spenser's literary materials and methods. A later and smaller item was "Spenser's Acrasia and the Circe of the Renaissance" (1943), a critical survey of the disreputable sisterhood so useful to major and minor poets.

Meanwhile Hughes had settled in the Miltonic domain (while paying occasional visits outside, to Donne or another). The early title, "Lydian Airs" (1925), might not have suggested the range and weight of the Miltonic studies that "Il Penseroso" was to produce in later years. Hughes's editions of *Paradise Lost* (1935) and *Paradise Regained, the Minor Poems, and Samson Agonistes* (1937) were the first fully annotated editions of Milton that were in the full current of the modern "history of ideas." This approach to Milton, which had been opened up by Edwin Greenlaw, J. H. Hanford, and A. H. Gilbert, was now being explored by multiplying younger scholars, and a new Milton was replacing the conventional stereotype. Hughes's editions have had a wide circulation and their fresh and learned apparatus has done much to place Milton in his ideological world and to enrich the comprehension of successive generations of students. The revised one-volume edition of 1957 was greatly enlarged by the inclusion of the "major prose," and the separate edition of *Paradise Lost* (1962) was still further revised. In 1962 Hughes edited the third volume of Milton's *Complete Prose Works* for the Yale edition; he had been partly prepared for that large enterprise by his own short studies of Milton's political thought as well as by his earlier editing. A still larger and more difficult enterprise is the sifting and ordering of scholarly and critical material on *Paradise Lost* for the projected *Variorum*

Commentary, the first variorum since Todd's of the early nineteenth century. In addition to his own formidable task, Hughes is chairman of the group who are dealing with the rest of the poetry for the *Variorum.*

This brief and factual summary has partly suggested the direction and strength of Hughes's scholarly work. (Of his academic career as a whole, of his local and general activities—including that of military historian—I am not qualified to speak.) As an editor and interpreter of Milton, Hughes has taken account of the varied products of current critical fashions, of the erratic along with the fruitful, but he has himself steadily pursued the historical mode of exegesis. He has not been concerned with source-hunting in the old sense (the kind of thing in which, again, his and my generation were brought up), but rather with the discriminating use of parallel or analogous ideas which place Milton in the traditions he lived with and enable us to place ourselves somewhere near him and understand both his traditionalism and his masterful originality. In his inquiries into Milton's use of ideas Hughes's scholarly and critical assets—intellectual curiosity, wide learning, and open-mindedness—have had the essential further asset of basic sympathy (in which his Quaker inheritance may have had a share).

The studies selected for the present reprint have to do with philosophical, religious, and aesthetic ideas and attitudes, chiefly in Milton's poetry. While synthesis and interpretation are here focused on the various topics, these topics inevitably spread out over the whole classical-Christian tradition. If Hughes's citing of a multitude of old authors, famous or obscure, makes many of us feel woefully ignorant, our sense of inadequacy is deepened by his active and apposite knowledge of a likewise wide array of modern scholars and critics; he has read them all. In the apparatus of his editions we may now and then wish that he were more given to asserting his own well-grounded view of a debatable matter—although such freedom from dogmatism commands respect from those of us who recognize the natural rightness of our opinions. In these separate essays and articles Hughes is more concerned with expounding a view of his own, but it is never a narrow or eccentric view; and he remains generous in welcoming the ideas of others and un-Miltonically mild in disagreement. At the same time he is not to be staggered out of his scholarly walking by the whiff of every new pamphlet.

This volume is published as a tribute to a scholar of solid authority who has helped greatly to spread understanding for many years past. Knowing his zeal and energy, we may be sure that he will continue to enlighten us, still searching what he knows not by what he knows, still closing up truth to truth as he finds it.

DOUGLAS BUSH

Abbreviations

ANCL	*Ante-Nicene Church Library* (Edinburgh Edition, 1886–90, 1890–1900)
CE	*The Works of John Milton*, ed. Frank Allen Patterson (18 Vols. Columbia University Press, 1931–38)
ELH	*English Literary History*
ES	*English Studies*
HTR	*Harvard Theological Review*
JEGP	*Journal of English and Germanic Philology*
JHI	*Journal of the History of Ideas*
JWCI	*Journal of the Warburg and Courtauld Institutes*
MLN	*Modern Language Notes*
MLR	*Modern Language Review*
MP	*Modern Philology*
NQ	*Notes and Queries*
PMLA	*Publications of the Modern Language Association of America*
PQ	*Philological Quarterly*
PR	*Partisan Review*
RES	*Review of English Studies*
SP	*Studies in Philology*
SEL	*Studies in English Literature*
SR	*Sewanee Review*
UTQ	*University of Toronto Quarterly*

✳ 1 ✳

Lydian Airs

One of Milton's many heresies from conventional ideas was his frank desire in *L'Allegro* to be lapped "in soft Lydian airs." Throughout the Renaissance the term "Lydian" was the standard reproach for everything thought to be vicious in music. Lydian airs were the "jazz" of the time, but the name had connotations much more definitely ugly than those commonly attached to modern syncopation. What those connotations were Giraldi Cinthio tells us in his *Dialogo Secondo della vita civile:*

> Non dico però questo, perchè alle donne la Musica non convenga, ma non questa molle, non questa non meno lasciva, che si fosse già la Lydia, che parue tanto abomineuole a Platone, che non la volle accittare a modo alcuno nella sua Republica come lasciva e guastratrice di gli animi di huomini, e delle donne parimente.[1]

It was probably from the volume of which this dialogue was a part that Shakespeare obtained his knowledge of Cinthio's *Novelle,* and M. Jusserand has given good evidence[2] that Spenser was familiar with this same dialogue

1. Second ed. Venice, 1580 (p. 36).
2. J. J. Jusserand, "Spenser's 'Twelve Private Morall Vertues as Aristotle hath devised,'" *MP, 3* (1906), 373–83.

of Cinthio. Certainly Spenser reflected its animus against
Lydian music in his picture of Malecasta's hall:

> And all the while sweet musike did divide
> Her looser notes with Lydian harmony.[3]

Ultimately this prejudice against Lydian music goes
back to the Platonic bigotry against all modes except the
Dorian and to the Platonic ideal expressed by Laches of
the perfect man who does not content himself only with
the most beautiful harmony on his lyre or on some frivo-
lous instrument, but who, in the reality of his life, invests
his words and deeds with harmony according to the Dorian
mode and not according to the Ionian, much less according to the Phrygian or Lydian.[4] Milton admitted Lydian
airs into his Tower of Ivory in defiance of their exclusion
from the ideal republic framed by the Platonic Socrates.
Why he did so is a question not very difficult, perhaps,
but interesting. He was perfectly familiar, no doubt, with
the passage in *The Republic* where Socrates condemns all
musical modes except the Dorian on the score of their
inaptness for the education of brave and temperate men,
and Plato's severe and exalted ideal of character to be set
before the educator coincided very closely with his own
ideal as expressed in the tractate *Of Education*.[5] Why,
then, did he differ from Cinthio and most of his humanist
predecessors and contemporaries who shared the Platonic
phobia against Lydian airs?

For this there were at least two reasons of quite different
kinds, and the best way to get at them is to analyze the
musical prejudice inherited from Plato. Cinthio simplified
it too much in making Lydian music synonymous simply
with sensual music. In *The Republic* Plato condemned Lydian music first because it was elegiac and expressed moods
of sadness and despair unbecoming in men devoted to the

3. *Faerie Queene*, III.i.40.
4. *Laches* 188d.
5. CE, *4*, 317.

defence of their country. He condemned it only secondarily because it seduced to sensuality.[6] "Because these modes (Mixolydian and Lydian) expressed sad and dissolute emotions respectively," said Plutarch, "Plato did well to reject them and to choose the Dorian mode as the only one convenient for warlike and temperate men."[7] The Lydian mode had been much employed in tragedy, and in excluding it Plato forbade music to express tragedy. For the Platonist all music had to be martial or else religious or didactic.

> "Of the harmonies," said Socrates, "I know nothing, but I want to have one warlike, which will sound the note which a brave man utters in the hour of danger or stern resolve . . . and another to be used in times of peace and freedom of action, when there is no pressure of necessity and he is seeking to persuade God by prayer, or man by instruction and advice; or on the other hand which expresses his willingness to listen to persuasion or advice and which represents him when he has accomplished his aim, not carried away by success, but acting moderately and wisely and acquiescing in the event. These two harmonies I ask you to leave . . . the strain of courage and the strain of temperance; these I say leave."[8]

It is not hard to understand why Milton, the young enthusiast over

> Thebes and Pelops' line
> And the tale of Troy divine,

should have balked at a theory of music which forbade expression, to take presumable examples, of the despair of Orestes, or of Lear.

6. *Republic* 3.10.a–c.
7. *De musica* 17.
8. *Republic* 3.10.c.

But Milton stood very much alone among his contemporaries in interpreting the Greek ideal of temperance or the well-poised life (sophrosyne) in a way to leave the tragic sense unhampered. Spenser's treatment of Temperance in the Second Book of *The Faerie Queene* had made grief and its concomitant anger almost as dangerous enemies of self-control as sensuality. Sir Guyon, the Knight of Temperance, moralizes:

> When raging passion with fierce tyranny
> Robs reason of her dew regalitie,
> And makes it servaunt to her basest part,
> The strong it weakens with infirmitie,
> And with bold furie armes the weakest hart:
> The strong through pleasure soonest falles,
> the weak through smart.[9]

The sage and serious Spenser was a better Platonist than Milton and in consequence of that fact *The Faerie Queene* lacks the tragic elements that might have raised it to the epic level.

Spenser's allegory of the pleasure through which "the strong soonest falles" is embodied in the stories of Phaedria[10] and of Acrasia's Bower of Bliss.[11] His less familiar allegory of the "smart" through which the weak fall is the story of Amavia,[12] the too-fond wife who killed herself for grief over her murdered husband. The angry scenes where Pyrochles, Furor, and Occasion appear[13] are extensions of this allegory, for under the influence of a tradition ultimately Stoic and wide-spread in both the Middle Ages and in the Renaissance, Spenser thought of grief and anger as having their psychological roots in the same "smart."[14]

9. *Faerie Queene,* II.i.57.
10. Ibid., vi.
11. Ibid., xii.
12. Ibid., i.
13. Ibid., iv.
14. The identification of fear with anger is a familiar dogma of orthodox modern psychology.

He gave more weight to anger than Socrates did because he lived after anger had been raised for several centuries to the rank of a very popular vice as one of the Seven Deadly Sins.

It is very far from my purpose to suggest that the Second Book of *The Faerie Queene* as a whole was a crystallization of orthodox Platonism. It is just a good illustration showing how strikingly the ethical principle underlying the Socratic prejudice against Lydian airs had gained ground during the Renaissance. Many other instances might be found. Almost every serious book written in England, France, and Italy between 1400 and 1600, when Europe was striving so self-consciously to bring in an herioc age, in some degree shared Spenser's inheritance of the Platonic Puritanism succinctly defended by Socrates in the passage already quoted from the Third Book of *The Republic.* The war of Reason against Passion was the universal theme which lasted in various forms until it was dissolved by the reactions of sentimentalism and romanticism late in the eighteenth century.

The most influential champions of the Platonic Puritanism during the Renaissance were educators. They did not, of course, share Plato's doubts about poetry, but they were inclined to think even less liberally than he did about music. They were as certain as was Socrates that contemporary popular music was, as it was put by Sassuolo, who taught music in Mantua in the first quarter of the fifteenth century, "inquinata, impudens, corrupta atque corruptrix."[15] On the other hand, they needed the example of Socrates to confirm their faith that music is a necessary part of education. Vergerius, writing at Padua in 1392, acknowledged that

> As to music, the Greeks refused the title of "Educated" to anyone who could not sing or play. Socrates

15. Cesare Guasti, *Intorno alla Vita e all'insegnamento di Vittorino da Feltre: lettere di Sassolo Pratese volgarizzate* (Florence, Sansoni, 1869), p. 69.

set an example to the Athenian youth by himself
learning to play in his old age; urging the pursuit of
music not as a sensuous indulgence, but as an aid to
the inner harmony of the soul. In so far as it is taught
as a healthy recreation for the moral and spiritual
nature, music is a truly liberal art, and, both as regards its theory and its practice, should find a place
in education.[16]

Aeneas Sylvius, in the Letter to Ladislas, King of Bohemia, in 1459, asked less certainly than Vergerius

whether we ought to include Music among the pur-
suits unsuited to a Prince? The Romans of the later
age seem to have deprecated attention to this art in
their Emperors. It was, on the other hand, held a
marked defect in Themistocles that he could not tune
the lyre. The armies of Lacedaemon marched to victory under the inspiration of song, although Lycurgus
could not have admitted the practice had it seemed
to him unworthy of the sternest manhood. The Hebrew poet-king need be but alluded to, and Cicero is
on his side also. So amid some diversity of opinion
our judgment inclines to the inclusion of Music, as a
subject to be pursued in moderation under instructors
only of serious character, who will rigorously disallow
all melodies of a sensuous nature. Under these condi-
tions we accept the Pythagorean opinion that Music
exerts a soothing and refreshing influence upon the
mind.[17]

This Pythagorean opinion of the soothing and refreshing effect of music was a betrayal of Platonic Philistinism,
though Vergerius was half unconscious of the fact and half

16. P. P. Vergerius, *De ingenuis moribus,* trans. W. H. Woodward in *Vittorino da Feltre and Other Humanist Educators* (Cambridge, the University Press, 1922).
17. Ibid., p. 239.

ashamed of it. As soon as music got a foothold as an accepted recreation it was on the way to reclaim its full character as an art, instead of remaining a mere discipline for boys or for men kept permanently immature by a purely military life. With its limited license only as a cure for tired and neurotic minds music was still a very elementary art, in theory at least, but it was on the high road to become the enthusiastically practiced art that we know it to have been in the home of John Milton, Senior, in Bread Street. The heresy that made music an art had a century of history already behind it among writers on education in England when Milton published his Letter *of Education* to Master Samuel Hartlib. Vives, the Spanish disciple of Erasmus who divided his time between England and the Low Countries and was as well acclimated in England as in Holland, justified music in a general discussion of the recreative value of all the arts in his *De tradendis disciplinis* (1531).[18] Returning to the subject for a fuller discussion, with an Aristotelian echo[19] he defended music again as a recreation by a skillful confusion of that value with the orthodox disciplinary value recognized by the rigorous Platonists.

> Let the pupil practice pure and good music which, after the Pythagorean mode, sooths, recreates, and restores to itself the wearied mind of the student; then let it lead back to tranquillity and tractability all the wild and fierce parts of the student's nature, as it is related in the ancient world . . . that rocks were moved and wild beasts allured by it.[20]

Vives' translator, Professor Foster Watson, compares him with Francis Bacon as a pioneer in the fields in which he

18. *Vives: On Education. A Translation of the De tradendis disciplinis,* by Foster Watson (Cambridge, the University Press, 1913).
19. Aristotle, *Politics* 8.6.1–9, 8.7.8–11.
20. Foster Watson, *Vives,* p. 205.

worked.[21] His influence, like Bacon's, was a solvent of traditional taboos and reverences. In *The Tractate of Education*
Milton echoed his justification of music on traditional disciplinary grounds and recommended "religious, martial or
civil ditties; which, if wise men and prophets be not extremely out, have a great power over dispositions and manners to smooth and make them gentle from rustic harshness and distempered passions." But music as a cure for
rustic harshness is a much more urbane conception than
music as a cure for distempered passions, and in Milton's
subsequent recommendation of music as "not inexpedient
after meat, to assist and cherish nature in her first con-
coction,"[22] the dilettante must have felt that at last the
orthodox Platonist among music masters had been put to
rout.

To musically sophisticated moderns this whole question
of the ethical bearing of music seems strange because we
do not understand what Milton meant when he said that
many wise men and prophets were strangely mistaken if
music did not have incalculable power to discipline the
passions. People who, like Mr. Carl Van Vechten, "know
the interchangeable values which Händel gave to secular
and sacred tunes" and who can deny that "minor keys are
sad and that major keys are always suggestive of joy,"[23]
may wonder how it was possible to compose music which
you could be sure would either incite to noble deeds or
sooth the disorder of the mind. That may be a lost art, but
we may be certain that it existed in the Renaissance, at
least in Utopia, for Sir Thomas More says so. "All their
Musicke," he wrote,

> bothe that they playe upon instrumentes, and that
> they singe with mannes voyce, dothe so resemble and

21. Ibid., intro., pp. xxi, xxxiv, liii, etc.
22. CE, *4*, 289.
23. Carl Van Vechten, *Music and Bad Manners* (New York, Knopf, 1916),
p. 183.

expresse naturall affections, the sound and tune is so
applied and made agreeable to the thinge, that whether
it bee a prayer, or els a dytty of gladnes, or patience,
of trouble, mournynge, or of anger; the fasshion of the
melodye dothe so represent the meaning of the thinge
that it doth wonderfullye move, stirre, pearce, and
enflame the hearers myndes.[24]

No one in the seventeenth century doubted Aristotle's
dictum that characters are affected by music or his proof
of it "by the power which the songs of Olympus and of
many others exercised; for beyond question they inspired
enthusiasm" and "enthusiasm is an emotion of the ethical
part of the soul."[25] Aristotle's certainty on this score had
been reinforced by every writer on music in the intervening
centuries and in Milton's mind it stood on a much surer
footing than did the contemporary notions about astronomy or any other branch of science.[26] In holding this view
and at the same time recommending the use for pleasure
of the whole gamut of vocal and instrumental music available in his time, Milton proved himself a rebel against
the ethical theory that had limited ideas about music
throughout the entire Renaissance.

There was one more aspect of the Platonic prejudice
against Lydian music which Milton definitely did not share.
It was the underlying preference for simple and archaic
types of melody, the fundamentally reactionary element

24. *The Utopia of Sir Thomas More: Ralph Robinson's Translation with Roper's Life
of More and Some of His Letters,* ed. George Sampson (London, G. Bell and Sons,
1910), p. 182.

25. *Politics* 8.5.5.

26. Aristotle's idea is stated without acknowledgment by Boethius in *De
Musica* 1.1, Patrologiae Cursus Completus . . . Series Prima . . . Accurante
J.-P. Migne (Paris, 1844-55. 217 vols.), Vol. 63, col. 1171: "Musicam naturaliter
nobis esse conjunctam, et mores vel honestare vel evertere." Summing up his
argument he concludes: "Quid quod cum aliquis cantilenam libentius auribus
atque animo capit, ad illud etiam non sponte convertitur, ut motum quoque
aliquam similem auditae cantilenae corpus effingat, et quod omnino aliquod
melos auditum sibi memor animus ipse decerpat?"

in Plato's feeling which made him resist the law of development in all of the arts which makes progress consist in ceaseless differentiation into new and more and more complex types. This side of Plato's feeling is veiled in *The Republic,* but Plutarch expressed it frankly enough. Soterichus' exposition of the history of music in the *De Musica* is motivated throughout by the belief that the innovations of recent centuries had ruined the art.

> "Music," he said, "is an invention of the gods and is therefore in all its aspects a respectable art. The ancients in their practice of it, as in their practice of all the arts, watched over its dignity; but the moderns, rejecting all its venerable qualities, have introduced into the theatres in the room of this virile and heavenly art that is so dear to the gods an effeminate and mechanized art."[27]

Soterichus regretted the innovation in recent centuries of more complex instruments and more complex rhythms and harmonies than had been known before the Attic stage reached the peak of its development. Readers of *The Republic* will know that in this Plutarch was expressing Plato's deepest prejudice. Milton's enthusiasm for the "skillful organist plying his grave and fancied descant in lofty fugues," and for "the whole symphony with artful and unimaginable touches adorning and gracing the well-studied chords of some choice composer,"[28] leaves no doubt that on the score of capacity to appreciate the law of evolution in music and its expression in recent inventions in the art Milton was no Platonist.[29]

27. Plutarch, *De musica,* sec. 15.
28. CE, *4,* 288.
29. Most English writers before Milton were pessimistic about the art and, like Plato, were *admiratores temporis acti.* Roger Ascham in *Toxophilus* has Nymphodorus talk as follows: "Therefore eyther Aristotle and Plato knowe not what was good and euyl for learning and vertue, and the example of wyse Histories be vainlie set afore vs or els the minstrelsie of lutes, pipes, harpes, and

On examination Milton's short discussion of music in the tractate *Of Education* proves to have been the protest of a mind aesthetically mature against the moralistic and reactionary elements in the Platonic tradition. In the frankly expressed taste for Lydian airs in *L'Allegro,* it is not fantastic to read Milton's claim that music should exercise poetry's right to be both sensuous and passionate.[30]

---

all other that standeth by suche nice, fine, minikin fingering (suche as the moste parte of scholers whom I knowe vse, if they vse any) is farre more fitte for the womannishnesse of it to dwell in the courte among ladies, than for any great thing in it, whiche shoulde helpe good and sad studie, to abide in the vniuersitie amonges scholers. But perhaps you knowe some great goodnesse of suche musicke and suche instrumentes, whervnto Plato & Aristotle his brayne coulde neuer attayne, and therfore I will saye no more agaynst it." *The English Works of Roger Ascham,* ed. William Aldis Wright (Cambridge, the University Press, 1904), p. 14.

30. Though this study puts Milton's attitude toward music against a background in the history of ideas about the art very different from that chosen to illuminate it by Sigmund G. Spaeth in *Milton's Knowledge of Music* (Princeton, 1913), it would not be understood as differing from his conclusion (p. 67) that the prevailing current of Milton's musical tastes was Doric rather than Lydian.

2

Milton and the Sense of Glory

Perhaps the least justified of the slights, deliberate and unconscious, to which modern critics have subjected Milton is Herbert Read's omission of him from the roster of names to which he dedicates the chapters of his *Sense of Glory.* He gives us the bright glory of the Middle Ages in Froissart's praise of Gaston de Foix. He rejoices in the worship ("active honor, magnanimity, *grandeur d'âme,* glory gained") of Malory's Gareth of Orkney "that was called Beaumains." But for Mr. Read the knell of glory began to toll when Descartes laid down his "first principle of dualism," which inevitably leads "to a denial of aesthetic values," since "beauty can only be a mechanical harmony, devoid of spiritual animation, deficient in the sense of glory."[1] Certain reincarnations of the sense of glory in recent centuries are recognized by Mr. Read, who is very far from agreement with Remy de Gourmont that "Literary glory was invented for children preparing for examinations,"[2] or that the idea of glory itself is but "one of the secondary and naïver forms" of "the general idea of immortality."[3]

1. Herbert Read, *The Sense of Glory* (Cambridge, the University Press, 1929), p. 71.
2. Remy de Gourmont, *Decadence and Other Essays on the Culture of Ideas,* trans. W. A. Bradley (New York, Harcourt, Brace, 1921), p. 69.
3. Ibid., p. 36.

For Mr. Read finds glory dead in Swift but renascent in Vauvenargues and in moderns as diverse as Sorel, Unamuno, and Henry James, the "calm, dominant, reticent and fastidious intellect, ordering the gathered forces of time to a manifestation of the most enduring glory."[4] But of the English sixteenth and seventeenth centuries, aside from an echo of Traherne's *Meditations,* to which Mr. Read responds in much the way that he might to Mr. Llewelyn Powys' *Glory of Life,* he says nothing.

Exclusion from even the most eclectic survey of the experience of glory in literature from medieval to modern times is strange treatment for Milton, whose theme in every major poem may be regarded on one of its facets as glory. The theme is stated in *Comus* when the Elder Brother declares that, though "Virtue may be assail'd," it is "never hurt," and anticipates the "fortunate fall" which enhances the glory of God in *Paradise Lost* by asserting that,

> even that which mischief meant most harm
> Shall in the happy trial prove most glory.[5]

If the dogmatic ethics and theology of these poems repel us, we may still respond to the authentic outpouring of the Renaissance passion for earthly glory by Satan in *Paradise Regained.* As documentation of the "modern idea of fame," which Jakob Burckhardt[6] traced from Dante to Machiavelli, nothing anywhere in European literature can excel Satan's panorama of the wealth, honor, arts, and arms in the ancient world and of all that he

> propos'd in life contemplative
> Or active, tended on by glory, or fame.[7]

4. *Sense of Glory,* p. 228.

5. *Comus,* 591–92.

6. Jakob Burckhardt, *The Civilization of the Period of the Renaissance in Italy,* trans. S. G. C. Middlemore (2 vols. London, C. K. Paul, 1878), *1,* pt. II, chap. 3.

7. *Paradise Regained,* IV.370–71.

Satan's appeal is charged with conviction deeper than that in Comus' temptation speech to the Lady. Modern readers who think it academic should compare it with Satan's cold but closely parallel appeal to the soul's lust of glory in Jeremy Taylor's *Contemplation of the State of Man*. In Christ's unqualified denial of Satan's values we are so prone to read a betrayal of Milton's own humanistic heritage that we lose sight of the devil's sincerity. To convince most moderns of it probably nothing would suffice short of a declaration by some twentieth-century Blake that the hero of *Paradise Regained* is Satan, and that Milton was of his party without knowing it. To worldly seventeenth-century readers such a suggestion might not have seemed invalid. Even on moral grounds it might have been alluring to men who chose to consider it in the light of Sofia's myth of Jove and fame in Giordano Bruno's *Lo Spaccio de la Bestia Trionfante:* "Jove," it seems, "commanded Justice that, subject to Law, it should never quench, but rather, to the limit of its power, enkindle the passion for glory in all human breasts because that is the one efficacious spur to rouse and impassion men to do the heroic deeds whereby commonwealths are enlarged, preserved and made strong."[8] In Bruno's allegory Fame is simply the innocent

> spur that the clear spirit doth raise . . .
> To scorn delights and live laborious days.[9]

There is no misgiving of it as the "last infirmity of noble mind"; no fear of it as the root of the perverted individualism that Burckhardt traced to it; no Augustinian sense of

---

8. "Giove . . . ha commandato al giudicio che, gionto alla legge, non estingua, ma, quanto si puo, accenda l'appetito de la gloria ne gli petti umani, perche questo è quel solo ed efficacissimo sprone, che suole incitar gli uomini, o riscaldarli a quelli gesti eroici che aumentano, mantegnono e fortificano le republiche." Giordano Bruno, *Opere Italiane,* ed. Giovanni Gentile (2 vols. Bari, Gius Laterza, and Figli, 1927), *2,* 90.

9. *Lycidas,* 70, 72.

the "hunter of glory" as the victim of the passion for power
and vulgar applause. Usually, however, the triumphs of
Fame, from Petrarch down, were shadowed by St. Augustine's doctrine that the "contempt of fame is a great vertue: because God beholdeth it, and not the iudgement of
man."[10] On the popular and aristrocratic levels, the humanistic and the religious alike, the Augustinian view was
to dominate Renaissance ethics. On the aristocratic level
we find it in terms of Aristotelian magnanimity in Piccolomini's *Della Institution Morale,* where the magnanimous
man proves himself by his conviction that the desert is
infinitely better than the enjoyment of honor.[11] On the
popular level we find it in la Primaudaye's appeal to the
pride of the humble not to "follow the fashion & maner
of life used by the multitude," and his assurance that "this
we shall do if we despise the glory, honor, praise and pride
of this world, and iudge nothing woorthy to be cared for
of us, but onely vertue, which is able to bring us to the
fulnesse of true glory, and of euerlasting felicitie."[12] Milton
followed a main-traveled road when he wrote that

Fame is no plant that grows on mortal soil . . .
But lives and spreads aloft by those pure eyes
And perfect witness of all judging Jove:[13]

10. St. Augustine, *Of the Citie of God: with the learned comments of Io. Lodovicus
Vives,* Eng. trans. J.H. (London, 1610), p. 225.
11. Alessandro Piccolomini, *Della Institution Morale* (Venice, 1569). Though
the work may not have had the influence on Spenser that J. J. Jusserand once
attributed to it, and may never have come under Milton's eye, he would have
approved of its treatment of honor, alone worth pursuit by the magnanimous
man: "Il quale honor se il magnanimo conoscerà che non gli sia renduto
secondo i meriti, non per questo si turberà: anzi, ridendosi dell'indignità di
coloro, che lo debbon rendere; a lui sia sol bastante il conoscer d'esserne degno:
come molto meglio sia l'esser degno dell'honor, che il riceverlo non sarà mai."
p. 269.
12. Pierre de la Primaudaye, *The French Academie, wherein is discoursed the
institution of maners,* Eng. trans. T.B. (London, 1586), p. 246.
13. *Lycidas,* 78, 81–82.

and when he echoed those words in Christ's definition of glory in *Paradise Regained:*

> This is true glory and renown, when God
> Looking on earth, with approbation marks
> The just man.[14]

Milton's lines are landmarks on the highway which—as Miss Irene Samuel reminds us—was first marked out by Plato in the *Symposium* and *Republic,* and which had been traveled by Spenser with the knights whose only ambition was to serve Gloriana.

Since in different ways *Lycidas* and *Paradise Regained* alike are bound by their subjects to a certain orthodoxy, their sincerity is open to question. Indeed, in the passage on fame in *Lycidas* Mr. Tillyard frankly says that he "does not get the impression of emotional conviction."[15] In thinking so he may not be entirely misled by the "personal heresy," for the essence of the drama in both *Lycidas* and *Paradise Regained* is the conflict between the personal and the impersonal—between the two loves to which St. Augustine traced the earthly and heavenly cities; "the first seeketh the glory of men, and the later desireth God onely as the testimony of the conscience, the greatest glory."[16] From Piccolomini to Vauvenargues, doubt and faith in the "greatest glory" were in strife. The skepticism of Vauvenargues' young correspondent is the foil for his faith that by the light of nature as well as grace the love of true glory fortifies the spirit against the world's contempt.[17] If the passage

14. *PR,* III.60–62. The Platonic basis of the passage is pointed out in detail by Miss Samuel in *Plato and Milton* (Ithaca, Cornell University Press, 1947), pp. 89–92.

15. E. M. W. Tillyard, *Milton* (London, Chatto and Windus, 1930), p. 83.

16. *Citie of God,* p. 531.

17. "Pratiquons la vertu; c'est tout," concludes Vauvenargues' *Premier Discours sur la Gloire.* "La gloire, mon très-cher ami, loin de vous nuire, élèvera si haut vos sentiments, que vous apprendrez d'elle-même à vous en passer, si les hom-

on fame in *Lycidas* is to move us, the skeptical mood must be no less disturbingly a part of it than the reply is reassuring when Apollo touches the poet's trembling ears.

If the reply fails to reassure us, we may be at fault by failing to see its structural importance and its relation, which Mr. Malcolm Ross has pointed out, to the attack on the corrupt clergy by the "prophet of the Galilean lake."[18] We should expect a poet with Milton's interest in Plato[19] as well as in Augustine to transform the noble thirst for immortality into a passion for social righteousness. Yet Mr. Ross's purpose is less to interpret *Lycidas* than it is to attack the "ethical, political and theological" in Milton, which in *Comus* "forgets charity for chastity, which is mere sexual prudence," in the *Ode* reduces the pagan gods to "mere victims of ethical persecution," and everywhere infects Milton's work with "a self-conscious ethical selectiveness . . . sterile to art, if no positive impulse appears powerful enough to absorb restrictive moral energies into activity on a different level."[20] Ross's reasoning is not easy to follow; it is as tortuous and arbitrary as was Mutschmann's in *Der andere Milton*, and it heaps crimes upon Milton's Puritanism and Protestantism that are almost as fantastic as those for which the German, writing *im felde* in World War I, blamed his Calvinism and Stoicism. Yet Ross appears to write with a sincerity that at least one reader never could credit to

mes vous la refusent: car quiconque est grand par le coeur, puissant par l'esprit, a les meilleurs biens; et ceux à qui ces choses manquent ne sauraient porter dignement ni l'une ni l'autre fortune" (*Oeuvres de Luc de Clapiers, Marquis de Vauvenargues,* in J. A. C. Buchin's *Choix de Moralistes français,* Paris, Panthéon littéraire, 1836, p. 552).

18. Malcolm Ross, in *UTQ 18* (1948), 353.

19. Cf. Plato's *Symposium* 208-09.

20. This is a strange sally in an article which refers respectfully to Professor A. S. P. Woodhouse's "The Argument of Milton's *Comus*," *UTQ 11,* (1941), 60, where the contention is "against the common view that it [*Comus*] is simple, unrelievedly austere, and negative in conception," and against the interpretation of chastity and virtue in the masque as amounting to a repudiation of "the order of nature" or to its absolute severance from "the order of grace."

Mutschmann. His violence is born of theological convictions like those which have led some critics to condemn Milton as a bad man and a worse theologian. Mr. Ross assaults him for abandoning the sacramental principle and for releasing "on the whole body of culture" his "sharpened Protestant ethic." Underneath these whirling words there seems to be an honest resentment against Milton for having deceived the world about his lack of what Mr. Eliot has called the poet's greatest faculty—the faculty to "see beneath both beauty and ugliness; to see the boredom, and the horror, and the glory."[21]

If we take some obvious passages in Milton's poetry and prose where he deliberately or unguardedly expresses his sense of glory and brings it to Joycean "epiphany," nothing is easier than to document the case made against him by Ross and Mutschmann even better than they do themselves. If we accept the naïvely dogmatic doctrine of Milton's full indentification of himself with the hero of *Samson Agonistes,* with the Satan of *Paradise Lost,* and the Christ of *Paradise Regained* which Mutschmann inherited from S. B. Liljegren,[22] it is indeed easy to blush as we read passages of hero-worship like the choruses in *Samson:*

> Nor do I name of men the common route,
> That wand'ring loose about

21. Quoted by R. P. Blackmur in "T. S. Eliot: From *Ash Wednesday* to *Murder in the Cathedral,*" reprinted by Leonard Unger in *T. S. Eliot: A Selected Critique* (New York, Rinehart, 1948), p. 247, to explain "this most magnificent statement about poetry" by Mr. Eliot on the ground that it may have arisen from his "insight into the nature of the Church's authority."

22. "Seit langer Zeit," wrote Mutschmann, "hat man schon im Samson des Dramas Züge Miltons erkennen wollen. Es wird jetzt notwendig sein, die Identifizierung gründlicher auszugestalten. Es blieb jedoch Liljegren vorbehalten, die Gleichnungen aufzustellen: Satan des Verlorenen Paradieses ist Milton; Christus des Wiedergewonnenen Paradieses ist Milton: Beides sind Bilder Miltonischer Wesensart, Miltonischer Seelenzustände. Man kann noch viel weiter gehen und, wie schon angedeutet, sagen: Wo immer der Dichter mit wahrer Leidenschaft und mit packendem Uberzeugungsvermögen redet, da spricht er in eigener Person" (Heinrich Mutschmann, *Der andere Milton,* Bonn and Leipzig, Schroeder, 1920, p. 19).

Grow up and perish, as the summer fly,
Heads without name no more remember'd,
But such as thou hast solemnly elected,
With gifts and graces eminently adorn'd
To some great work, thy glory.[23]

If we seriously take the Christ of *Paradise Regained* as a
self-portrait by Milton, the entire epic rises to a peak of
absurdity when its hero crowns his proud humility with
condescension to the whole rout of ancient poets and philosophers, even including "poor Socrates," whom he has
recognized as "Equal in fame to proudest conquerors"[24] because he had suffered an unjust death "for truth's sake."
And in *Paradise Lost* it is hardly less damaging to Milton to
regard him as a kind of Byronic exhibitionist twisting the
Marlovian conception of *virtù* into a Satan of purely narcissistic design.[25]

All three of these narcissistic views of Milton's creation—
of Samson, Satan in *Paradise Lost,* and Christ in *Paradise
Regained*—are closely bound up with epiphanies of glory in
the three poems, and deserve separate examination. Of the
three figures the Christ is obviously the least narcissistic,
though this may reveal most of its creator's spiritual experience in a long and disappointed life. Of course, in
actual fact, the Christ of *Paradise Regained* is no more a
piece of self-portrayal than is the Christ of *The Christian
Doctrine* (II.9), where he stands as he does in the poem with
Job as an example of the Aristotelian virtue of magnanimity, or the "acceptance or refusal of riches, advantages,

23. *Samson Agonistes,* 674–80.
24. *Paradise Regained,* IV.99.
25. In this connection Mutschmann's section on "Die 'Tugend' als Fantasma
bei Milton" is relevant—especially his statement that "Im Verlorenen Paradies
spielt der Begriff der Tugend eine wesentlich andere Rolle. Sie ist hier der
Marloweschen Entschlossenheit verwandt, und tritt besonders unter dem
Namen 'fixed thought,' fester Entschluss, auf. Dieser Kommt dem Luzifer und
seinem Genossen zu, und verleiht ihnen höchste Kraft des Widerstandes"
(*Der andere Milton,* pp. 90–91).

or honors" in accordance with the individual's "own dignity, rightly understood." To Milton there was nothing stranger in associating the humiliations of Job and Christ with the perfection of the pagan virtue of magnanimity than there was in justifying Job's final restoration "to health and prosperity," when he "did not disdain the congratulatory offerings of his friends." Similarly at the close of *Paradise Regained,* though Christ

> unobserv'd
> Home to his mother's house private return'd,

he did not refuse the ministry of the angels when

> they the Son of God our Saviour meek
> Sung victor.

Here the underlying thought was familiar to Milton's readers, for it was simply the Christian belief in a humility for the reward of which earthly honors cannot suffice. In *The Christian Doctrine,* where some of Aristotle's virtues are integrated into Milton's Christian ethic, there is an implied appeal to merely human values as justifying the magnanimous preference for the desert to the enjoyment of honors. Beyond the human level Milton doubtless maintained a life-long, dogmatic faith in

> all judging Jove,
> As he pronounces lastly on each deed.

In *The Christian Doctrine,* in the closing words of the First Book, "perfect glorification" is defined as consisting "in eternal life and perfect happiness, arising chiefly from the divine vision," and involving "the renovation of heaven and earth, and of all things therein adapted to our service or delight, to be possessed by us in perpetuity."

   The dogma of immortality that is implied in Milton's doctrine of Perfect Glorification is rather prone to fall into a false perspective for modern readers. To some it is unacceptable, and they may read him so carelessly that, like a recent correspondent of *The Times Literary Supplement,* they believe that in *The Christian Doctrine* he "denied the immortality of the soul."[26] Surely Denis Saurat[27] and George Williamson[28] have made it abundantly clear that it was the separate existence of the soul that Milton and the Mortalists denied while they passionately affirmed "the resurrection of the body and the life everlasting." Milton's chapter on "The Death of the Body"[29] is perfectly explicit on the point. To doubt it is to misunderstand Milton altogether and to isolate it as if it were something to consider by itself, like trying to understand the heart or the brain apart from the body. For to most of the theologians of the Renaissance the immortality of man—whether or not they believed in a soul capable of existence separate from the body—was so intimately bound up with the beatific vision that they quite subordinated the idea of eternal life to that of the vision of God as a part of human experience in the life to come and, fragmentarily, in the life that we now know. The reasoning was essentially Platonic, and it remained the same in men who differed as widely as Marsilio Ficino and Milton did about the nature of "the soul." If we can accept Kristeller's view of the matter, Ficino, like Plato, was so much inclined to think of "pure contemplation (or the knowledge of God)" as "the highest activity of the human Soul," that, "to be consistent, he must consider the knowledge of God and the enjoyment connected with it the real content of the future life. And if this future contemplation is to be conceived as perfect, it

26. Richard Flatter, *Times Literary Supplement* (August 7, 1948), p. 443.

27. Denis Saurat, *La Pensée de Milton* (Paris, Alcan, 1920), pp. 154–59; *Milton: Man and Thinker* (2d ed. London, 1944), pp. 119–23.

28. George Williamson, replying to Saurat in "Milton and the Mortalist Heresy," *SP, 32* (1935), 553–79.

29. The *Christian Doctrine,* I.13.

must . . . possess all the positive qualities whereas it must
remain free from all limitation. . . . It must be communicated to as large a number of Souls as possible as a per-
manent, eternal possession."[30] The point of Kristeller's
study is his insistence that the contemplative basis of Ficino's thinking about immortality was deeply involved in
his inner experience. It so ramified through all his thought,
his ideas about life and even about the physical constitution of the universe, that it can be said of him—as Arthur
Barker says of Milton—that his view of both the phenome-
nal world and of Christianity "permitted no strict segregation of the spiritual and the natural."[31] If the beatific
vision could be realized in even the smallest authentic degree in the life that men knew, then the immortality of
the soul followed as an obvious corollary.

Immortality regarded as beatific vision and as a natural
outgrowth of life on the human level is much more satis-
factory than the doctrine of either immortality or the vision
if they are regarded as a kind of judicial reward of virtue.
Although the latter view is sympathetically stated in *The
Christian Doctrine,* Milton's tone is very far from that of such
a popular divine as William Perkins, who promised the
saints that a part of the glory rewarding their earthly piety
in Heaven would be "that they shall still beholde the face

30. Paul Oskar Kristeller, *The Philosophy of Marsilio Ficino,* trans. Virginia
Conant (New York, Columbia University Press, 1943), p. 333. In substance
Ficino's thought hardly differs from that of popular evengelical writers like
Bishop Joseph Hall when he wrote in *Heaven upon Earth* (London, 1606), pp.
126–27: "And if our perfect fruition of God be our compleat heaven, it must
needs be, that our inchoate conversing with him is our heaven imperfectly,
and the entrance into the other: which (mee thinks) differs from this, not
in the kind of it, but in the degree." By "a daily renuing of heavenly familiarity," Hall continued, "the minde so communicates it selfe to God, and hath
God so plentifully communicated unto it, that hereby it grows to such a habit
of heavenlinesse, as that it now wants nothing, but dissolution, of glory."

31. Arthur Barker, *Milton and the Puritan Dilemma* (Toronto, University of
Toronto Press, 1942), p. 259.

of God, which is his glorie and maiestie. Rev. 2 and 4."[32]
And Milton is almost silent about those other rewards of
heavenly bliss that look so much like bribes to the bar-
gaining Christian, not only in Perkins but also in a great
Anglican writer like Jeremy Taylor when he pleads in a
chapter on the beatific vision: "what honour shall it then
be, when God shall give to them that served him, not only
to tread upon the stars, to inhabit the palaces of heauen,
to be lords of the world, but, transcending all that is created, and finding nothing among his riches sufficient to reward them, shall give them his own infinite essence, to
enjoy, as a recompense of their holiness, not for a day, but
to all eternity."[33]

Milton's reticence about the glory of the saints in heaven
contrasts strikingly with the expansiveness of Perkins and
Taylor. His silence can hardly have been accidental, for
he was as familiar as any divine with the heavenly visions
of the apocalyptic books and with the "facile but inscrut-
able phrases"[34] of St. Paul about the glorification of the
saints. His agnosticism or indifference about "the state of
the elect after iudgement," about which Perkins was un-
reservedly explicit, was probably a reaction against the ex-
tremes to which some Catholic writers had gone in the

---

32. William Perkins, *The Order of the Causes of Salvation and Damnation* in
The workes of that famous minister of Christ in the Universitie of Cambridge (2 vols.
Cambridge, 1612), *I*, 95.

33. *The Whole Works of Jeremy Taylor,* ed. Reginald Heber, rev. C. P. Eden
(10 vols. 1847–54), *3*, 486–87. Puritan divines might, like Robert Bolton, in
his *Last and Learned Worke of the Foure Last Things* (London, 1635), p. 140, deplore
the Scholastic tendency to "audaciously undertake to define without any good
ground or sound warrant, many particulars [about heaven's sensual joys] not
without much absurdity and unspiritualnesse"; but even Bolton himself, in
A Discourse about the State of true Happinesse (London, 1611), p. 129, regarded the
"high perfection of heauenly beautie, glory and blisse" as a judicial reward
for "the fire of affliction" endured by the saints on earth.

34. William Haller, *The Rise of Puritanism* (New York, Columbia University
Press, 1938), p. 88.

description of heaven. It is not hard to imagine Milton's contempt, if ever he saw Henry Vaughan's translation of St. Anselm's *De felicitate sanctorum dissertatio,* for its pages on the "great sufficiencie of all accommodations in the life to come."[35] There, we learn, the righteous are to be accommodated with a beauty which "shall shine equally with the sunne," with an activity rendering them "equall for swiftnesse with the very Angels of God," with a strength such that "nothing can have power to resist the saints," with "an equal liberty with the Angels in heaven"; health which "shall fill the whole man with such an immutable, inviolable, and inexpressible sweetnesse and solace, as shall utterly repel and forever drive away all thoughts of infirmities," and pleasure so intense as to be comprehensible only as the inversion of the agony of "a naked man with hot and flaming irons thrust into the apples of his eyes, and into every part and member of his body, his veines, nerves and muscles, so that neither his marrow, nor his entrails, nor any of the most inward and tender parts were free from the anguish and immanity of the torment." Though Milton might not have been prepared to deny any of St. Anselm's statements here, we may be sure that he would have been far less attracted by the *De felicitate sanctorum dissertatio* than was Vaughan. Milton was content to think of the glorification of the saints in terms of the beatific vision simply, or in terms of the fame that only all-judging Jove awards. If he could not fancy the joys that St. Anselm described, he could have approved Jeremy Taylor's pleasure in the "honour which the just receive in heaven: for if we look upon him who honours, it is God; if with what, with no less joy than his own divinity . . . if before whom, before the whole theatre of heaven."[36] To Milton this kind of meed in heaven would have seemed as

35. *The Works of Henry Vaughan,* ed. L. C. Martin (Oxford, Clarendon Press, 1914; 2d ed. 1957), pp. 191–210.

36. *Works of Jeremy Taylor, 3,* 490.

appropriately a part of the beatific vision as it did to
Taylor.

In fairness both to Vaughan and to Milton we should
digress for a moment to note that both men were good
enough theologians to see many implications of the idea
of the beatific vision—implications both logical and psychological—and that both men were stirred by it as poets.
We recognize it in Vaughan's "world of light" and less
satisfactorily in Milton's heaven where under God's throne

> all the Sanctities of Heaven
> Stood thick as stars, and from his sight receiv'd
> Beatitude past utterance.[37]

We fail to recognize it in paradoxical inversion when Milton founds his whole dark picture of hell upon those mysterious flames which, giving

> No light, but rather darkness visible
> Serv'd only to discover sights of woe,
> Regions of sorrow . . .[38]

Here Milton was simply thinking of a tradition going back
to Origen and St. Gregory and St. Basil the Great which,
in Taylor's words, opposed "that infernal fire, without
light," to the "celestial light" that "is to penetrate the
bodies of the blessed, and fill them with an incomparable
delight and sweetness."[39] Or, as Vaughan said of "those
furious and unquenchable burnings of hell . . . though
they be of such an *intense heat,* as to work upon *spirits,* and
the most subtile Essences, yet do they give no light at all,
but burn blacker then *pitch, Cremationem habet, lumen verò non
habet.* (Greg. Mor. c. 46.)."[40] Our point would hardly be
worth making but for the fact that no critic has seen far

37. *Paradise Lost,* III.60–62.
38. Ibid., I.63–65.
39. *Works of Jeremy Taylor, 3,* 505.
40. *Works of Henry Vaughan,* 169.

enough into Milton's conception of hell to recognize that
he was doing in conscious reverse with darkness what
Dante did with the light of the blessed spirits in Paradise
when, despairing of expressing it, he wrote:

> Perch'io lo ingegno, l'arte e l'uso chiami,
>   sì nol direi, che mai s'imaginasse,
>   ma creder puossi, e di veder si brami.[41]

It is strange that Milton's treatment of hell's darkness has
not been generally recognized as the play of his imagination upon the reversal of heaven's glory, yet current opinion seems to concur with Mr. Eliot in seeing nothing more
in it than an unfortunate result of his visual ineptitude.
Mr. Eliot is content to say of the famous passage simply
that "it is difficult to imagine a burning lake where there
was only darkness visible."[42] He seems unfamiliar with an
idea that was so common among Milton's contemporaries
that it could be a casual oath in the mouth of one of Fulke
Greville's characters:

> By fires of hell, which burne and have no light;
> I sweare . . .[43]

41. *Paradiso*, X.43–45.

42. T. S. Eliot, "Milton," *SR, 56* (spring 1948), 204.

43. Alaham, cursing Caine, in *Alaham*, III.2, for the murder of Mahomet.
Poems and Dramas of Fulke Greville, ed. Geoffrey Bullough (2 vols. New York,
Oxford University Press, 1945), *2*, 181. Popular curiosity about the lightless fires
of hell was satisfied by Thomas Milles in his translations from the works of
Pedro Mexia, Francesco Sanseverino, Anthony du Verdier, and others, under
the title *The Treasurie of Auncient and Moderne Times, &c.* (2 vols. London, 1613), in a
chapter devoted to the subject. After injecting into a rendering of Job 10:21–22
the words "the light is there as darkness," which are hardly justified by the
Vulgate reading, Milles wrote, *1*, 17: "Now whether this Fire be incorporeall or
no, that only is best knowne to God, and yet Origen (*Whether this Fire be incorporeall or no*. Orig. in Hom. 9.) prooves it to be inuisible by the iudgement of the
Apostle: *This Fire is of such substance, that being constitued inuisible, it yet burneth
uisible thinges, according as the Apostle saith.* For the things which men see, are
Temporal; and those which bee not seene, are Eternall. If then this Fire be
Eternall where with they are punished that separate themselues from God: it
falleth then vpon necessitie, that it must be also inuisible, because of the
opinion of the Apostle, that onely thinges Inuisible, are Eternall."

Thus far we have been interested in the ethical and theological sides of Milton's sense of glory to the exclusion of the political and sectarian side of it to which we saw Malcolm Ross objecting no less seriously. It is of course rather to the political element in Milton's thinking that Ross objects than to the essentially humanistic ethic which put the highest value upon the Aristotelian virtue of magnanimity, though it was given final sanction by the glory of the saints in heaven. Milton's humanism undoubtedly was limited—perhaps impoverished—as well as potently heightened because, as Professor Barker insists, it "was fused with and qualified by the sectarian idea of the rule of Christ through the Spirit in the hearts of the regenerate."[44] The foundation of Milton's reforming faith—as Professor Barker acknowledges in his masterly analysis in *Milton and the Puritan Dilemma*—was an aristocracy of grace. Though it had its universal and perhaps democratic aspect in the "natural equality of the regenerate in a true Christian commonwealth,"[45] it uncompromisingly postulated and condemned a host of enemies outside itself. While we may not agree with Mr. Ross that it was suicidally sectarian, we surely cannot deny Mr. Barker's finding that it was increasingly Millenarian as time went on; that its ideal was always "the Holy Community, in a temporal sense, which was the chief distinguishing mark of Puritan thought"; and that, like other "sectarian radicals," Milton transferred the privileges of the Holy Community "from the spiritual to the natural sphere" and restricted them "to the aristocracy of grace."[46]

In the Holy Community and the Aristocracy of Grace, as Milton understood them, there may be a sectarian vice so radical as to render those conceptions quite alien to the Augustinian "City of God." In Augustine's city Mr. Ross would probably see ample room for the communion of

44. Barker, *Milton and the Puritan Dilemma,* p. 228.
45. Ibid., p. 324.
46. Ibid., p. 303.

saints, a doctrine and a principle against which Milton
seems to him to offend. And he would doubtless find the
offense at its worst in the spirit (if not always in the letter)
of passages like those in *Paradise Lost* where the glory of
God is declared to be augmented by the devils' spite,[47]
and He laughs at the rebel angels while the Son congratu-
lates Him on penetrating their "vain disguises"—

> Matter to me of glory, whom their hate
> Illustrates . . .[48]

To accept such passages it is necessary to see the historical process from the world's creation to its end as begun
for the glory of God and ending in the glory of both man
and God, as the creeds of the Calvinist churches affirmed,
and as their theological books asserted in diagrams that
were even more unforgettable than the Shorter Catechism.[49] We have the inevitable end of the process at the
close of Michael's apocalyptic revelation to Adam of the
Saviour

> in the clouds from heav'n to be reveal'd
> In glory of the Father, to dissolve
> Satan with this perverted world . . .[50]

So we have its traditional justification in the idea of
"the fortunate fall," when Adam declares to Michael that
"thereof shall spring To God more glory"[51] as well as
greater happiness for men than could ever have otherwise
been.

The enhancement of God's glory by man's sin had been

---

47. *PL,* III.385–86.

48. Ibid., V.737–39.

49. Three such diagrams are to be found in Perkins' *Order of the Causes of
Salvation and Damnation,* one of which (opposite p. 95) purports to represent the
process "as the Church of Rome would have it."

50. *PL,* XII.545–48.

51. *PL,* XII.477.

declared by several theologians and poets before Milton,[52] and once Christ's atonement for that sin has been accepted, the enhancement of God's glory and the justification of his ways to man ineluctably follow. Whether man's final happiness seemed to Milton greater in consequence of Adam's sin than it would have been had he lived according to God's first plan and seen his body

> at last turn all to Spirit,
> Improv'd by tract of time, and wing'd ascend
> Ethereal,[53]

like the bodies of the angels, is a question that can be safely left to Mr. Diekhoff.[54] For our present purpose the importance of the fall on the human side was the split of mankind into the children of light and darkness, the City of God, the Holy Community, or the Aristocracy of Grace and their opposites, those who were "ingrafted in Christ"[55] and those, probably a majority, who remained outside "the mystical body called the Invisible Church," whereof Christ was not only the head but also—if we can trust M. Saurat[56]—the physical substrate. The result was a sectarian reading of history, a sectarian sense of glory. Mainly history is the record of

> The brute and boist'rous force of violent men
> Hardy and industrious to support
> Tyrannic power, . . . raging to pursue
> The righteous and all such as honour truth.[57]

Rarely a Samson arises,

52. Cf. A. O. Lovejoy, "The Fortunate Fall," *ELH, 4* (1937), 161–79.

53. *PL,* V.497–99.

54. John S. Diekhoff, *Milton's "Paradise Lost": A Commentary on the Argument* (New York, Columbia University Press, 1946), pp. 126-31.

55. See the *Christian Doctrine,* I.21, "Of being ingrafted in Christ, and its effects."

56. Saurat, *Milton: Man and Thinker,* pp. 146–48.

57. *Samson Agonistes,* 1273–76.

> With gifts and graces eminently adorn'd
> To some great work, [God's] glory,
> And people's safety.[58]

Rarely, he thought, history records the granting of the prayer of the disciples in *Paradise Regained:*

> . . . arise and vindicate
> Thy glory; free thy people from their yoke.[59]

And, as every reader of his prose is aware, Milton looked upon the Puritan Revolution as one of those rare moments of fulfillment of the disciples' prayer. Characteristically, at the close of the *Second Defense of the English People,* he referred to the Cromwellian Commonwealth as "a harvest of glory."

In Milton's controversial writing it must be acknowledged that the national note is strong, especially when, as in *Areopagitica,* he covets for England the glory of reforming its neighbors,[60] or when, as in *A Declaration against Spain,* he incites his countrymen to war rather than the peaceful selling "away [of] the precious opportunities which God hath put into their hands for his glory, and the advancement of the Kingdom of Christ."[61] Our attitude toward the national sense of glory in Milton's tracts is apt to vary with our own national commitments or sympathies. Probably most of us are more or less responsive to the "prophetic" note which Sir Herbert Grierson hears in the tracts, though not all of us would agree with the revolutionist, Georges Sorel, that in the struggle of the Protestant sects and its literature there is true "sublimity."[62] A majority of Milton's readers, however, probably concur

58. Ibid., 679–81.
59. *PR,* II.47–48.
60. CE, *4,* 340.
61. Ibid., *13,* 562–63.
62. Georges Sorel, *Reflections on Violence,* trans. T. E. Hulme (New York, Huebsch, 1914), p. 244.

with his latest popularizer[63] in regarding him as "unjust
to his opponents" in his tracts and more or less tolerantly
excuse him on the ground that it "was a penalty that could
hardly be escaped by a man of such passionate convictions." But excuses cannot save Milton, and his admirers
face a challenge that goes to the root of his nationalism
by insisting upon the fact that everywhere in his poetry
his politics and ethics emerge openly—in Mr. Diekhoff's
words—as "not separate disciplines, but parts of one."[64]

Because—aside from its soundness—Mr. Diekhoff's book
is a polemic against Milton's challengers, all parties to the
debate can accept his account of the part played by ethics
and politics in *Paradise Lost,* for it serves the purposes of
all alike. At heart, though most of us may agree with Mr.
Eliot's halting surmise that poetry has "something to do
with morals, with religion, and even with politics," the
majority go along most willingly when he adds that "we
cannot say what."[65] The profound objection to *Paradise
Lost* that has been taking form since Sir Walter Raleigh's
book on Milton in 1900 is perhaps less potently expressed
by the scattered observations of critics like Mr. Eliot than
it is in more imaginative writing. Perhaps, as Foster Damon
indicated in 1929,[66] we should read it in the correspondence between Milton's epic and Joyce's *Ulysses.* Though
Mr. Damon hardly implied Milton's eclipse by Joyce, his
readers are now likely to concur in Mr. Davis' recent regret
that he failed (at least in the original form of his essay) to
discuss "Joyce's complete negation of the Protestantism,
moralism, and political responsibility which underlay Mil-

63. F. E. Hutchinson in *Milton and the English Mind* (London, Hodder and
Stoughton, 1946), p. 186.

64. *"Paradise Lost" . . . the Argument,* p. 142.

65. T. S. Eliot in the preface to the new edition of *The Sacred Wood* (London,
Methuen, 1928), p. iv.

66. S. Foster Damon, "The Odyssey in Dublin," in *The Hound and Horn* (fall
1929), reprinted by Sean Givens in *James Joyce: Two Decades of Criticism* (New
York, Vanguard Press, 1948), pp. 203–11.

ton's work."[67] And Mr. Davis goes on more in general to point out the disruptive relation of "the comic monomyth in *Finnegan's Wake* to the Protestant, Christian sense of a moral and meaningful human history."

The reply to Mr. Davis and to Joyce was written to the satisfaction of those of Milton's admirers who are still living in the seventeenth century by Mr. C. S. Lewis, in 1942. With a sure scent for the real peril, Mr. Lewis saw a supreme danger to Milton's literary reputation in the public response to Joyce. But Milton's reputation cannot be retrieved by upbraiding the public for thinking that it is "the special function of poetry to remove the elaborations of civility and get at 'life' in the raw," instead of admiring *Paradise Lost* for having organized our "elementary passions into sentiments."[68] The reply, if there is any sufficient reply, to modern distrust of Milton, must make room for modern acceptance not only of his "moralism and political responsibility" but also of his "meaningful human history" culminating for the Holy Community and its citizens in "perfect glorification," which consists in "eternal life and happiness, arising chiefly from the beatific vision."[69]

Though the modern world may not be able to accept the dogma and the sense of glory to which all Milton's thought tended, it may pause to compare him with two of his early contemporaries who contrasted sharply in their views of the communion of saints. One of them was the anonymous writer of the first Moravian tract in English,[70] and the other, Henry Ainsworth, the spokesman of a severely disciplinary ideal of communion. His treatise, *The Communion of Saints*, went into six or more editions between 1607 and 1649, most of them printed in Amsterdam

67. Robert Gorham Davis, reviewing Givens' *James Joyce* in *PR*, *15* (1948), 1017.
68. Clive S. Lewis, *A Preface to "Paradise Lost"* (London, Oxford University Press, 1942), p. 131.
69. The *Christian Doctrine*, I.33. The closing words of the book.
70. *A Repayring of the Breach; Wherein is shewed the benefit that comes by a Christian Communion among the Saints* (1639).

because it was a weapon in the hands of Puritans whose "revolutionary techniques"[71] had long included the identification of the Catholic doctrine of the Communion of Saints with their own Holy Community in its struggle with the Stuart kings and Anglican bishops. Ainsworth took pleasure in pleading that, because the kingdom of Christ was "no earthly Monarchie," it was "therefore . . . able to beat down, break in pieces, and grind to powder all adverse power and domination; whether of this world, or the spirituall wickednesses which are in high places."[72] In Ainsworth's later chapters the belligerent spirit narrows into reckless insistence upon vigilance among the Holy Communicants themselves. They were to be relentlessly sensitive and merciless to heretics within their own ranks. Ainsworth stands out as one of the leaders who thwarted Cromwell's hope of political union among the Separatists and "insisted upon the ineluctable division of all men into a band of regenerate saints and a multitude of unregenerate sinners." The attempt of Ainsworth and his kind "to regiment the multitude according to a code of specious righteousness," as Professor Haller observes,[73] "destroyed whatever influence they may have had with the public and has given them and their kind a bad name to the present day."

In contrast with Ainsworth it is worth while to recall the anonymous Seeker who wrote or translated the first Moravian tract in English, *A Repayring of the Breach; Wherein it is shewed the benefit that comes by a Christian Communion among the Saints.* With a tolerance of spirit surpassing Milton's, the Moravian pled that love could "assimilate" all

71. Cf. M. M. Knappen's chapter on "Revolutionary Techniques" in *Tudor Pragmatism* (Chicago, University of Chicago Press, 1939).

72. Henry Ainsworth, *The Communion of Saints: A Treatise of the fellowship that the Faithfull have with God, his angels, and one with another: in this present life* (Amsterdam, 1640), p. 161.

73. William Haller and Godfrey Davis, *The Leveller Tracts* (New York, Columbia University Press, 1944), p. 50.

men. "It did assimilate Christ unto us, and now if we will entertaine it . . . it will assimilate our Soules to his, and bring us into the perfect state of true felicitie."[74] The writer went on to preach the "resolution, that we will not live to our selves, but unto the Communion of Saints";[75] he was sure that, though their "adversaries . . . ayme at an universall overthrow of all Protestants," their "mutual preservation" was sure through "a reall conjunction of spirits in the fundamentals of the Gospell, and the principles of true learning."[76] The unknown Moravian's principles might finally have been acceptable to Milton, as they ultimately became to the more extreme revolutionary, John Lilburne, but they were—it cannot be denied—more optimistic and more mystical than anything to be found in the *De Doctrina Christiana* or *Paradise Lost*.

Milton's position was between the schools of thought represented by Ainsworth and the anonymous Moravian, but he was much closer to the latter than to Ainsworth. If he was not a mystic in the Moravian, or even in the religious sense, we must concede with M. Saurat that there was an approach to mysticism in his conception of the communion of saints as meaning an immortality of participation in the life of the spirit, or of reason, by its initiates in all ages.[77] Inseparably bound to his conception was his sense of glory in the communion of saints, though he subordinated it to the kind of individual glory that he discussed in his chapter on "Partial Glorification" in the *De Doctrina* and explained as the individual's mastery of himself. Glory was a matter of private ethics—of the self-discipline that can ignore the applause that is "but the blaze of fame, the people's praise," and can tell a dictator that peace hath victories more renowned than war.

74. *A Repayring of the Breach,* p. 7.
75. Ibid., p. 8.
76. Ibid., p. 9.
77. *Milton: Man and Thinker,* p. 149.

3

The Christ of *Paradise Regained* and the Renaissance Heroic Tradition

The curve of modern criticism seems to be sweeping toward the conclusion that Milton's Christ, whose deeds in *Paradise Regained* were to be "Above Heroic, though in secret done" (I. 15), is interesting only as the self-portrait of a defeated old man. In that poem, said Sir Walter A. Raleigh in one of his fleeting glances at it, "is heard . . . the voice of a high Stoical philosophy, strong in self-sufficiency, rich in illustrations drawn from the experience of the ages, and attributed, by this singular poet, to the Christ."[1] Even Professor Grierson, to whom, "seen in a proper perspective," it appears a "noble and intriguing poem," condemns it as "preeminently the poem of Miltonic Puritanism. What Milton failed to apprehend," he writes, "is that the restrictive virtues in themselves are somewhat cold and negative. They too," he pleads, "must have their root in passionate love of God and our fellow men. 'The treasures of heaven are not negations of passion, but realities of intellect from which all the passions emanate uncurbed in their eternal glory.' We miss in Milton's Christ the note of passionate, self-forgetting love. He is too serene

1. Walter Raleigh, *Milton* (London, Edward Arnold, 1900), p. 163.

35

and forbidding, if noble and imperturbable."[2] What the
Scottish critic says gently is roundly said by the German,
Herr Josef Reck, who sees in the Christ of *Paradise Regained*
a monstrous exaggeration of an inhuman, Stoic ideal and
a monument of Milton's pride and moral fanaticism.[3]

Still more damaging criticism of Milton's Christ comes
from one of his most sympathetic students, Mr. Tillyard,
who finds that the figure is "in fact, partly allegorical"
and "partly Milton himself, imagined perfect."[4] The latter
remark is not an echo of the common charge of crude egotism. It is a suggestion that in Christ's denial of Satan's
appeal to him to throw himself into a life of action for the
redemption of Israel we have a bitter confession from Milton that at last he understood the futility of his own share
in the defence of the Parliamentary cause. Mr. Tillyard
corroborates his suggestion by treating Milton's whole management of the second temptation as a kind of palinode.[5]
Seventeen years before *Paradise Regained* was issued, in the
Defensio Secunda, Milton had been rash enough to speak of
his defense of the regicide Commonwealth as fulfilling his
early purpose to raise an epic argument of some kind to
the glory of England. As a retractation of the boast in the
pamphlet, the poem gains great but adventitious interest.
However clear the note of disillusion and repentance may
be, it cannot clear Milton's hero of the charge that he is
"hardly a success artistically"[6] and that he moves in "an
allegorical twilight"[7] through a series of pageants which
were at least partly conceived in the medieval spirit of the

2. Herbert J. C. Grierson, "John Milton," *Criterion, 7* (1928), 254.

3. Josef Reck, *Das Prinzip der Freiheit bei Milton* (Erlangen, 1931), p. 27.

4. Tillyard, *Milton,* pp. 305-06.

5. Ibid., p. 309. Grierson confirms the point about *Defensio Secunda* in *Milton and Wordsworth* (New York, Macmillan, 1937), pp. 70–73.

6. Saurat, *Milton: Man and Thinker,* p. 234.

7. *Milton,* p. 318.

morality plays. To test the prevailing critical view of Milton's Christ as a self-portrait of an aging Puritan taking refuge in Stoicism, it will be worth while to try the historical approach and go a step further than anyone has yet gone toward recognizing the contribution of the Middle Ages to Milton's conception of his hero.

Long before the poem was written, it may be argued, a conspiracy of historical forces was at work to attenuate the heroes of both medieval and Renaissance romance and epic into something like the allegorical Christ of *Paradise Regained.* In the first place, as Professor Thornbury has suggested in her study of the epic tradition against which Fielding was the first successful rebel, the arch-conspirator was the Church. The monks, we are told, brought it about that "chivalrous heroes became more and more monastic"[8] and that in the later legends only a sinless Galahad or a penitent and ascetic Parsifal could achieve the Grail. Shocked though Milton might be at the thought of owing anything to Catholic tradition, he could hardly deny that his "allegorical atmosphere" owed something to "the lofty fables and romances," which were the reading of his early youth, as he tells us in the *Apology for Smectymnuus,* and to Malory's *Morte Darthur* in particular.[9] There is more of Malory in *Paradise Regained* than appears on the surface. "The fiend" who tries "in likeness of a man of religion" to bring Sir Bors into "error and wanhope"[10] is perhaps the first of the many patterns to which we can trace the Satan whom Milton brings to Christ in the wilderness beyond Jordan, masked like "an aged man in rural weeds" (I.

8. Ethel M. Thornbury, *Henry Fielding's Theory of the Comic Prose Epic,* University of Wisconsin Studies in Language and Literature, 30 (1931), 24.

9. *Milton,* p. 319.

10. Thomas Malory, *Le Morte Darthur,* Book XVI, chap. 13 (2 vols. London, Dent, 1912), *2,* 230.

314).[11] Still more striking is the resemblance of the close
of this episode to Satan's mysterious fall, "smitten with
amazement" (IV. 562), at the climax of Milton's story.
When Sir Percivale has resisted all his wiles, Malory's fiend
goes away at last "with the wind roaring and yelling,"[12]
into that region of middle air which is the "old Conquest"
(I. 46) of Satan's cohorts, just as the "Table and Provision"
in Milton's banquet scene no less suddenly

> vanish'd quite
> With sound of Harpies' wings and Talons heard.
> [II.402–03]

The end of another of Malory's temptations by the Evil
One in disguise—this time with Sir Bors as the victim—
suggests the scene where Christ's final triumph results in
Satan's fall from a pinnacle of the temple in Jerusalem.
Sir Bors has a glimpse of the Tempter on "an high battle-
ment," appealing to him in the form of a queen with many
ladies-in-waiting about her. "And anon he heard a great
noise and a great cry, as though all the fiends of hell had
been about him, and therewith he saw neither tower, nor
lady, nor gentlewomen."[13] At bottom, though Malory of-
tener disguised the Evil One as a queen than as a hermit,
his legends of the Grail have something in common with

---

11. More immediate "sources," of course, are Spenser's picture of the devil's
emissary—or of the devil himself, whichever we take Archimago to be—imposing
on the Redcross Knight as

> An aged Sire, in long blacke weedes yclad,
> His feete all bare, his beard all hoarie gray.
> *Faerie Queene*, I.i.29.

And Giles Fletcher's Satan tempting Christ as an "aged Syre" who comes

> slowly footing; every step he guest
> One of his feete he from the grave did drawe.
> *Christ's Victory and Triumph*, stanza 15.

12. *Morte Darthur*, Book XIV, chap. 9 (*2*, 204).
13. Ibid., Book II, chap. 12 (*2*, 228).

Milton's treatment of the Temptation. The bond is frankly confessed when Milton's Satan appears with the demon servitors who resemble

> Ladies of th'*Hesperides,* that seem'd
> Fairer than feign'd of old, or fabl'd since
> Of Fairy Damsels met in Forest wide
> By Knights of *Logres,* or of *Lyones,*
> *Lancelot,* or *Pelleas,* or *Pellenore.*   [II.357–61]

The conquest of Satan in personal encounter and renunciation of the world sums up the ideal which patterns the knights of Malory's account of the quest of the Grail. The same formula applies to the hero of *Paradise Regained.* *Contemptus mundi* was never carried further by medieval pope or doctor of the Church than it was by Milton in this poem. Disillusion like his may have been possible only in the twilight of the Renaissance; and perhaps the denunciation of ancient culture that consummates Christ's refusal of even the noblest earthly glory could have come only from a spirit stripped of its faith in the renewal of the vision of ancient civic liberty that is painted in *Areopagitica.* Satan's retort is to exclaim that, if he is fit for life on terms only of such absolute *contemptus mundi,* Christ should withdraw into some private world of Arcadian retreat:

> Since neither wealth, nor honour, arms nor arts,
> Kingdom nor Empire pleases thee, nor aught
> By me propos'd in life contemplative,
> Or active, tended on by glory, or fame,
> What dost thou in this World? the Wilderness
> For thee is fittest place.   [IV.368–73]

Puritanism is so generally blamed for Christ's unworldliness that a burden of proof rests heavily upon one who looks in it for any vestige of medieval otherworldliness. Most modern readers regard him as a figure more Stoic than Christian. Since Mr. S. B. Liljegren's *Studies*[14] was published in 1919, it has become almost a dogma that Milton's Christ was the projection of a proud spirit, *naturaliter stoicus,* and nourished partly on Calvinism (which he so feelingly criticized in the *Treatise on Christian Doctrine*), partly on Machiavellism, but mainly on the residue of the movement in France which Leontine Zonta has traced in *La Renaissance du Stoicisme au XVIᵉ Siècle.*[15] I should like to plead that Milton's treatment of Christ as an ideal figure "above Heroic" (I. 15) and his integration of that conception with both his theology and cosmology resulted from a complex of historical forces of which the "budge doctors of the *Stoic* fur" were one of the least. Among the greatest of those forces was the effort of the preceding centuries to Christianize the Aristotelian ideal of the magnanimous man—the effort which came to a head in the Arthur of *The Faerie Queene,* whom Professor H. S. V. Jones reminds us that Spenser regarded as a link uniting his "several virtues to God."[16] We may look first at that influence on Milton, for it played a decisive part in the *contemptus mundi* of the hero of *Paradise Regained.*

Thirty years before the publication of his short epic, in the exordium of the Second Book in *Of Reformation in England,* Milton appealed to the *Nicomachean Ethics* and *Politics* of Aristotle to plead that a king should be "a spirit of greatest size and divinest mettle." He concluded that an English prince should be a fountain of "magnanimity," for he was Peripatetic enough to believe that "the grounds and causes . . . of single happiness to one man" are identical with those of "a whole state, as Aristotle, both in his Ethics and Politics, from the principles of reason, lays down."[17] Though the pamphlet professed what Milton at the time of

---

14. S. B. Liljegren, *Studies in Milton* (Lund, C. W. K. Gleerup, 1919).

15. Paris, 1918.

16. H. S. V. Jones, "*The Faerie Queene* and the Medieval Aristotelian Tradition," *JEGP, 25* (1926), 293.

17. CE, *3,* 38.

writing took to be his sincere loyalty to "the free and un-
tutored monarch"[18] that Charles I was perhaps destined
to become, its real devotion was to "our Saviour Christ,"
whom "Pilate heard once . . . professing that 'his kingdom
was not of this world.' "[19] The First Book opens with a
picture of the author meditating in apocalyptic mood upon
"our Saviour Christ," now no less than when he was incarnate on earth "triumphing to the highest pitch of glory
in the spirit."[20] Years later—later, perhaps, than the composition of *Paradise Regained*—in *De Doctrina Christiana*,[21] he
reverted to Christ's rejection of the world as a triumph of
the spirit and made it an example of the magnanimity
which Aristotle called "a crowning ornament of all the virtues."[22] In the *De Doctrina* Milton defines the pagan virtue
altogether in Christian terms. It is shown, he says, "when
in seeking or avoiding . . . riches, advantages, or honours,
we are actuated by a regard for our own dignity, rightly
understood."[23] After several examples of it from the Old
Testament, his final instance is that of "Christ in rejecting
the empire of the world, Matt. iv, 9. 'all these things will
I give thee, if,' &c." No wonder, then, that in *Paradise
Regained* renunciation should be the climax of Christ's speech
refusing Satan's offer of the kingdoms of this world and the
glory of them, or that his justification of his great refusal
should be simply to say that "to lay down" such honours

> hath been thought . . .
> Far more magnanimous than to assume.
> [II.483]

The readiest answer to the question why, both as thinker
and artist, Milton should have imagined Christ as a su-

18. Ibid., p. 63.
19. Ibid., p. 42.
20. Ibid., p. 1.
21. Book II, chap. 9 (CE, *17*, 241).
22. *Nicomachean Ethics* 4.3.16.
23. CE, *17*, 241.

preme exemplar of Aristotle's magnanimity is suggested by
an anonymous digest of the *Nicomachean Ethics* which Mr.
Leo Strauss has found among the Hobbes papers at Chatsworth and which he believes had a considerable influence
upon the development of the theories which took final form
in *Leviathan*.[24] Hobbes, it will be remembered, probably over
twenty-five years before *Paradise Regained* was written, had
reacted violently against the conception of magnanimity
which the poem embodies, and for this Mr. Strauss is inclined to credit the anonymous Aristotelian commentator.
That man, whoever he was, confessed that he was guided
by the *Della Institution Morale* of Alessandro Piccolomini.[25]
This treatise became interesting to workers in the field of
Comparative Literature a few years ago when the late M.
Jusserand identified it as a part of Spenser's philosophical
background.[26] It was particularly Piccolomini's views of
magnanimity and of "heroic virtue"[27] which concerned the
anonymous commentator on the *Ethics*. In the first of the
two chapters which are in point, Piccolomini is true to
Aristotle in describing the great-souled man as setting a
justly high value upon himself and preferring the esteem of
intelligent contemporaries to riches, noble birth and all
the goods of fortune. Even here, however, there is a trace
of the renunciation of the world by Milton's Christ, of his
contempt for the "people's praise" and for the

> herd confus'd,
> A miscellaneous rabble, who extol
> Things vulgar and, well weigh'd, scarce worth
>   the praise.   [III.49–51]

---

24. Leo Strauss, *The Political Philosophy of Hobbes*, trans. from the German
manuscript by Elsa M. Sinclair (Oxford, Clarendon Press, 1936), pp. 46 ff.

25. Alessandro Piccolomini, *Institution Morale* (Venetia, appresso Giordano
Ziletti, 1569).

26. Jusserand, "Spenser's 'Twelve Private Morall Vertues as Aristotle hath
devised,'" *MP*, *3* (1906), 373–83.

27. *Institution Morale*, Book VI, chap. 9, and Book VIII, chap. 17.

But Piccolomini out-Aristotled Aristotle by exaggerating the aristocratic aspect of the matter and pointed toward Hobbes's "extreme accentuation of the concept of aristocratic virtue in the *Leviathan.*"[28] If Dr. Strauss's analysis is sound, Hobbes was reacting against Aristotle via the *Institution Morale* when he twisted his version of magnanimity into a mainstay of that "Hobbism" which became, "after the Restoration, an almost essential part of the fine gentleman."

It would be a paradox if, on the genealogical tree of historical ideals, Milton's Christ were to prove to be even distantly related to the pattern of "greatness of mind" which Hobbes's sympathizer, Davenant, could discover only in "Courts and Camps."[29] In fact, the two ideals were closely enough related to be felt even in the third quarter of the seventeenth century as actively at war. Their conflict took its most significant form in the *Dialogue de la Gloire* of Jean Chapelain, whose first encounter with it had been on a more imaginative level, when, in *La Pucelle,* he tried to reconcile nationalistic with religious motives in the story of Jeanne d'Arc. Like *Paradise Regained,* the *Dialogue* has been judged "banal au fond";[30] and its modern editor, M. Fidao-Justiniani, defends it on the ground that, in an age which despises glory, we are in no position to understand either the emotional or the philosophical importance of the subject in the times of Louis XIV.

Chapelain introduces two speakers: M. d'Elbène, "a man of honour" who, though no stranger in courts and camps, has embraced ideals altogether inimical to both; and the Marquis de Montausier, a veteran of twenty-five wars, of whose notions of glory Hobbes and Davenant would have

28. *Hobbes,* p. 54.

29. Preface to *Gondibert,* ed. J. E. Spingarn in *Critical Essays of the Seventeenth Century* (3 vols. Oxford, Clarendon Press, 1908), 2, 14.

30. Collas, quoted by J. E. Fidao-Justiniani in *L'Esprit classique et la preciosité au XVIIe siècle* (Paris, 1914), p. 144.

approved. Like Milton's Christ in his dialogue with Satan, M. d'Elbène condemns the passion for every kind of glory short of the honor which is due Reason's votaries. "La gloire," he says, "à l'égard des gens de raison," in comparison with such fame as Milton thought "the intelligent" and "the wise"[31] among men too few to secure for those who deserve it, "n'est plus attrayante ni plus douce. Il suffit à la vertu pour se faire passionément aimer, de sa pureté, de sa solidité, de sa gravité, de sa majesté, de sa lumière qui n'éblouit point de sa grandeur qui ne trompe point, de sa fermeté qui ne change point."[32] As if intending to intimate explicitly that his *Dialogue* belongs in the tradition to which both the second temptation of Milton's Christ and the ordeal of Spenser's Knight of Temperance in the delve of Mammon and the court of Philotimé belong,[33] Chapelain made M. d'Elbène use Spenser's term. "Cette philautie," he says, using the word for which Spenser was ultimately indebted to Aristotle,[34] "est la matière éternelle du combat du Sens avec la Raison: au secours de laquelle," he adds, in a figure that recalls Milton's

> sage Philosophy . . .
> From Heaven descended to the low-rooft house
> Of Socrates,   [IV.273–74]

"la Philosophie est descendue des cieux et en faveur de laquelle elle déploie ses forces heureusement jusques à lui faire remporter la victoire."[35]

In the end Chapelain himself reluctantly judges the debate, and his decision, though a nominal triumph for the soldier, is a moral one for the champion of Reason. If only

31. Milton's words in *Paradise Regained*, IV.58–59.
32. *L'Esprit classique*, p. 159.
33. This relation of Milton to Spenser was admirably studied by Professor Edwin A. Greenlaw in "A Better Teacher than Aquinas," *SP*, *14* (1917), 196–217.
34. *Nicomachean Ethics* 2.7.8.
35. *L'Esprit classique*, p. 162.

the world were capable of M. d'Elbène's idealism, he says,
even kings might dispense with the motive of glory. His
conclusion appeals to the "Eden rais'd in the waste Wilderness" by Milton's Christ, though it is only an idyllic fancy,
unlike the "paradise within thee" which Michael promises
Adam shall be "happier far"[36] than the garden in Eden.
At last Chapelain convinces the Marquis of Montausier of
the very Miltonic opinion that, if the temptations of glory
could be banished from the world, "les siècles ne seraient
plus de fer mais d'or, et les peuples reglant leurs actions et
leurs pensées à ce niveau-là, seraient leurs rois à eux-mêmes
et n'auraient point besoin de princes pour les régler ni
pour les régir."[37] Chapelain's dialogue, it should be observed, is no pietist's tract. His spirit was much like Montaigne's, when he praised the life of solitude for which a
man prepares by outgrowing every worldly ambition, or
when he closed the essay *De la Gloire* with the maxim:
"Toute personne d'honneur choisit de perdre plustost son
honneur, que de perdre sa conscience."[38]

Through his sympathy with military and aristocratic
ideals like those of Chapelain's marquis, Hobbes, as Dr.
Strauss observes, reached "a final theory of magnanimity
(which) assumes a complete break with Aristotelianism,"[39]
In opposition to Hobbes the Cambridge Platonist, Henry
More, built a popular treatise on ethics, the *Enchiridion
Ethicum,* upon a sheerly Christian interpretation of the Aristotelian principle. His little book ends with the conclusion
that "Magnanimous (men) look on the world with contempt."[40] When, in the *De Doctrina Christiana,* Milton
dressed the Greek virtue in Hebrew as well as Christian

36. *PL,* XII.586–87.

37. *L'Esprit classique,* p. 176.

38. *Oeuvres complètes de Montaigne,* ed. Jean Plattard (6 vols. Paris, Fernand
Roches, 1931–32), Book 2, chap. 16, Vol. 4, p. 46; Book 1, chap. 39, Vol. 2,
p. 150.

39. *Hobbes,* p. 53.

40. Henry More, *Enchiridion Ethicum,* reprint of the English translation of
1690 (New York, Facsimile Text Society, 1930), p. 257.

garb and discerned it in Abraham's refusal of the gifts of the king of Egypt, he was following in the main track of Catholic Christianity. The difference between him and Hobbes went deep, because the latter, like the unknown writer of the digest of the *Ethics* of Chatsworth, neglected Aristotle's noetic virtues and deliberately ignored his famous apology for the theoretic life at the close of his tenth book. Hobbes chose to contemn the contemplative ideal which was the heart of Aristotle's thought as Saint Thomas Aquinas had transmitted it to the western world.

In Milton's times and even in his own life, in spite of their opposition, the aristocratic and religious conceptions of magnanimity sometimes passed into each other. In his pamphleteering days he had shared the faith of the high Renaissance in the active life as the way to a transcendental magnanimity and "heroic virtue." In his youth he must have sympathized with the faith which Castiglione made the Lord Octavian express in *The Fourth Book of the Courtier:* "He who shall bee most wise, most continent, most temperate, most manly and most just," as the creed runs in Hoby's translation, "hee shall be most glorious and most dearely beloved to God . . . through whose grace hee shall attaine unto that heroicall and noble vertue, that shall make him passe the boundes of the nature of man, and shall rather be called a demy God, than a man mortall."[41] Yet never, it seems, could Milton quite abandon himself to the active life. Under the surface, as we know from what he tells us in *The Reason of Church Government,* its appeal, though gilded with millenial hopes, could hardly make him "leave a calm and pleasing solitariness, fed with cheerful and confident thoughts, to embark in a troubled sea of noises and hoarse disputes, put from beholding the bright countenance of truth, in the quiet and still air of delightful studies."[42]

    41. Baldassare Castiglione, *The Book of the Courtier. Done into English by Sir Thomas Hoby* (London, Everyman, 1928), p. 276.
    42. CE, *3,* 241.

When he wrote those words Milton was, he said, in search among the knights of the old romances for a hero for a short epic which was to be modeled, as, in part *Paradise Regained* was modeled, upon the Book of Job. He was embarrassed, he said, by the doubt whether any "king or knight, before the conquest, might be chosen in whom to lay the pattern of a Christian hero."[43] Already, perhaps, his reading of British history had made him feel that the true Arthur fell far short of his imaginary namesake in *The Faerie Queene*. By referring in the same passage of *Church Government* to Tasso, he glanced at the *Jerusalem Delivered* and at Tasso's profession that there, in the figures of Godfrey and Rinaldo, the two principles were reconciled. His suggestion—immediately preceding—that he might model a short epic upon the Book of Job must mean, however, that already he was in quest of a subject

> Not less but more Heroic than the wrath
> Of stern Achilles.

It may well be that in 1641 he was planning a poem of which either Job or Christ was to be the hero—perhaps planning the framework of very much the *Paradise Regained* that we know. Structurally, his debt to the Book of Job has been recognized, but, conceptually also, he was indebted to it. His poem as we have it makes no fewer than five allusions to Job, all parallelling him to Christ because he was given up to Satan "To prove him, and illustrate his high worth";[44] although nothing in the Bible story quite justifies such a view, Job had come to be recognized as the greatest human exemplar of the Christian version of Aristotle's high-mindedness or magnanimity. In a popular, contemporary, Italian compilation of traditional lore, the *Selva Novissima di Concetti* of Alessandro Calamato,[45] he appears in the chapter on "Ambitione, e suoi danni" linked

43. Ibid., p. 237.
44. Ibid., cf. *1*, 147, 425; *3*, 64–67, 95.
45. Venice, 1648 (p. 50).

with Christ and several pagan exemplars of the magnanimity which spurns earthly glory.

From the time when he wrote *Church Government* until he
completed *Paradise Regained,* Milton must have been concerned over the conflict of the contemplative with the active ideal and in its possible solution by some heroic spirit,
in art, if not in life. In the background was Catholic Christianity, standing for the priority of the contemplative principle. Closer to him was the Renaissance, with its challenge
to the life of action. Throughout that movement and after
it, in Italy at least, the conflict between the two ideals
was a constant preoccupation of poets as well as moralists.
Tasso's profession to have embodied both in the *Jerusalem
Delivered* may not signify much, but it is significant that
all his life he was interested in the question as to which
of them, in theory, ought to determine the character of an
epic hero. Doubtfully, in his discourse *Della Virtù Eroica e
della Carità,* he decided for the active type;[46] but the essence of his heroic virtue he believed to be a perfect fusion
or equilibrium of the two ideals. On that point critics
generally agreed. Interpretation of the ancient epics became a highly successful search for that balance in heroic
incarnations. Julius Caesar Scaliger, in the *Poetics,* solemnly
pronounced Aeneas the most perfect of epic heroes because
he had every mark of the contemplative character and lived
the active life in obedience to Reason as it was revealed
in the commands of the gods. For a critic believing that
"the perfection of man is consummate in contemplation,"[47]
no other view was possible. Tasso, in his discourse *Del
Poema Eroico,* took much the same view of Aeneas as the
supreme epic hero and completely magnanimous personality, possessed of contemplative and active virtues alike.

46. *Le Prose Diverse di Torquato Tasso,* ed. Cesare Guasti (2 vols. Florence, Suc-
cessori Le Monnier, 1875), 2, 194.

47. J. C. Scaliger, *Poetices Libri Septem* (2nd ed., Heidelberg, 1581), p. 228
(Book III, chap. 12).

In the seventeenth century the theory reached absurd lengths. Sir William Alexander, in a passage which recalls the rejection of the heroes of the classical epics in the opening lines of the Ninth Book of *Paradise Lost,* complained that Scaliger exaggerated Virgil's power to "provoke Magnanimity." "The Praise of an *Epick* Poem," Alexander insisted, "is to feign a Person exceeding Nature, not such as all ordinarily be, but with all Perfections whereof a Man can be capable; every Deficiency in that imaginary Man being really the Author's own."[48]

Italian theories of the epic hero bear directly upon Milton's Christ, for his critical temper—as the late W. P. Ker said of its expression in the preface to *Samson Agonistes*— "belongs to the Italy of one hundred years before; it is like the solemn sermons before an Italian learned society, in which the doctrines of poetry used to be expounded more gravely than any text of Saint Thomas."[49] In one such literary sermon, which was delivered before the Florentine Academy by Benedetto Varchi and later found its way into a popular collection of such eloquence, Milton could find Aeneas exemplifying the contemplative ideal side by side with its favorite symbols in Christian tradition; Rachel in the Old Testament and Mary in the New.[50] Although Tasso appealed to Aristotle to justify his faith in an Aeneas magnanimous enough to incarnate both principles, his pagan terms were not intended to disguise his very Christian thought. Aeneas, he said, might rate as a supreme example of Aristotle's σπουδαιοί (*uomini eccelenti*), men possessed of a high seriousness which he regarded with no less transcendental earnestness than Matthew Arnold did two centuries afterwards.[51]

48. From *Anacrisis,* ed. Spingarn, in *Critical Essays, I,* 183–84.
49. Essays of John Dryden, ed. W. P. Ker (2 vols. Oxford, Clarendon Press, 1900), *I,* xxviii.
50. Francesco Sansovino, comp., *Orationi Volgarmente Scritte da Molti Hvomini Illustri de Tempi Nostri* (Venice, 1575), Pt. I, p. 129.
51. Tasso, *Prose Diverse, I,* 116.

Although, as we shall see, it had become deeply involved in Christian and Neo-Platonic cosmology, Tasso traced his doctrine of heroic virtue finally to Aristotle. His discourse makes capital of its bare mention in the *Nicomachean Ethics*,[52] where it is a vague hypothesis on the frontier of the empirical, Greek system of morals—something described in a few words as opposite to bestiality and godlike and therefore not, properly speaking, a human quality at all. In the *Politics* of Aristotle Tasso thought that he found warrant for his account of heroic virtue as "an excess and perfection of the good, something which has nothing to do with moderation, as the moral virtues have,"[53] something really divine and only distinguishable from Christian charity or the passionate love of God because its object is earthly honor rather than heavenly glory. The finest earthly honor, he said, belonged to Roman worthies like the Curzii, Decii, and Marcelli, but the heroic spirit of such men he treated as merely "a shadow and a figure"[54] of the divine love which Christ brought into the world. The words of Milton's Christ about the founders of Rome's greatness are intelligible only in the light of Tasso's theory and we should remember it when we read Christ's reply to Satan's challenge to him to emulate them:

> Among the Heathen (for throughout the World
> To me is not unknown what hath been done
> Worthy of Memorial) canst thou not remember
> *Quintius, Fabricius, Curius, Regulus?*
> For I esteem those names of men so poor
> Who could do mighty things, and could contemn
> Riches though offer'd from the hand of Kings.
> [II.443–49]

Conventional discussions of the contemplative ideal, like

52. *Nicomachean Ethics,* 7.1.1.
53. *Prose Diverse, 2,* 200.
54. Ibid., pp. 196, 200.

that by Benedetto Varchi to which I have referred, canted endlessly about the noble old Romans. Here, incidentally, Milton protests against that sort of thing. Though he had provocation in much contemporary Neostoic propaganda, like the *Wise Stoick* of Anthony Legrand,[55] he did not fall into cant of the opposite complexion, as Dick Steele did in *The Christian Hero*, when he demanded, "In a word, why is it that the Heathen struts, and the Christian sneaks in our Imagination?"[56]

Tasso's doctrine of heroic virtue was a part of the natural science as well as of the literary theory which England took from Italy. Piccolomini's chapter on the subject integrates the conception with a complete cosmology. His psychology is, in general, what Milton himself accepted, for—as Miss Nicolson has pointed out—he followed the standards of his time in the theory that man is constituted of three spirits: natural, vital, and animal, the latter (from *anima*, the soul) being his true spirit, which excels the brutes in the faculty of Reason, though he shares with them his physical processes, his sense perceptions, and his intelligence. Because, "in Milton's psychology and ethics, the *natural* order of man's faculties is all-important,"[57] Miss Nicolson observes that his account of Adam's fall is crystallized in terms of the reversal of that order:

> For Understanding rul'd not, and the Will
> Heard not her lore, both in subjection now
> To sensual Appetite, who from beneath
> Usurping over Sovran Reason claim'd
> Superior sway.[58]

Piccolomini's account of heroic virtue can be read as a

55. *Man without Passion: Or, the Wise Stoick*, trans. G.R. (London, printed for C. Harper, 1675).

56. Richard Steele, *The Christian Hero*, ed. Rae Blanchard (Oxford, the University Press, 1932), p. 15.

57. Marjorie H. Nicolson, "Milton and Hobbes," *SP, 23* (1926), 422.

58. *Paradise Lost*, IX.1127–31.

reversal of these lines. He defines it simply as the extinc-
tion of appetite by Reason and draws the corollary that
the hero is on a footing of equality with the most "exalted
and abstract"[59] beings in the universe. Implicit in what
he says is the assumption of that "great chain of being"
which, in the imagination even of the men upon whom
the new science and cosmography had come with all their
force, stretched from the highest creatures in heaven to the
lowest beneath the moon, and of which "the middle link"[60]
was man. Ascent to the heroic regions above the human
level he regarded as possible by that fusion of natural and
spiritual law which Raphael expounds to Adam—the doctrine of "various degrees of substance" in the universe,

> Each in thir several active spheres assign'd,
> Till body up to spirit work.[61]

As a supreme example of the heroic virtue which masters passion to the point of working body up to spirit, Piccolomini mentions Hercules. Readers of the Neoplatonic
poets of the French Renaissance will remember that the
twelve famous labors were often transcendentally interpreted to mean that the hero, like Christ in Milton's exordium to *Of Reformation in England,* triumphed "to the
highest pitch of glory in the spirit, which drew up his
body also."[62] So, in a fine sonnet, Joachim du Bellay interpreted the story of Hercules' self-immolation as a tale
of

> Alcmena's strong, unconquered son, who dared
> Wrest freedom from the hated flesh by fire,
> Making himself immortal on his pyre.[63]

59. Piccolomini, *Institution Morale,* pp. 380–81.
60. A. O. Lovejoy, *The Great Chain of Being* (Cambridge, Mass., Harvard University Press, 1936), p. 103.
61. *Paradise Lost,* V.477–78.
62. CE, *3,* 1.
63. In love with intellectual beauty, the poet is transformed into that

It was the Neoplatonic habit of treating Hercules as a supreme example of heroic virtue which led Milton to compare Christ's mysterious final triumph over Satan to one of Hercules' most familiar triumphs. Satan has placed Christ on a pinnacle of Herod's temple and challenged him to keep that impossible footing. Then, suddenly, he has fallen himself. Instantly the simile follows, interpreting the scene for those who could read the allusion to the familiar, allegorical interpretation of the myth:

> Satan smitten with amazement fell
> As when Earth's Son *Antaeus* (to compare
> Small things with greatest) in *Irasa* strove
> With *Jove's Alcides,* and oft foil'd still rose,
> Receiving from his mother Earth new strength,
> Fresh from his fall, and fiercer grapple join'd,
> Throttl'd at length in th'Air, expir'd and fell.
>
> [IV.562–68]

Echoes of the heroic virtue of which Hercules was a symbol and Tasso and Piccolomini were exponents are heard in several of Milton's contemporaries. In Sir William Temple's pretentious essay on the subject they are muted to a "perfection of natural reason" which implies "the perfection of body and mind."[64] More sonorously we hear them sounding through Sir Thomas Browne's *Christian Morals* (III, 14), as in the famous preachment: "Fill thy Spirit with Spirituals, with the mysteries of Faith, the magnalities of Religion, and thy Life with the Honour of God; without which, though Giants in Wealth and Dignity,

---

Que se monstroit l'indomté fils d'Alcmème,
Qui dedaignant nostre figure humène,
Brula son corps, pour se faire immortal.

Quoted by R. V. Merrill in *The Platonism of Joachim du Bellay* (Chicago, University of Chicago Press, 1925), p. 44.

64. *The Works of Sir William Temple, Bart.* (4 vols. London, Longman and Co., 1814), *3.* 333.

we are but Dwarfs and Pygmies in Humanity, and may hold a pitiful rank in that triple division of mankind into Heroes, Men, and Beasts."[65] Sir Thomas Browne's triple division is an essentially religious conception; but, by the middle of the seventeenth century, humanitarian tendencies had begun to modify the idea of the heroic. It betrays itself in Temple's stammering pronouncement that, "indeed, the character of heroic virtue seems to be, in short, the deserving well of mankind."[66] Joseph Glanvill kept close to Piccolomini's statement and yet adumbrated the modern faith in heroes of science, when he wrote that "those illustrious Heroes, *Cartes, Gassendus, Galilaeo, Tycho, Harvey, More, Digby*" were "in great part freed from the entanglements of a drossie Vehicle" and "imploy'd like the Spirits above, in taking a survey of Nature's Riches."[67]

Henry More, the Cambridge Platonist, to whom Glanvill's list of heroes refers, would have subscribed to his notion of heroism and so, to some degree at least, would the Milton who fancied looking through "the glass of Galileo" at "Imagin'd Lands and Regions in the Moon." Yet More and Milton, no less than the Catholic Tasso, conceived the heroic character as contemplative, i.e. as possessing an enlightenment which was intellectual in consequence of being rationally ethical and (thanks to a touch of the emotion which Matthew Arnold said turns ethics into religion) religious. At bottom, the conception remained that of the virtue which the Roman Catholic Church has long regarded as the beginning of sanctity, and proof of which is the first step in the process of canonization. The Church defines "heroicity" mainly in terms of patience and constancy—in short—of those restrictive virtues which Professor Grierson finds too prominent in *Paradise Regained.*

---

65. *The Works of Sir Thomas Browne,* ed. Geoffrey Keynes (4 vols. London, Faber and Faber, 1927, rev. 1964), *1,* 280.

66. *Works of Sir William Temple, 3.* 333.

67. Joseph Glanvill, *The Vanity of Dogmatizing* (London, 1661), p. 240.

Anyone who takes the trouble to examine the three volumes of Benedict XIV's *Treatise on the Beatification and Sanctification of the Servants of God* which deal with "Heroic Virtue" will find that unromantic conception of heroism spread on every page.

If we turn to the most romantic of all the books about the heroic which the Renaissance produced, Giordano Bruno's *De gli Eroici Furori,* we find it expounded there in terms no less religious than Benedict's, although they are more or less Platonic. Bruno made nothing short of the vision of the divine beauty[68] and truth[69] the goal of the "spirito eroico." Bruno's cosmology, like Piccolomini's, corresponded with his ethics and his theory of the heroic. He thought of a chain of being with Reason or Wisdom penetrating it like sunlight from above and of man as microcosm of that cosmos, standing at its centre. Nature, we are told, had created inferior and superior orders in both the macrocosm and its counterpart, man; and the heroic soul is passionately determined to maintain nature's arrangement. The thought, in this passage,[70] is colored by the analogy in Plato's *Republic* between the disorderly soul and the disorderly state; but the emotion which fires the thought is biblical, for Bruno twice admonishes the reader to heroism with the Psalmist's *sursum corda.*

Another Neoplatonist, Leo the Jew, on a page which parallels Christ's speech at the close of the Second Book of *Paradise Regained,* describes the heroic nature Platonically

68. Bruno, *Opere Italiane,* 2, 434.

69. Ibid., p. 498.

70. Social as well as natural degrees, says Bruno, are necessary, if there are to be any spirits "eroici simili a gli dei. Però a che doviamo forzarci di corrompere il stato della natura il quale ha distinto l'universo in cose maggiori e minori, superiori ed inferiori, illustri ed oscure, degne ed indegne, non solo fuor di noi, ma ed ancora dentro di noi, nella nostra sustanza medesima, sin a quella parte di sustanza che s'afferma immateriale; come delle intelligenze altre son suggette, altre preminenti, altre serveno ed ubidiscono, altre commandano e governano?" Ibid., pp. 464-65.

as attained only after "sensuality has quite ceased to disturb virtuous reason."[71] The hero is the man who "vanquishes himself." Leo completes the thought with an allusion to the verse in Proverbs (16:32) which says that "he that ruleth his spirit [is better] than he that taketh a city." So Milton's Christ combined the same proverb with Plato's thought in the *Republic:*

> he who reigns within himself and rules
> Passions, Desires and Fears, is more a King;
> Which every wise and virtuous man attains:
> And who attains not, ill aspires to rule
> Cities of men or head-strong Multitudes,
> Subject himself to Anarchy within,
> Or lawless passions in him which he serves.
>
> [II.466–72]

"Redemption" in *Paradise Regained,* says M. Saurat, "is the return to Reason."[72] He does not explain how Reason is to be understood, but would give it no merely restrictive or Stoic force. The central question in criticism of the poem is whether Reason shall include the value which Milton all his life set upon the passions and how it shall correspond with the disillusioned magnanimity of Christ. The final answer must wait until one more tradition in the historical background of his Christ—both as a symbol of the return to Reason and as an epic hero—has been recognized. Perhaps in the end the poem may seem no more moving than it did before our examination began; but its epic quality—if, with Mr. Lascelles Abercrombie, we take "an immediate response to some general and instant need in its surrounding community" as the criterion of " 'authentic' epic"[73]—will hardly be deniable.

71. Leone Ebreo, *Dialoghi d'Amore,* ed. Santino Caramella (Bari, Gius. Laterza. and Figli, 1929), pp. 17–18.

72. Saurat, *Milton: Man and Thinker* (New York, Dial Press, 1925), p. 171.

73. Lascelles Abercrombie, *The Epic* (London, Secker, 1914), p. 21.

That Christ should be Milton's symbol for the return to Reason was due, in a general way, to the entire Protestant tradition. More directly, it was due to the faith of representative Reformers like Luther's contemporary, Hans Denck, who "had drunk deeply at the well of the fourteenth and fifteenth century mystics" and "believed that there was a spark of the divine nature in man, an Inner Word . . . and that man could always keep true to this inward monitor, who was none else than Christ."[74] Milton's thought was in their line of descent when, in *De Doctrina Christiana*,[75] he said that Christ has a "prophetical function" which involves "the illumination of the understanding." Hans Denck and his kind were ill fitted to dominate the Reformation, but their appeal to Christ as the Word of the Fourth Gospel, though less popular than the principles of Luther and Calvin, became the common faith of sensitive minds of all communions and of no communion. The Lutheran, Philip Melancthon, writing in the *De Anima* more as a psychologist than as a theologian, spoke the universal language of Christians who were above the strife of creeds, when he said: "Vocamur enim ad instaurationem naturae, et proponitur nobis filius Dei. . . . Hanc Evangelii vocem cum audimus, et fide amplectimur, ipse filius Dei, λόγος aeterni patris accendit lucem in mentibus nostris, et Spiritu suo sancto corda inflammat, ut in Deo acquiescant et laetentur, diligant eum, et obedire incipiant."[76]

In theologians of many camps passages like this might be found. They represent a cumulative movement of thought by which the Inner Word became identified with the "Word, the Filial Godhead"[77] who creates the world in

74. Thomas M. Lindsay, *A History of the Reformation* (2 vols. New York, Charles Scribner's Sons, 1928), *2*, 436.

75. Book I. chap. 15 (CE, *15*, 289).

76. Philip Melancthon, *Opera*, ed. C. G. Bretschneider (28 vols. Halle, 1846), *13*, 157.

77. *Paradise Lost*, VII.175.

Paradise Lost. Recently the effect of Milton's conception of Christ as the creative Reason or Word on his cosmology has been a good deal stressed. Its effect on the hero of *Paradise Regained* is no less important, for it explains the emergence of Milton's Christ as the culmination of a theological doctrine and simultaneously of the conception of the hero "as a great example, as a highly significant object-lesson, a figure of solemn and inspiring didacticism,"[78] which a recent Warton lecturer regards as the mark of the distinctively Renaissance epic.

Viewed as the climax of an epic tradition stretching back to Petrarch, Milton's Christ gains immensely in interest. He gains no less when he is viewed at the same time as the final symbol of a religious faith which was based upon the conception of the Son as the Word and Image of God. The hold of that conception upon Milton's thought and emotion was not in the least impaired by his Arianism.[79] Too much has been said about that heresy of his and we have suffered too many groans like those of Hilaire Belloc, who protests that Milton "denies with close and serried argument the divinity of Our Lord."[80] In reality, the *De Doctrina Christiana* is instinct with vital, albeit qualified, faith in a uniquely divine Christ. When Milton says— as he does again and again in various ways—that "there

78. E. M. W. Tillyard, *The English Epic Tradition,* Warton Lecture on English Poetry (London, British Academy, 1936), p. 10.

79. Arianism, if it figured at all in the thought of the Neoplatonist Marsilio Ficino, seems to P. O. Kristeller (in *The Philosophy of Marsilio Ficino,* New York, Columbia University Press, 1943, pp. 168-69) to have yielded to his desire to minimize his Plotinian inheritance of "a sharp difference between the two divine substances" (the absolute One and the divine Mind), in order to justify the orthodox Christian conception of the Trinity. But Ficino's influence did much to build up the idea of Christ as *exemplar virtutum,* which he presented in his mature work *De Religione Christiana* (1474), cap. 16, in contrast with that of Christ the sacrificial redeemer. In *Milton and Wordsworth,* pp. 98-100, Grierson deprecated the exaggerated interest in Milton's "Arianism" which had figured in recent criticism of his later poems.

80. Hilaire Belloc, *Milton* (Philadelphia, J. B. Lippincott Company, 1935), p. 292.

is in Christ a mutual hypostatical union of two natures,"[81] he is as much in earnest as is Bunyan's Great-Heart, that final popularization of the magnanimous ideal, when he tells the pilgrims that Christ "hath two natures in one person, *plain to be distinguished, impossible to be divided.*"[82]

Milton's "Arianism" ought not to enter this discussion, for his conception of Christ as the Word or Reason which creates and preserves the world was shared by most orthodox Protestants. For example, the Huguenot, Duplessis-Mornay, whose work on Christian evidences Sir Philip Sidney began to translate, wrote that God's creative "Worde hath in it the seedes of all things; That he hath distributed to every of them their severall natures; and that he is the invincible bond of the whole world, and of al things therein."[83] The Huguenot stated this in a context of passionate, trinitarian orthodoxy; while Milton reconciled a similar conception with a unitarian faith which saw the creation as an act of absolute Reason, in which God and the filial Word had no more free choice than men have in obeying the laws of thought. In all this M. Saurat sees a grand reflection of Milton's private world, where his liberty-loving passions were given the form of Reason. With a touch of respectful irony, M. Saurat adds that "hence came what is peculiarly his religion: regeneration through Reason, Christ being the incarnation of divine Reason coming to tame passion."[84] But Milton's Christ was by no means his own invention. Melancthon's redemptive Logos[85] or Image of God and Duplessis-Mornay's

---

81. Book I, chap. 14 (CE, *14*, 229).

82. John Bunyan, *The Pilgrim's Progress,* ed. James Blanton Wharey (Oxford, Clarendon Press, 1928), p. 222.

83. Philippe Duplessis Mornay, *A Woorke concerning the trewnesse of the Christian Religion, written in French: Against Atheists, Epicures, Paynims, Iewes, Mahumetists and other Infidels* (London, 1587), p. 81.

84. *Milton: Man and Thinker,* p. 106.

85. In his Commentary on Genesis, Melancthon wrote: "Praeterea et Christum disces, cum scribitur ad similitudinem et imaginem Dei conditum esse hominem, cui imagini nos restituit Christus, qui fuit nativa et propria imago Patris," *Opera, 13,* 772.

"Worde that hath in it the seedes of all things" are conceptions too closely allied for there to be any doubt that
Milton's Christ was a universal possession of contemporary
minds, less popular, no doubt, but no less powerful as a
stimulant of religious emotion and of theological speculation than the Christ of *Piers Plowman,* the exemplar of
Charity and the expounder of Holy Trinity.

First of all, however, Milton's Christ is an epic hero,
and his attributes as the creative and redemptive Word
must fit that character. To Milton's mind they did so, I
believe, because more or less consciously he compared him
with his Platonic prototype, the "World-Artificer" of the
Timaeus,[86] who is "not a Creator, in the strict sense, that
is to say, he does not make things *ex nihilo,* but only im-
poses order and system on a preexisting Chaos,"[87] as the
Son of God does in the account of the Creation in *Paradise
Lost.* Like Milton's Christ Plato's Demiurge controls the
world by his goodness, or by being, in some not altogether unambiguous way, the "idea" of absolute good. So
it is by his perfection that the Son of God reigns as the
first of all created things in *Paradise Lost* and vanquishes
Satan in *Paradise Regained.* At the turning point in the
second temptation Satan recognizes Christ as at once the
ideally magnanimous man and the absolute pattern of the
good. His reply to Christ's refusal of his offer of the world's
wealth opens the Third Book with a kind of formal acknowledgment of the hero's greatness of soul. "Thy actions," says the devil,

> to thy words accord; thy words
> To thy large heart give utterance due, thy heart
> Contains of good, wise, just, the perfect shape.
> [III.9–11]

86. In general, the resemblance of Milton's Son of God to the Demiurge of
the *Timaeus* has been traced by Herbert Agar in *Milton and Plato* (Princeton,
1928).

87. R. G. Bury in his introduction to the Loeb Classical Library Edition of
the *Timaeus* (London, Heinemann, 1929), p. 7.

The word "shape" which sounds almost meaningless to modern ears, meant the absolute perfection of the thing—its form, in the Baconian sense—as it does in the strikingly parallel situation in *Paradise Lost,* when Satan's insolence is rebuked by the angel Zephon and

> abasht the Devil stood,
> And felt how awful goodness is, and saw
> Virtue in her shape how lovely.   [IV.846–48]

To feel the force of these two scenes may be impossible today. A contemporary reader, turning the pages of Alexis Carrel's *Man the Unknown,* is unlikely to sympathize when he finds the Catholic Church praised for its recognition of the saints because they have been "virtuous in a heroic manner." He may agree, but he may not be moved, when he reads that "moral beauty is . . . a very striking phenomenon" and that "this form of beauty is far more impressive than the beauty of nature and of science. It gives to those who possess it a strange, inexplicable power. It increases the strength of the intellect. It establishes peace among men. Much more than science, art, and religious rites, moral beauty is the basis of civilization."[88] Dr. Carrel speaks what he knows will be to many of his readers the language of obscurantism. His words compare instructively with the language of enlightenment as it was confidently spoken in the best English counterpart of those discourses before the Italian academies which charmed the young Milton.[89] The best commentary on his Christ is Sir Philip Sidney's citation of the "saying of *Plato* and *Tullie* . . . that who could see Vertue would be wonderfully ravished with the love of her beauty."[90] For Sidney and

88. Alexis Carrel, *Man the Unknown* (New York, 1934), pp. 130–31.

89. The point is made by Kenneth Myrick in *Sir Philip Sidney as a Literary Craftsman* (Cambridge, Mass., Harvard University Press, 1935), chap. 2, "*The Defence of Poesy* as a Classical Oration."

90. *An Apology for Poetry,* ed. G. Gregory Smith, in *Elizabethan Critical Essays* (2 vols. Oxford, Clarendon Press, 1904), *I,* 179.

Milton alike the great, polarizing purpose of heroic poetry was the evocation of that vision. All his life, as he put it in *The Reason of Church Government,* Milton was concerned with "the very visible shape and image of virtue, whereby she is not only seen in the regular gestures and motions of her heavenly paces as she walks, but also makes the harmony of her voice audible to mortal men."[91] In his antiepiscopal pamphlets he all but identified that "visible shape and image of virtue" with the Christ who "came down amongst us to be a teacher."[92] To modern taste his Neoplatonic faith in virtue in her redemptive "shapes" and "images" may ring as false as the cry of the benighted Lady in *Comus:*

> O welcome . . .
> . . . thou unblemish't form of Chastity,
> I see ye visibly.   [213–16]

What the Lady saw may have been colored by recollection of a tinsel virtue in a court masque. Recent criticism has been severe in its psychoanalysis of the idealism of *Comus.* But psychanalysis can tell us very little that is not obvious about the forces which went to the creation of the hero of *Paradise Regained,* for they are better understood in the light of general, cultural history than in that of Milton's development in his old age. His Christ was the culmination of the faith of the Reformers in an exemplar Redeemer, the Word of Saint John's Gospel, as it fused with the craving of the critics and poets of the later Renaissance for a truly exemplary hero in epic poetry.

91. CE, *3,* 185.
92. *Animadversions upon the Remonstrants Defense against Smectymnuus* (CE, *3,* 165).

✳ 4 ✳

Milton and the Symbol of Light

In the last decade *Paradise Lost* and the *Divine Comedy,* those once supposedly "waning classics,"[1] have become the Meccas of the most modern critical pilgrims: the analysts of structure, imagery, and symbol, the typologists, and the historians of ideas. The change is due to the discovery of some new varieties of critical experience. New directions have led to new horizons with alluring—sometimes deceptively alluring—points of view upon the world's classics. The somewhat ragged symphony of their analysts drowns the dissonance of the prophets who once condemned some of them in the name of enlightenment.

No study of the role of light in *Paradise Lost* should be attempted without an understanding of the major part which it has played in analysis of its imagery by scholars with interests as diverse as those of D. C. Allen, T. H. Banks, J. I. Cope, Phyllis MacKenzie, and Arnold Williams. And no such study can afford to ignore the traditional material in J. A. Mazzeo's chapters on "Dante's Sun Symbolism" and "Light Metaphysics,"[2] or disregard

1. Albert Mordell, *Dante and Other Waning Classics* (Philadelphia, Acropolis Publishing Co., 1915).
2. J. A. Mazzeo, *Structure and Thought in the* PARADISO (Ithaca, Cornell University Press, 1958) and *Medieval Cultural Tradition in Dante's* COMEDY (Ithaca, Cornell University Press, 1960).

Mlle Yvonne Batard's magnificent and meticulous survey of his light imagery.[3] The limitations as well as the powers of Milton's control of metaphor emerge by contrast with her revelations of the psychological character of the main images which Dante regarded as "found, not created,"[4] and her recognition of the fusion of theology with imagery "dans le ciel, où la lumière est un rire de ceux qui ont trouvé 'le bien de l'intelligence.'"

It has, of course, been understood for a long time that, "Manifestly, Beatrice is identified, in some sort, with light (*la verace luce*) and love"[5]—the conclusion reached by J. B. Fletcher in his *Symbolism of the Divine Comedy* in 1921. About the same time Ida Langdon put it on record that "Milton's allusions to light, in the main, directly or indirectly, express his theory of form."[6] In her preceding paragraph she reduced his formal theory simply to his very un-Dantean technique in portraying Satan's deformity by progressively darkening his figure instead of making him the traditional monster with three faces and large, flapping wings "in form and texture like a bat's." As a key to Milton's "theory of form" this contrast of his devil with Dante's is not helpful. Hazlitt had said as much and made the contrast extend pertinently to Tasso's Satan.

In closing her paragraph, however, Miss Langdon made a statement which, while perhaps not strictly original, certainly points the way toward our present perception of the importance of light in the metaphorical structure of *Paradise Lost*. She pointed out that the function of Milton's ever-darkening Satan is to display the richness of the sym-

3. Yvonne Batard, *Dante, Minerve et Apollon: Les Images de la Divine Comédie* (Paris, Les Belles Lettres, 1952).

4. Ibid., p. 373, Dante "parlant de quatre espèces d'opérations de la raison, dit de certaines d'entre elles que 'nous n'en sommes pas à proprement parler les créateurs, mais, les trouveurs': c'est un Autre qui les a ordonnées; c'est un plus grand créateur qui les a faites."

5. New York, Columbia University Press, 1921 (p. 156).

6. Ida Langdon, *Milton's Theory of Poetry and Fine Art* (New Haven, Yale University Press, 1925), p. 21.

bolic "single phenomenon" which he "chose to denote the greatest moral excellence and spiritual good." How distinctly she saw what these words might imply is hard to tell. Though she remarked that the pervading light imagery "gives added meaning to the entreaty of the poet for light in his darkness," her sketch of its landmarks in the design of the epic mentions only the physical and moral darkness of Hell and Chaos which contrast with the glory of Heaven. Her most interesting link with more recent criticism is her final remark that the significance of light in *Paradise Lost* is proved by the many "passages containing such words as *light, lustre, radiant, shining, dark, gloom,* and *night.*"

In 1921 Miss Langdon's little list of words denoting light and darkness in *Paradise Lost* passed unnoticed. Something like a revolution of our sensibility had to occur before true esthetic response to such words was possible. Striking evidence of the beginning of the change was Josephine Miles's note in 1945 on "the sparks of fire and of soul" which give characteristic "brightness" to the metaphysicals, and on "the emblazoned mass of glittering terms of sensory power" which make "the great array of the world bright for the brightness' sake" in Milton's poetry.[7] Challenging the tendency to regard his dark scenes as a "mere conceptual opposite" to his empyreal "world of high angelic stations and essences" and to his glowing earthly garden in Eden, Miss Miles reduced the dark elements to a subordinate and purely esthetic role. By a kind of panoramic, visual view of *Paradise Lost* she saw its dark landscapes and dark spirits only as foils for the bright ones. And so "in ocean, waste, descent, foundation, den, and womb, with wild and dreary, and dismal, obscure, and silent, and in 'dark, unbottom'd, infinite abyss,'" the shadows in the cosmic scene become what Miss Miles calls "the nether portion of bright" and the means to "vivify it scenically."

7. Josephine Miles, "From Good to Bright: A Note on Poetic History," *PMLA, 60* (1945), 766–74.

At a time when Milton's visual effects had never been
seriously scrutinized, and when it was fashionable to deny
that he had any visual imagination, Miss Miles produced
her statistical evidence that in *Paradise Lost* "descriptive
detail, sensuous and scenic detail, became a chief material
of poetry," appearing "consistently and abundantly enough
to be recognizable as a chief quantitative force," making
"depth and height, air and mass, light and shadow" visibly
sensible. But though she saw the visual effects as determining the character of the epic, she took only the first step
towards recognition of their metaphorical importance.
"Extensive" though she called them, she anticipated later
recognition of their importance in the structure of the
poem only by remarking that they are "far more structural
than the Elizabethan cloud before the sun."[8]

A long step toward recognition of the metaphorical elements in the structure of *Paradise Lost* was taken in 1946
when Phyllis MacKenzie[9] put her finger on the link between the paradoxical image of the flames of hell, which
yield "No light, but rather darkness visible" (I.63) and the
no less paradoxical address of the angels to the omnipotent
Father

> Thron'd inaccessible, but when thou shad'st
> The full blaze of thy beams, and through a cloud
> Drawn round about thee like a radiant Shrine,
> Dark with excessive bright thy skirts appear,
> Yet dazzle Heav'n, that brightest Seraphim
> Approach not, but with both wings veil thir eyes.
>   [III.377–82]

After remarking on "the impetus of a developing emotion"
in these lines, Miss MacKenzie turned to a passage which
inverts the process which has intensified Heaven's glory.

8. Ibid., p. 669.
9. Phyllis MacKenzie, "Milton's Visual Imagination: An Answer to T. S.
Eliot," *UTQ, 16* (1947), 22.

There is equal momentum in several passages "involving the progressive degradation of beauty, light, and goodness."[10] Her choice illustration is the "Darken'd . . . Archangel whose

> form had not yet lost
> All her Original brightness, nor appear'd
> Less than Arch-Angel ruin'd, and th'excess
> Of Glory obscur'd: As when the Sun new ris'n
> Looks through the Horizontal misty Air
> Shorn of his Beams, or from behind the Moon
> In dim eclipse disastrous twilight sheds
> On half the Nations, and with fear of change
> Perplexes Monarchs. Darken'd so, yet shone
> Above them all th'Arch-Angel; but his face
> Deep scars of Thunder had intrencht, and care
> Sat on his faded cheek.   [I.591–602]

The heart of the passage is the exploding image of the eclipsed sun, "shorn of his beams" and shedding "disastrous twilight . . . On half of the Nations." The fading glory of the fiend finally implicates half of mankind. The argument of the entire poem is there, and so is its metaphorical structure in little.

Discerning readers have always seen the "strong moral connotations" which Professor Banks declared in 1950 to be characteristic of the great majority of Milton's "images of brightness."[11] By that time such readers were beginning to feel the esthetic and organic importance of those connotations, though a year earlier not very many of them had reacted strongly to Professor Barker's reasoning that *Paradise Lost* should "be read as a metaphor of spiritual evolution."[12] The time was not quite ripe for study of the

10. Ibid., p. 26.
11. Theodore Howard Banks, *Milton's Imagery* (New York, Columbia University Press, 1950), pp. 125–26.
12. Arthur Barker, "Structural Pattern in *Paradise Lost*," *PQ, 28* (1949), 30.

scene of the epic as "mimesis of the argument." Before its
continually unfolding metaphors of light and darkness,
height and depth, could be made part of the common
experience of many readers, they had to digest Professor
Brooks's recognition of the simile in Book I, lines 587–602,
as "a microcosm of the whole poem,"[13] and Professor
Allen's panoramic vision of the "motion in full brightness
[which] enlarges the extended descriptions of the epic."[14]
Meanwhile, many readers were doing collateral work under
Jung's guidance in the mysteries of the archetypal quater-
nion of harmonized division and union of Good and Evil,
Spiritual and Material ("the dark chthonic world"),[15] as
indigenous in man's racial and individual psyche. The
collateral also included Cassirer's theory that the "development of the mythical feeling of space always starts from
the opposition of *day* and *night, light* and *darkness.*"[16] The
trails blazed by Jung and Cassirer had to be trodden by
many pilgrims before an audience was ready for Mrs.
MacCaffrey's foundation of a book-length interpretation
of *Paradise Lost* largely upon the fact that for Milton, "as
for Spenser and Shakespeare, the dark/light antithesis
embodied profound intuitions of value."[17]

Mrs. MacCaffrey's work, however, is a tributary rather
than a distinct current in the main stream of interpretation
of the poem in terms of its dark/light imagery. Her prime
interest is in the reflection of primeval human experience
in the myths which Jung and Cassirer have taught us to
recognize in the world's primary epics. Her purpose is to

13. Cleanth Brooks, "Milton and the New Criticism," *SR, 59* (1951), 10.
14. Don Cameron Allen, *The Harmonious Vision* (Baltimore, Johns Hopkins
Press, 1954), p. 106.
15. *Psyche and Symbols: A Selection from the Writings of C. G. Jung,* ed. Violet
S. de Laszlo (Garden City, N.Y., Doubleday, 1958), pp. 33, 53.
16. Ernst Cassirer, *Philosophy of Symbolic Form,* trans. Ralph Manheim (3 vols.
New Haven, Yale University Press, 1953–57), *2,* 96.
17. Isabel Gamble MacCaffrey, *Paradise Lost as "Myth"* (Cambridge, Mass.,
Harvard University Press, 1959), p. 105.

reveal those myths in the themes and scenes of *Paradise Lost*, and so to plumb the psychological mysteries of its creation in the poet's mind and its hold upon modern readers of all degrees of sophistication. Though her chapters on the language and imagery of the poem are richer than any earlier discussion of either subject, they are ancillary to her central psychological interests in Cassirer's identification of spatial with moral dimensions and in Jung's conception of the epic hero's dark journey, which she sees inverted in the expedition of the anti-hero of *Paradise Lost* from Hell to Earth and back again.

The main stream of interpretation of the poem in terms of its imagery has finally debouched into Professor Cope's study of its metaphoric structure.[18] His penultimate chapter on its "scenic structure" displays its strategy and design as resting upon the contrast and interplay of scenes of physical darkness and brilliance in an increasingly symbolic drama. The structural value of their contrast first emerges clearly when the action moves from the darkness of Hell and Chaos as Satan catches sight of "th'Empyreal Heav'n" and "This pendant world."[19] Then Book III opens with the salute to "holy Light," which is an overture to the glory of its scenes at the divine throne, "dark with excess of bright."[20] The "middle books of innocence between the fall of Satan and the fall of man"[21] develop a constant and sometimes paradoxical interplay of the two principles. In Book IV the bright day in Eden has as its background Satan's recrimination against the sun whose light he abuses to spy on its innocent inhabitants. Books V and VI, respectively, begin with an earthly and a heavenly dawn culminating in the victory of the Son in his symbolic

18. Jackson I. Cope, *The Metaphoric Structure of Paradise Lost* (Baltimore, Johns Hopkins Press, 1962).
   19. *PL*, II.1047–52.
   20. Ibid., III.380.
   21. *Metaphoric Structure*, p. 118.

"Panoply . . . Of radiant *Urim*"[22] over the rebel hosts of
Satan in Heaven. In Book VII the murk of Chaos is in-
vaded by the command "Let there be light" from the lips
of the conqueror who has just cast Lucifer into Hell's darkness visible. Book VIII probes the mystery of the sunlit
and starlit skies before its dialogue is shadowed by warnings against the tempter. Though he will seduce Eve at
the hour of noon, Book IX is keyed for the act of darkness
by the opening scenes of Satan's second entry into Eden
at midnight and of his quest—"wrapt in mist / Of midnight vapour"[23]—for the serpent in which he must "incarnate and imbrute"[24] his essence. Here the dark/light
imagery links with the Christian version of Eve's seduction
by the serpent. In Book X those two traditional symbolisms
again emerge together when Satan descends through the
darkness of Chaos and Hell to report his triumph in Eden
to the "dark Divan" in Pandemonium and there finds himself and his "great consulting Peers"[25] turned suddenly
into serpents. In Book X there is little light after the Son
leaves "his radiant Seat . . . Of high collateral glory"[26] to
judge Adam and Eve, but it is in the last three books of
Paradise Lost that Professor Cope finds his best illustrations
of the structural importance of "Milton's paradoxical symbolic [in which] light carries the potentiality of darkness,
as sight carries the potentiality of blindness."[27] The false
light cast upon the Tree of Knowledge by Lucifer in Eden
and upon human affairs universally in Michael's revelation
to Adam of their future course is finally cleared away when
he can say to the angel: "I find / Mine eyes true op'ning,
and my heart much eas'd."[28] In this "blindness-and-sight

22. *PL*, VI.760–61.
23. Ibid., IX.158–59.
24. Ibid., IX.166.
25. Ibid., X.456–57.
26. Ibid., X.85–86.
27. *Metaphoric Structure*, p. 128.
28. *PL*, XII.273–74.

imagery," which is most obvious and moving in the invocation to Book III, but is everywhere latent throughout the
poem, Professor Cope finds the heart of its most important
structural metaphor.

Overemphasis of the structural aspect of Milton's
light/dark and spatial imagery may easily obscure its value
for hasty readers. Neither Professor Cope nor Mrs. Mac-
Caffrey nor Professor Summers in his pioneering essay
"Grateful Vicissitude"[29] has ever been in danger of losing
sight of the trees in their discovery of the patterned walks
through the wood. It was by close analysis of the esthetic
effects of many passages in *Paradise Lost* that Summers per-
ceived the pivot of its light/dark imagery in one centrally
placed passage:

> There is a Cave
> Within the Mount of God, fast by his Throne,
> Where light and darkness in perpetual round
> Lodge and dislodge by turns, which makes through
>   Heav'n
> Grateful vicissitude, like Day and Night. . . .
>   [VI.3–7]

The recognition of various metaphoric designs in *Paradise Lost* has been a valid critical experience. It began with
the pleasure of some experienced and sensitive readers in
Milton's dark/light imagery. Recognition of it as structurally interesting was a natural development. Thereafter
it was not surprising that the cosmic spaces which Miss
Nicolson had surveyed from the point of view of seventeenth-century astronomy should be absorbed into Mrs.
MacCaffrey's larger vision of the spatial imagery of the
entire poem as structurally fundamental. Since the publi-

29. Joseph H. Summers, *The Muse's Method* (Cambridge, Mass., Harvard University Press, 1962), pp. 71–86. The essay appeared in *PMLA, 69* (1954), 251–64.

cation of Professor Svendsen's *Milton and Science*,[30] most
criticism has focussed upon the effort to validate the metaphorical unity of the poem. His interpretation of the dialogue on astronomy in Book VIII as "the *central* image in
the dualistic and ambivalent design and mode and double
plot of the poem" has been attacked,[31] but less on the
ground of his attempt to find a central image than on that
of his assumption that the design is ambivalent and the
plot double. His reviewer readily agrees that scientific
imagery "is one of the ingredients integrated into the
structure, theme, and mood of the poem." Actually the
integration of such imagery into the design as it is seen by
Professors Summers and Cope is quite possible as long as
no exclusive claims are made. Cope's remarks on its closing
scene (XII.641–44) recognize the same interworking of the
"symbols associated with Satan earlier in the poem"[32]
which Svendsen regards as making the gate of Paradise,
"Waved over by that flaming Brand" and "With dreadful
Faces throng'd and fiery Arms"[33] simply "a metaphoric
resolution of the apparent contradiction raised by the
final images of Adam and Eve hand in hand, and a reas-
sertion of the central theme correspondent to the paradox
of the fortunate fall."[34]

There are, of course, also dangers in a too triumphant
assault upon *Paradise Lost* on the converging lines of metaphor and structure. The most obvious is that of over-
emphasizing the few emergences of scenic light/dark
imagery and of vertical spatial imagery in Adam's vision
of humanity's future. Here, in Book XI and also in XII,
time becomes the main dimension. But throughout the
entire poem time is important in the design—particularly

30. Kester Svendsen, *Milton and Science* (Cambridge, Mass., Harvard University Press, 1956).

31. By R. H. Syfret in *RES,* n.s. *9* (1958), 324.

32. *Metaphoric Structure,* p. 147.

33. *PL,* XII.643–44.

34. *Milton and Science,* pp. 106–07.

in the careful preparation for the accounts of the war in heaven and of the creation. Professor Colie has illuminated that obvious though neglected fact in her discussion of the action and structure of the poem as exemplifying "divine metaphysical truth (i.e. God's foreknowledge and providence in and from eternity)."[35] Her study of the most conspicuous of the figures in Milton's carpet—his means "to assert Eternal Providence"[36]—came surprisingly late in an age of space/time equation. More esoteric explorations of Milton's time patterns than hers have since come fast in Professor Cope's observations[37] on the noon/midnight polarity of events like Satan's revolt at midnight in Book V and Eve's fall at noon in Book IX, and Professor Cirillo's brilliant exploration of Milton's "double time scheme whereby events that are being expressed in temporal terms—in sequential action—are simultaneously occurring in the eternal present which is the central setting of the poem."[38] Metaphors of time as well as space now interplay with those of light and dark to establish a complex unity. There is no straining of the internal evidence by either Professors Cope or Cirillo, and there is no distortion of the scriptural and patristic passages on the meridian demon[39] which are behind Milton's timing of crucial events. They fall into their proper perspective behind the peaks of his epiphanies of light, one of which, the opening lines of the invocation of light in Book III, has recently come to be regarded by several of his best interpreters as, in the full sense of the word, a theophany.

If *Paradise Lost* achieves a theophany, its clearest peak of manifestation for most readers is the proem to Book III.

35. Rosalie L. Colie, "Time and Eternity: Paradox and Structure in *Paradise Lost*," *JWCI, 13* (1960), 138.

36. *PL,* I.25.

37. *Metaphoric Structure,* pp. 130–41.

38. Albert R. Cirillo, "Noon-Midnight and the Temporal Structure of *Paradise Lost*," *ELH, 29* (1962), 373.

39. Psalms 91:6.

Yet the early editors were blind to it and its perception has been a work of time. Bishop Newton echoed Addison's fear that "Our author's address to light, and lamentation of his own blindness, may perhaps be censur'd as an excrescence or digression not agreeable to the rules of epic poetry."[40] It could be defensible only for its "many beauties" and because "it acquaints us so much with the circumstances and character of the author." Even for Masson, whose note on the proem in 1874 recognized it as marking the emergence of the action from Hell's darkness to Heaven's brilliance, its "peculiar interest" was as "Milton's grand lamentation on his blindness." Only recently have better defenses for the proem been found than admiration for its beauties and sympathy for the blind poet "from the cheerful ways of men / Cut off," sitting in the "ever-during dark" where there could be no return of

> Day, or the sweet approach of Ev'n or Morn
> Or sight of vernal bloom, or Summer's Rose,
> Or flocks, or herds, or human face divine.

[III.41–43]

But now defense of the grand lamentation is confident, sophisticated, many-sided, and invulnerable to any attack except the personal aesthetic condemnation of "the famous opening of Book III" by Mr. Leavis[41] as a capital example of the monotony and insensitivity of Milton's verse. The defense is sophisticated because it depersonalizes the poet's voice. On the basis of style the proem to Book III has been marked by Professor Stein as a perfect example of the impersonal epic vioce speaking "because the poet is there, performing the office of his mystery and being absorbed

40. Newton's note on the first line of Book III in his Variorum Edition (1749) was repeated verbatim in Todd's Variorum (1801) and remained unchanged in its fourth and last revision (1842).

41. F. R. Leavis on "Milton's Verse," in *Revaluation* (London, Chatto and Windus, 1936), pp. 43–44.

into his part of it."[42] He is not concerned with himself
personally even on the high heroic level of the two sonnets
on his blindness. But it took over half a century for Masson's observation that the proem floodlights a great structural bridge in *Paradise Lost*[43] to develop into Tillyard's
recognition that the proems of Books I, III, VII, and IX
were not excrescent but were rather "clear marks of the
stages of the story, indications of the shifting point of
view."[44] From Tillyard's vantage-ground Professor Diekhoff went on to recognize the serious rhetorical function of
all four prologues as "ethical" appeals in the Aristotelian
sense,[45] like the openings of the tracts where Milton seeks
the approval of his readers for himself and for his themes.
In *Paradise Lost* (as Professor Daiches also says of the proem
to Book I), the function of the invocations is that "of estab-
lishing his status as a poet inspired by God."[46] They are
all essentially true prayers for illumination of "the public
defender of Providence" in the conduct of the "great argument" of the poem.

Of the four prologues the invocation in Book III is a
simple prayer for inspiration. In the last of them (Book IX),
the answer to the prayer seems long since to have become
secure in the established experience of the "nightly visita-
tion" of a "Celestial Patroness" who is hardly distinguishable from the "Celestial light" of Milton's earlier prayer to

> Shine inward, and the mind through all her powers
> Irradiate, there plant eyes, all mist from thence

42. Arnold Stein, *Answerable Style* (Minneapolis, University of Minnesota
Press, 1953), p. 134.

43. David Masson in his first note on Book III in his edition of *The Poetical
Works of John Milton* (3 vols. London, Macmillan, 1890).

44. Tillyard, *Milton,* p. 246.

45. John S. Diekhoff, "The Function of the Prologues in *Paradise Lost,*"
PMLA, 57 (1942), 697–704. Cf. his *"Paradise Lost"* . . . *The Argument,* pp. 17–18.

46. David Daiches in *The Living Milton,* ed. Frank Kermode (London, Routledge and Paul, 1960), pp. 63, 65.

Purge and disperse, that I may see and tell
Of things invisible to mortal sight.   [III.51–55]

To give a personal or theological name to the "Celestial light" is difficult, even though it seems to be explicitly identified with the Spirit that prefers "Before all Temples th'upright heart and pure" (I.18), and to be the same spirit that brooded "on the vast Abyss" at creation and made it "pregnant." But the seemingly obvious course of identifying Milton's Muse with the Holy Spirit is closed because, as Professor Kelley points out,[47] in *De Doctrina Christiana*[48] he explicitly withheld sanction of any invocation of the Holy Spirit.

Before any theological points are made about Milton's "Celestial light" Professor Chambers[49] suggests that his thought about that perhaps significantly uncapitalized "light" depends upon the lines (40–50) which are usually read as a personal digression with slight bearing upon what follows them—the lines on his blindness to the changes from night to day and from season to season, and to "flocks, or herds, or human face divine." Sympathy for the blind poet has made the passage seem simply autobiographical —a lovely and legitimate private digression. But at a time when the "Book of Nature" was familiarly regarded as

47. Maurice Kelley, *This Great Argument* (Princeton, the University Press, 1941), pp. 109 ff.

48. CE, *14*, 392–94. Still more to the purpose is Kelley's discussion of Milton's explicitly differing uses of the word "spirit." Debate about it goes back beyond St. Augustine's identification of the spirit which moved upon the face of the waters in Genesis 1:2 with the Holy Spirit who purges men of the uncleanness of their spirits. Most Renaissance Neoplatonists inclined to Pico's view in his *Heptaplus* I.1 (Pico della Mirandola, *De hominis dignitate, Heptaplus, De ente et uno*, ed. Eugenio Garin, Florence, Vallecchi, 1942, pp. 210–12) that the "Spirit of God" in Genesis 1:2 signified the organ of the divine working skill (artist) in the way that the human spirit is the organ of the human soul.

49. A. B. Chambers, "Wisdom at One Entrance Quite Shut Out," *PQ, 42* (1963), 114–19. For a different but no less valid critical purpose Arnold Stein links these passages of Plato and Aristotle with *PL*, III.37 ff. in *Answerable Style*, p. 152.

one of God's lesser epiphanies, Chambers points out that men thought of sight as the sense which "best helps us to know things," as Aristotle called it at the very beginning of the *Metaphysics*. But Aristotle had been anticipated in a Platonic passage where Chambers finds a striking verbal resemblance to *Paradise Lost* (III.41–43), in the reflection that our "sight of day and night, of months and revolving years, of equinox and solstice, has caused the invention of number and bestowed on us the notion of time and the study of nature and the world; whence we have derived all philosophy. . . . For the god invented and gave us vision in order that we might observe the circuits of intelligence in the heaven and . . . reproduce the perfectly unerring revolutions of the god and reduce to settled order the wandering motions in ourselves."[50]

Cut off from God's physical epiphany in the Book of Nature, the poet's only hope of divine illumination must be that of the poets and seers who were stricken blind in antiquity:

> Blind *Thamyris* and blind *Maeonides,*
> And *Tiresias* and *Phineus* Prophets old.
>
> [III.35–36]

Professor Allen[51] has opened the Christian background of Milton's parallel of his own case to those of Homer and the rest. To the Christian humanist they were the first to tread the way which led to the light-metaphysic of the Pseudo-Dionysius and on to St. Bonaventura's discovery that "to see, one must become blind: *Excaecatio est summa illumi-natio.*" Allen's study is one of the essential keys to the dark/light imagery of *Paradise Lost.* In the proem to Book III it opens the door between the visible world of nature from which Tiresias was cut off when he beheld Pallas

50. *Timaeus* 47a-c.

51. Don Cameron Allen, "Milton and the Descent to Light," *JEGP, 60* (1961), 626–27.

naked and the life of prophetic vision which the goddess granted him in compensation for his blindness. Such is the form given to the myth in Callimachus' *Hymn for the Bath of Pallas*.

By a Renaissance Neoplatonist like Pico della Miran-dola, Callimachus' Pallas Athene was easily treated as an emblem of the meaning of the Uranian Aphrodite or Heavenly Venus of Plato's *Symposium* (180e). In Pico's Com-mentary on Benivieni's *Canzone d'Amore*[52] Aphrodite Urania (in contrast to Aphrodite Pandemos, the goddess of vulgar passion) is Plato's heavenly goddess whose love is "precious both for public and private life" (185c). For Pico it was natural to treat the Uranian Aphrodite and Pallas Athene as equally established emblems of the heavenly beauty and wisdom which were revealed impartially to Homer and to St. Paul in visions which cost them their physical sight.

The Neoplatonic element in the proems to *Paradise Lost* is easily exaggerated or minimized, according to a reader's predilections. It cannot be dismissed on the ground that Milton invokes a "Heav'nly Muse" who is to carry him up to regions far higher than Mount Helicon,[53] or that he prefers to call her "Celestial light"[54] and his "Celestial Patroness,"[55] or that when once he names her it is only to ask her doubtfully whether he may call her Urania and then instantly declare that he is invoking "The meaning, not the Name":

> for thou
> Nor of the Muses nine, nor on the top
> Of old *Olympus* dwell'st, but Heav'nly born,
> Before the Hills appear'd, or Fountain flow'd,
> Thou with Eternal Wisdom didst converse,

52. Book II, chap. 25.
53. The "Aonian Mount" of *Paradise Lost*, I.15.
54. *PL*, III.51.
55. Ibid., IX.21.

Wisdom thy Sister, and with her didst play
In presence of th'Almighty Father, pleas'd
With thy Celestial Song.   [VII.5–12]

The Urania of this passage is surely not the simple
patroness of the science of astronomy in the Greek tradition, however that science may have been charged with
philosophical and theological implications by Plato in the
Timaeus. But it is equally clear that Milton's Urania is not
simply the Christianized Muse whom Professor Campbell
has traced in the English and Scottish translations and
imitations of Du Bartas' *La Muse Chrestiene.*[56] By far the
most famous of the poems to be influenced by Du Bartas'
Muse is Spenser's *An Hymne of Heavenly Beautie,* which,
however, Miss Campbell regards as deriving its central
figure, Wisdom or Sapience, from Marsilio Ficino's Commentary on Plato's *Symposium.*

The Sapience of Spenser's *Hymne,* "The soveraine dear-
ling of the Deity" (line 183), is not fundamentally a Christianized Pallas Athene. Most obviously she is the Wisdom
which Solomon quoted as saying that before the creation
she was with God "as one brought up with him, . . . was
daily his delight, playing always before him,"[57] and so she
understood "how the world was made."[58] Spenser's Sapience is clearly in the Hebrew-Christian tradition. Yet, as
Professor Osgood's variorum notes on *An Hymne of Heavenly
Beautie*[59] make abundantly clear, her Christian avatar is
also Neoplatonic and helps to explain the appearance of
Wisdom as the sister of Urania in *Paradise Lost* (VII.10).
They seem like twin daughters of God, for, says Milton,

56. Lily Bess Campbell, *Divine Poetry and Drama in Sixteenth Century England*
(Cambridge and Berkeley, 1959), pp. 75–80, 97–99.
57. Proverbs 8:30.
58. Wisdom of Solomon 7.
59. *The Works of Edmund Spenser: The Minor Poems,* ed. Edwin Greenlaw, Charles
Grosvenor Osgood, Frederick Morgan Padelford, Ray Heffner (2 vols. Baltimore,
Johns Hopkins Press, 1943), *1,* 548–70.

they both played "In presence of th'Almighty Father"[60] before the world was made.

Spenser's Sapience shares her mixed Biblical and Neoplatonic nature with the Wisdom who appears in the proem of Book VII of *Paradise Lost* as a sister of Milton's Urania. There he makes the sisters seem like identical twins. Using Osgood's notes on Spenser's Sapience as a clue to a theological identification of the Voice which Milton hesitantly calls Urania, Professor Hunter[61] proposes to identify Milton's Urania-Wisdom of Book VII with the "Spirit" whom he invokes in Book I.17, and with the "Celestial light" of Book III and the "Celestial Patroness" of Book IX by identifying all of them with the Son of God. Hunter adopts Osgood's ambivalent treatment of Spenser's Sapience as an eclectic figure in some ways suggesting the Holy Spirit and in others the Son of God as the Son was understood and symbolized by several Greek Fathers of the Church. Discussion of their symbolism must be deferred. Here it is important to notice that Osgood rounded out his theological background for Spenser's Sapience by quoting from Saurat's identification of her with the creative Wisdom of the Cabbalists, the Shekhina, and from Jefferson B. Fletcher's overconfident identification of her with the third Person of the Christian Trinity as it was conceived by the Greek Fathers Theophilus of Antioch and Saint Gregory Thaumaturgos. Writing under the influence of Philo Judaeus, they conceived the second and third Persons in their Trinity, the Son or Logos and the Holy Spirit or Sapientia, as emanating involuntarily from the absolute, nameless deities of both Hebrew and Neoplatonic tradition.

Like all Neoplatonic versions of the "trinity" of the

60. *PL,* VII.11.
61. William B. Hunter, "Milton's Urania, Some More Heresies," *Studies in English Literature, 4* (1964), 38–39.

Timaeus (the unnamed Deity, the creating Demiurge, and the created Soul of the world[62]), the early Patristic trinities tended to be emanational and were rather unsatisfactory in their naming of the subordinate second and third Persons. In a passage to which J. W. Bennett has drawn attention, and which Osgood quotes from Pico della Mirandola's *Commentary* (I.4.5) on Benivieni's *Canzone d'Amore,* the Neoplatonic Sapience of the Fathers is carefully distinguished from both the Holy Ghost and the second Person in the Christian Trinity. For Pico the Son is "in everything equal, creator and not creature," not emanative from or subordinate to the Father. Presumably Pico was even better aware than Milton was of the heresy latent in the Neoplatonic trinities and in their Christian derivatives which treated the second Person, the Nous or Logos or Son, as an emanation existing first within the unknowable Father and later emerging as a subordinate creative spirit endued with the virtue and power of the absolute Being. In the Sapience of *An Hymne of Heavenly Beautie* it is impossible not to recognize resemblances to the Neoplatonic Nous or Logos and to the third person, the world soul (psyche) of the *Timaeus,* the rational ruler of Plato's cosmos, which reappeared as Sapience or Wisdom in some patristic versions of the orthodox Trinity.

With the confused biblical and Neoplatonic background of the noncommittal theology of the *Hymne* in mind, Osgood has balanced the evidence for identifying Spenser's Sapience with either the Son of God or the Holy Spirit against her simple identification with the Platonic Heavenly Beauty which is the subject of the *Hymne.* His con-

---

62. Or—as in the first Neoplatonic version fusing Neoplatonic with Hebrew thought, that of Philo—the unknowable God, who is both a Hebrew and Platonic conception; the Logos or Mind of God, which exists first within him as a universe of ideas; and later as an emanation from Him which becomes "the Author of this ordered frame," the visible universe.

clusion is the modest one that final proof is impossible
and that, as for Spenser's intention, "he did not care."[63]
But now in a probable non-Christian influence upon
Spenser's *Hymne* (the *Dialoghi d'Amore* of Pico's acquaintance, the expatriate Spanish Jew, Leone Ebreo), Professor
Ellrodt finds what may be interpreted as strong support
for Osgood's hesitant identification of Spenser's Sapience
with the second Person of the Trinity. In the Godhead of
his *Dialogues,* though any distinction of persons is denied,
Leone invited "a Christian interpretation"[64] by imper-
sonally distinguishing the wise (il sapiente) and the beautiful (il bello) from wisdom (la sapientia) and beauty (la
bellezza). The supremely wise, beautiful deity is made
one with the wisdom and beauty of his essence by love,
which is also a part of His trinal nature. Filone, Leone's
voice in the third Dialogue, explains that the pure, divine
unity is in no sense divided in any way. In perfect simplicity
it contains the nature of a beloved (amato), of a lover
(amante), and of the love that unites them, just as the sun
contains the essences of the various lights and colors in its
simple and supreme brightness.[65]

In so short a summary of the long dialogue there may
seem to be no justification for Ellrodt's view that any
Christian poet, reading Leone's work, "would be inclined
to identify Leone's 'sapience' and 'beauty' with the second
Person of the Christian Trinity." His best evidence that
Spenser had both read Leone and made that identification
is the several close correspondences between the texts from
Canticles, Proverbs, and the Book of Wisdom which Spen-

63. *Minor Poems, 1,* 561. Going further with doubt of any possible final proof
in *The Poetry of Edmund Spenser* (New York, Columbia University Press, 1963),
pp. 114–15, William Nelson finds Spenser deliberately unspecific about his
Sapience because he thought of her simply as possessing "all the Wealth and
Wisdom of which the world's riches and knowledge are only a token."

64. Robert Ellrodt, *Neoplatonism in the Poetry of Spenser* (Geneva, Droz, 1960),
pp. 190–91.

65. Leone Ebreo, *Dialoghi d'Amore,* p. 255.

ser applied to Sapience in the *Hymne,* and which are similarly applied to the Sapience of Leone's *Dialogues.* Ellrodt sees Spenser as probably deliberately Christianizing Leone's thought by identifying the beloved (l'amato) of the *Dialogues* with God the Son, and at the same time as identifying the Son with "the 'sapientia amata' that Leone discerned in God."

In Ellrodt's theory of Leone's influence upon Spenser's Sapience there are other features which may encourage Hunter's recourse to Spenser's figure in order to explain the mixed biblical and Neoplatonic origin of the Wisdom of the proem to Book VII of *Paradise Lost* as the twin of Milton's Urania. The close association of the sisters is as vital to Hunter's theory of the meaning of Milton's Muse as is the identification of the Wisdom of Proverbs and the Book of Wisdom with the Son of God in the Christian Trinity. Indeed, though he declares that it "is not clear exactly how the sisters Urania and Wisdom are to be interpreted," he suggests that Milton "may be using 'sister' as a metaphor for self-identity: the Greek Heavenly Beauty is the sister of the Greek Wisdom in that both had been used to express the Second Person of the Trinity in two different cultures." In Pico della Mirandola's Commentary on Benivieni's *Canzone d'Amore* we have a hardly less striking collocation of figures representative of the two cultures. Homer and St. Paul are brought together as having shared a common poetic and prophetic vision of the heavenly love and beauty symbolized by Athene in Callimachus' *Hymn for the Bath of Pallas.*

Far in the background of Pico's allegory is a passage in Plato's *Cratylus* (407b) where—as Hunter recalls—Homer is said to have represented Athene as mind (nous) or intellect (dianoia). Socrates then half-seriously suggests that the true etymological meaning of her name is "the mind of God." Picking up this suggestion, Hunter regards this title "as exactly comparable to the title of Mind or Intellect which had been the interpretation of Aphrodite Urania." And then by adding that "in a quite literal way the two goddesses are sisters, for both were born from Zeus and neither had a mother,"[66] he confirms the aptness of Milton's metaphor to reduce them to simple identity. And to cap his demonstration of their oneness Hunter quotes Cudworth's saying that "God was also called Athena or Minerva, as wisdom diffusing itself through all things; and Aphrodite Urania, the heavenly Venus or love."[67]

Ellrodt's exploration of Leone's *Dialogues* was limited by his Spenserian interest. In the context of the passages on Wisdom which he quotes, however, there is a rabbinical interpretation of the opening words of Genesis—"In the beginning God created the heaven and the earth"—which beautifully confirms Hunter's view of Wisdom and her "sister" Urania in Milton's proems. A part of the Mosaic lore expounded by Leone is an interpretation of the "beginning" as meaning wisdom, the supreme wisdom which is also the primal beauty, and is to be identified with the creative, world-ruling Wisdom of Solomon's Proverbs.[68] So—presumably—the Wisdom of Moses was in Milton's mind when in asking for illumination from the "Heav'nly Muse" he declared:

66. In "Milton's Urania"; p. 38.

67. Ralph Cudworth, *The True Intellectual System of the Universe,* ed. J. Harrison (3 vols. London, Thomas Tegg, 1845), 2, 279.

68. Filone is speaking: "Le prime parole che Moise scrisse furono: 'In principio creò Dio il cielo e la terra'; e l'antica interpretazione caldea disse, onde noi diciamo in principio, 'con sapienza creò Dio il cielo e la terra': e perché la sapienza si dice in ebraico principio (come disse Salamone), principio è sapienza, e la dizione in può dire cum. Mira come [per] la prima cosa ne mostra che 'l mondo fu creato per sapienza e che la sapienza fu il primo principio creante, ma che 'l sommo Dio Creatore mediante la sua somma sapienza, prima bellezza, creò e fece bello tutto l'universo creato: si che li primi vocabuli del sapiente Moise ne denotarono li tre gradi del bello, Dio sapienza e mondo. E il sapientissimo re Salamone, come seguace e discepulo del divino Moise, dichiara questa sua prima sentenza ne li *Proverbi* discendo: 'Il Signor con sapienza fondò la terra, compose li cieli con somma scienzia; col suo intelletto l'abissi fúrno rotti e li cieli stillano la rosata'." *Dialoghi d'Amore, pp.* 351–52.

Thou from the first
Wast present, and with mighty wings outspread
Dove-like satst brooding on the vast Abyss
And mad'st it pregnant: What in me is dark
Illumine. . . .   [I.19–23]

There is, of course, no reason to suppose that Milton
had read Leone, but—as Professor Williams has noted—
he may have found Leone's interpretation of "the beginning" in several early hexameral commentaries on the Ara-
maic version of Genesis in the Targum Jerusalem. There
"in wisdom" is the translation of the Hebrew phrase which
the King James Bible renders as "In the beginning." Williams adds that some commentators linked the Targum
rendering with Proverbs 8:27: "When he prepared the
heavens, I was there." And Williams hazards the guess
that it was "probably natural that the speaker in Proverbs
should be understood [by Christian interpreters], not as
Wisdom, but as the Word of John 1:1: that is Christ."[69]

In general, there is good reason for assuming that Milton would have had an even greater interest in rabbinical
lore than he had in classical mythology as supplementing
or at least paralleling (though often distorting) the ultimate
truths which a Christian epic must present. Professor
Fletcher was the first to establish the rabbinical interest
as a fact, and by his analysis of Ben Gerson's commentary
on Proverbs to anticipate Hunter's conviction that in all
of the proems of *Paradise Lost* the same Person is invoked.[70]
His identification of that Person as the third Person of the
Trinity is set aside by Hunter on the basis of Milton's
assertion in the *Christian Doctrine* that the Holy Spirit is
not to be invoked.[71] Yet in a study of "The Holy Spirit

69. Arnold Williams, *The Common Expositor* (Chapel Hill, University of North
Carolina Press, 1948), p. 40.
70. Harris Francis Fletcher, *Milton's Rabbinical Readings* (Urbana, University of
Illinois Press, 1930), pp. 109–20.
71. Cf. n. 47, above.

and the Preëxistent Christ"[72] Professor Wolfson has drawn
upon a much broader range of rabbinical literature for
evidence of two kinds to which both Fletcher and Hunter
might appeal. There is encouragement for Hunter's identification of the traditional figure of Wisdom with Christ, or
the Logos of St. John's Gospel, in Wolfson's opening demonstration that St. Paul and several patristic writers identified Christ the Logos with the promised Messiah of the
Old Testament who was associated in rabbinical literature
with the hidden Wisdom of God. Hunter's case is strength-
ened if the Messiah is recognized as an aspect of the biblical Wisdom who is twinned with Urania in the proem
to Book VII of *Paradise Lost.* But there is specious support
for Fletcher's view in Wolfson's concluding account of the
identification or confusion of the pre-existent wisdom and
Messiah with the "Spirit of the Lord" and the "Holy
Spirit" in Wisdom 1:4–7, 7:24, 9:10, and 17. In those passages there is ground for the thesis which Wolfson advances in his following chapter on "The Holy Spirit as
the Begetter of Jesus."

If we now turn with Professor Daiches to Milton's chapter on the Holy Spirit in the *Christian Doctrine,* we find
Milton interpreting the word "spirit" in the Bible as sometimes signifying God the Father Himself (Genesis 6:3),
sometimes as signifying "that light which was shed on
Christ himself," as in the prophecy that "the Spirit of
Jehovah shall rest upon him, the Spirit of wisdom and
understanding . . ." (Isaiah 11:2), sometimes as meaning
the Son of God through whom the Father has created all
things—the meaning which Milton expressly says is to be
seen in Genesis 1:2: "The Spirit of God moved upon the face
of the waters." Of all the meanings of the words "spirit"
and "Holy Spirit" which Milton quoted from Scripture in

---

72. Harry A. Wolfson, *The Philosophy of the Church Fathers* (Cambridge, Mass.,
1956), pp. 155–67.

the *Christian Doctrine,* Daiches is surely right in thinking that the most relevant to the proem of the first Book of *Paradise Lost* is "that impulse or voice of God by which the prophets were inspired."[73] In the light of the *Christian Doctrine* (I.6), it hardly seems justifiable to insist that in a strict theological sense Milton was consciously praying in the proem of Book I for the afflation of the Son of God as something to be distinguished from "that light which was shed on Christ himself" and upon Moses and the prophets.

Similarly, a lay reader may be forgiven if he doubts whether in all his proems Milton was consciously appealing to the inspiring Voice of God strictly conceived as the two-stage Logos whose emergence from rabbinical sources into Philo's thinking, and whose development in the early Patristic conceptions of the Trinity, Wolfson traces in later chapters. Hunter draws upon these extensively, though he does not mention those on the pre-existent Messiah and on the Holy Spirit as the begetter of Jesus. But before considering the evidence for such a conception of the Son in the opening lines of Book III, where Hunter, especially, finds evidence for it, we must look briefly at two other unrelated dogmatic interpretations of the meaning of "light" in the proem to Book III.

The first of the two dogmatic theories to be considered lies on the borderline between theological interpretations of the second Person of the Trinity with which Milton was certainly familiar and the Christology of Robert Fludd's pseudo-scientific theory of the nature of light, which the late Professor Saurat thought that Milton took rather seriously just as he found it in Fludd's chaotically eclectic cosmographical works.[74] On various other grounds to which Saurat drew attention, it seems certain that Mr. Broadbent

73. Daiches, "The Opening of *Paradise Lost,*" in *The Living Milton,* p. 64.
74. Saurat, *Milton: Man and Thinker,* pp. 262–64.

is right in assuming Milton's interest in Fludd as a "speculative theologian."[75] Saurat was intensely interested in Fludd's theory of inchoate primary matter as (1) a part of God, who is the material as well as the efficient and the final cause of all things, (2) as being in its real nature light of various kinds, the grossest of which is the aboriginal fire from which the Stoics derived the other mundane elements, and (3) as existing in three phases: (a) uncreated and invisible in God the supreme Creator, (b) illuminant and procreant in the Son, and (c) ardent in the Holy Spirit.[76] Reasoning from Fludd's treatment of the Trinity as an aspect of his materialistic and pantheistic theory of light, Saurat assumed that in the opening line of the third book of *Paradise Lost*

> "Offspring of Heav'n first-born" is certainly a designation of the Son, from whom all things are made, and therefore of the divine matter out of which they are made. So Milton seems to adopt the Fluddian theory of light as a *materia prima,* at least poetically, for the moment. And he emphasizes the point by adding "since God is light." And we know that all things are of God. "Offspring of Heav'n first-born" goes well with "ab ea increata creatam," but Milton adds at once: "Or of th'Eternal Coeternal beam," which recalls "vel increatam lucem": "Bright effluence of bright essence increate." And Milton hesitates and goes back to "pure Etherial stream, Whose fountain who shall tell?"[77]

75. J. B. Broadbent, *Some Graver Subject* (London, Chatto and Windus, 1960), p. 141.

76. Writing in *Milton et le matérialisme chrétien en Angleterre* (Paris, Rieder, 1928), p. 72, Saurat quoted Fludd's *De Macrocosmi Historia* (1617), I.1, as follows: "Concludimus igitur, lucem esse vel increatam, scilicet Deum omnia naturantem, (nam in ipso Deo Patri est vera lux, deinde in Filio ejus illustrans splendor et uberans et in Spirito Sancto ardens fulgor) vel ab ea increata creatam."

77. *Milton: Man and Thinker,* pp. 262–63.

A main flaw in this reasoning, which Saurat candidly recognizes, is the fact that Milton "was quite definitely committed to the doctrine that the Son was not co-eternal," but an equally serious flaw which Saurat overlooked is Milton's repeated assertion in the *Christian Doctrine*[78] that, in the words of John (1:3) and of the writer of Hebrews (1:2), it was *by* (not *from*) the Word (Logos) or Son that God made the worlds. Nor did it occur to Saurat that what Milton actually had in mind was the whole light-metaphysics tradition which Mazzeo traces[79] to Augustine's distinction between uncreated light, the light which is born of God and is his Wisdom, and all created light either incorporeal or corporeal.[80] God is the supreme uncreated light of which Wisdom is born, but there was never a time when God's Wisdom did not exist. Augustine's conception was anti-materialistic, for he was bitterly opposed to the materialism of the Manichees. Creation, for him, was the miracle of the making of the created lights and of the visible universe whose illumination and nutrition was their work. To Milton's readers (many of whom were familiar enough with the light-metaphysical tradition to identify Wisdom with the second Person of the Trinity), his opening questions about the naming of the eternal-coeternal beam would be much less likely to recall Fludd's theories than to awaken memories of Augustine's passage and the many discussions of it by orthodox Christian writers.

78. CE, *14*, 180–82.

79. Mazzeo, *Medieval Cultural Tradition in Dante's* COMEDY, pp. 60, 220–21.

80. In *De Genesi ad litteram imperfectus liber*, 5.20, Augustine distinguishes between the created lights which are either intelligible (found only in the consciousness of creatures or physically visible to them) and the uncreated lights, one of which is identifiable with God himself while the other is His offspring: "Dei Sapientia . . . non creata est, sed nata; nec sine luce Deus fuisse putetur priusquam istam, de qua nunc agitur, condidisset . . . Alia est lux, de Deo nata, et alia lux quam fecit Deus: nata de Deo lux, est ipsa Dei Sapientia; facta vero lux est qualibet mutabilis sive corporea sive incorporea." *Patrologia Latina, 34*, col. 228.

Aware of the improbability of anything like reflection of Fludd's ideas *as Fludd's* in Milton's proem, Saurat conveniently assumed that he "obviously did not care to contradict Fludd on the subject of light, and as he does not make a particular point of light being the *materia prima,* he let Fludd have it his own way." But it is most likely that, even if Milton for a moment thought of Fludd's pantheistic light-theology, his interest would not have been in its materialistic metaphysic, but in Fludd's constant justification of it by appeals to Pythagoras and the Zoroastrians and to the many Neoplatonic writers, both pagan and Christian, whose thinking finally went back to Plato's great metaphor of the Good as the sun of the intelligible world. In the long run Augustine's thought stemmed from that metaphor. Debate about the theological implications of the Christian assertion that "God is light" (I John 1:5), which Augustine took literally, though in no physical sense, had been going on in Augustinian terms for over a thousand years before Milton was born. Fludd was naïve enough to reduce the metaphor to a scientific dogma which (with the help of some of his schematic illustrations) his readers might visualize.

Though Milton's acquaintance with Fludd can hardly be taken for granted on Saurat's ground that "every educated man of the time knew Fludd,"[81] it must be conceded that the appearance of Gassendi's polite volume refuting his philosophy in Paris in 1630–31 must have encouraged a sense of his importance in England, however much they hurt his reputation with critical scientific thinkers all over Europe. But in spite of his following among readers of greater philosophic curiosity than knowledge, there is no real evidence that Milton regarded him as anything better than one of "the more discreetly fantasti-

81. *Milton: Man and Thinker,* pp. 261, 248.

cal"[82] of the tongue-wagging English theosophists—as Henry More called him. His main expositions of his theory of light as a divine primary substance run through his repetitious folios—*Utriusque Cosmi Historia* (2 volumes, 1617 and 1623), *Philosophia Sacra* (1623), and *Mosaical Philosophy* (posthumously published in 1659). Their figures of a geocentric universe were supplemented with drawings illustrating his essentially traditional conception of the four mundane elements lying stratified under a beaming sun in the ethereal heaven. Above it the empyrean heaven stretched up to the foot of God's throne. For convincing proof of his cosmic views, however, Fludd relied heavily upon ancient, medieval, and contemporary writers. Among them the "platonicks" were prominent. Commentators on *De Augmentis Scientiarum* have thought that Bacon had Fludd in mind when he said that premature conclusions in mathematics and physics had led some "Platonists to treat light superstitiously, as if it were something half way between things divine and things natural."[83]

Fludd's works are not a key to the proem of *Paradise Lost,* III. His diagram featuring the sun as the seat of Divine Light in a precisely bounded ethereal heaven may help a modern reader with Miltonic images like the sun's "Lordly eye" (III.578) and with Adam's apostrophe: "Thou Sun, of this great World both Eye and Soul" (V.171). But Fludd's medieval Hell conceived as Satan's lair at

82. In *Milton and the Angels* (Athens, University of Georgia Press, 1955), p. 37, Robert H. West quotes More's words from *The Second Lash of Alazonomastix* (London, 1655), p. 204.

83. "Tractatio autem de Luce et causis ejus in Physicis rursus superstitiosa fere est, tanquam de re inter divina et naturalia media; adeo ut quidam ex Platonicis eam Materia ipsa antiquiorem introduxerint: cum enim spatium esset difflatum, id primum lumine, postea vero corpore impletum fuisse, vanissimo commento asseruerunt; quando tamen Scripturae Sacrae massam coeli et terrae tenebrosam, ante lucem creatam, diserte posuerint." *The Works of Francis Bacon,* ed. James Spedding, R. L. Ellis, and D. D. Heath (15 vols. New York, Hurd and Houghton, 1869), *2,* 356.

the earth's center is far remote in space and in spirit from
Milton's Hell in the depth of Chaos. Though—as Professor Duncan points out[84]—several passages in *Paradise
Lost* are consistent with Fludd's essentially Stoic theory of
light or fire as the prime creative substance or power, such
scattered resemblances to the notions of an eclectic writer
fall far short of proof that Milton was his disciple. As a
gloss to the theology of the poem, Fludd's works can hardly
be taken more seriously than they can as a gloss to its
metaphysics. Saurat's assumption that Milton's unorthodox
conception of the Son of God was specifically Fluddian,
and was definitely in Milton's mind when he wrote the
proem to Book III, cannot stand up against the fact, as
quoted by Professor Dickson, that "Milton's metaphors of
light for Divinity inevitably reflect the thought as well as
the phraseology of the orthodox past, and all his labori-
ous . . . rejections of Trinitarianism in the explicit prose
of the *Doctrine* remain less memorable than the poetic
figures of his epic, which are his hostages, willynilly, to
Christianity."[85]

These words are a reminder that the proem to Book III
is fabricated of metaphors which Neoplatonizing theologians had developed from the image "God is light" (I
John 1:5) and from the image of Christ the Word, the
Logos, who was with God "in the beginning," as "the
light of men" (in the Gospel according to John 1:1–4).
Fludd treated such statements literally and took the Jo-
hannine figure of God as light in a pseudo-scientific sense
which was literal in a way very different from Augustine's
when he declared God to be *vera lux*. Naïve literal interpretation of Milton's proem led Saurat to misunderstand

---

84. Edgar H. Duncan, "The Natural History of Metals and Minerals in the
Universe of Milton's *Paradise Lost*," *Osiris, 11* (1954), 416.

85. David W. D. Dickson, *Milton's Son of God: A Study in Imagery and Orthodoxy,* Papers of the Michigan Academy of Science, Arts, and Letters, 36 (1950),
281.

its metaphors, of all of which light is the vehicle while the tenor is God—understood simply or variously as one or another of the Persons of the Trinity.[86] If the metaphors are taken literally, tenor and vehicle are confused. Then the "holy Light" of the first line of the proem is mistaken for the Person of the Trinity who seems to the reader to be described as "offspring of Heav'n first-born." Because the light is called "holy," its divine character is assumed, and the reader ignores Professor Kelley's belief that here light is invoked in the physical sense that is unquestionably implied for it in lines 8–12 and 21–24 below. He also ignores the fact that Milton is saluting the physical light whose "sacred influence" (*Paradise Lost*, II.1034) Satan has just seen for the first time as—with Milton and with the action of the story—he has just emerged from Hell's darkness into that visible light. Milton is using the classical epithet as he does again when he speaks of the shining of the "sacred Morn" (*Paradise Lost*, VI.748) on the third day of the battle in heaven and of the dawning of "sacred Light" (IX.192) on the morning of Eve's temptation. The light was holy to the blind poet with the poignancy that it was holy to Sophocles' Antigone when she took her last leave of the bright day.[87] But before Sophocles light had been sacred in the language of drama and epic.

Milton was also following classical tradition when he invoked the light in the fear that he might not be "unblamed" when he hazarded its description as co-eternal with "th'Eternal" and as an "Etherial stream" from an ineffable fountain. From Bentley to Verity, all commentators on *Paradise Lost* compared the second of those questions with Horace's salutation to the opener of heaven's

86. On Saurat's confident and Sewell's wavering interpretation of the Light of the poem as the second Person of the Trinity, see Kelley, *This Great Argument,* pp. 92–94.

87. *Antigone* 878–80.

gates, the god Janus: "Morning father, or dost thou prefer
to be called Janus?"[88] But still more striking is Milton's
use of this figure of speech[89] in his proem to Book VII,
where Urania is asked whether she will accept that name
as rightly given to the Voice whose inspiration he is seeking. Milton is making a solemn inquiry of the kind that
Socrates makes in playful earnest about the meaning and
justification of the names of the gods in the *Cratylus*.[90]

The tradition at work in the poet's mind went beyond
the mere recollection of Horace's offer of a choice of titles
to a minor deity. His schooldays had made him familiar
with many titles for the god of light, whose darting solar
rays entitled him to Homer's name of the far-darter or
worker from afar, and to Herodotus' name for him, Loxias,
the giver of hard prophecies. Or he might be called Delius
because he was born on the island of Delos, or because—
as the mythographer Conti said—he revealed mysteries.[91]
But he was best known as Phoebus because of his glorious
radiance, which—as Ficino explained—made him the symbolic leader of the Muses, the inspirer of all the arts, and
the symbolic link between the physical light of the sun
and the divine intelligible light to which it owes its creation and to which men owe their spiritual illumination.

The figure of "the questioner" (*erotema*) which links Milton's invocations of his inspiring "Voice" in *Paradise Lost*,
III and VII, may well be regarded as supporting Hunter's
doctrine that in all four of his invocations the same Person

88. "Matutine pater, seu Jane libentius audis?" Horace, *Satires* 2.6.20. Verity
compares *Damon's Epitaph*, lines 207–10, where Milton asks whether Damon
prefers that pastoral name or his real name of Diodati. Cf. *PL*, VIII.357.

89. *Erotema* (or the "questioner," as Puttenham called it), chap. 19 of his
Second Book of Poets and Poesie.

90. *Cratylus*, 401b–408e.

91. Cf. n. 17, p. 223. *Natalis Comitis Mythologiae . . . Libri decem* (Frankfurt,
1596), Book IV, chap. 10, p. 366.

is invoked. It seems odd, then, to find a shrewd critic[92]
ignoring the absence of anything like that figure and discerning an "analogue" to Milton's proem to Book III in
Tasso's very explicit address to the three Persons of the
Trinity in the opening lines of *Le sette giornate del mondo
creato:*[93]

> Padre del Cielo, e tu del Padre eterno
> Eterno Figlio, e non creata prole,
> De l'immutabil mente unico parto:
> Divina imago, al tuo divino essempio
> Eguale; e lume pur di lume ardente;
> E tu, che d'ambo spiri, e d'ambo splendi,
> O di gemina luce acceso Spirto,
> Che sei pur sacro lume, e sacra fiamma,
> Quasi lucido rivo in chiaro fonte,
> E vera imago ancor di vera imago,
> In cui se stessa il primo essempio agguaglia,
> (Se dir conviensi) e triplicato Sole,
> Che l'alme accendi, e i puri ingegni illustri;
> Santo don, santo messo, e santo nodo,
> Che tre Sante Persone in un congiungi,
> Dio non solingo, in cui s'aduna il tutto,
> Che 'n varie parti poi si scema, e sparge:
>   [lines 1–17]

It is no less odd that Milton's eighteenth-century editors, who were fond of spotting resemblances to the *Gerusalemme liberata* in *Paradise Lost,* should have ignored what
seem to some twentieth-century analysts of Milton's thought
and style to be clear correspondences between *Paradise
Lost* and the *Mondo creato.* It was only in the fourth edition
of Todd's Variorum (1842) that the *Mondo* was mentioned
in connection with Milton's invocation to light. Very casu-

92. Broadbent, in *Some Graver Subject,* p. 140.
93. Quotation is from Torquato Tasso's *Il Mondo creato,* ed. Giorgio Petrocchi (Florence, Felice le Monnier, 1951).

ally, Todd suggested that it might be compared with
Tasso's address to light, which comes not at the beginning
of his *Primo Giorno,* but not far from its end:

> E qual carro più bello e più veloce,
> O bellissima luce, o luce amica
> De la natura e de la mente umana,
> De la divinità serena imago,
> Che ne consoli e ne richiami al cielo,
> Potea intorno portar virtuti e doni
> Celesti in terra a' miseri mortali
> Da quei tesori, e da quei regni eterni,
> Ch' a noi dispensa con sì larga mano
> De' lumi il Padre, e 'l donator fecondo?
>
> [lines 561–70]

Hurrying on to quote a moralizing salute to light of
Du Bartas, Todd dropped Tasso without a word about
his preceding passage on the creation of visible light, "the
joy of earth and heaven, the delight and glory of the
mind and senses, the revealer of things both mortal and
eternal." It did not occur to Todd to compare Milton's
"holy Light, offspring of Heav'n first-born/Or of th'Eternal
Coeternal beam" with Tasso's lines (498–503) which assert
that "There was an uncreated light before the world and
perhaps also a created light," and that "before it there
unrolled thousands and thousands of lustra and flying centuries. Virtual eternities (if so it may be said) preceded
the world and time." As Tasso's modern editor Petrocchi
points out in his footnote on the lines, though they may
seem to be based upon Saint Augustine's distinction between uncreated and created light, they actually are a
paraphase of a passage in Saint Basil's *Hexameron* (2.5),
which declares that both an uncreated and a created light
existed before the creation of the visible light that is called
the first thing created by God in Genesis 1:3.

But neither Tasso nor Saint Basil was necessarily the source of Milton's proem to *Paradise Lost*, III. Its vast source was the ocean of hexameral writers of whom Professor Williams[94] reminds us that over a score had been extensively quoted by Benedictus Pererius in his *Commentariorum et disputationum in Genesin*, Tome I (Rome, 1589) as having substantially contributed to the interpretation of God's command in Genesis 1:3: "Let there be light." Stylistically, as Professor Prince[95] declares, Milton's blank verse was encouraged and in some ways probably shaped by Tasso's *versi sciolti*. Prince speaks of the first seventy-seven lines of the *Giornata Prima* as an "invocation to the Holy Spirit" and as one of the best passages in a poem which "is the work of an oldish poet, one who has suffered many afflictions, and whose tiredness and inability to concentrate his thoughts are often revealed in his writing." These weaknesses are of the kind which Mr. Leavis regards as prevalent in the verse of *Paradise Lost*, and of which he has pointed to "the famous opening to Book III"[96] as a conspicuous example. Valuations of Milton's "grand style" and of Tasso's "stile magnifico" vary with the centuries and with the critics. Petrocchi—in his Introduction to the *Mondo* (p. xlv)—agrees with other recent commentators on the poem who regard its unrhyming hendecasyllables as constituting a "stile forte" rich in its preservation of an appropriate tone amid an infinitely varying amplitude of rhythm corresponding to the varying scenes of the narrative. In contrast to Leavis, who sees only a supreme instance of Milton's late anchylotic style in the proem to *Paradise Lost*, III, Professor Daiches reproduces it in its entirety as an expression of "the strong emotion with which

94. Arnold Williams, *The Common Expositor*, p. 15.
95. F. T. Prince, *The Italian Element in Milton's Verse* (Oxford, Clarendon Press, 1954), pp. 54–55.
96. Leavis, *Revaluation*, p. 44.

he proceeded to the more daring part of his work, the description of God in Heaven,"[97] after that of the scenes in Hell. Judgment of the esthetic value of the styles of the *Mondo creato* and *Paradise Lost* may have to be left to individual distastes. Agreement is, however, possible on the fact that both poems were the work of oldish men. There is no reason to disagree with Professor Gilbert[98] that the proem to Book III is a late work and may even have been inserted when the poem was virtually complete.

To most readers there may seem to be one crucial difference between the two proems, however, for Tasso's betrays a dogmatic spirit which Cope attributes to his "urge to identify himself with the wave of authoritarian devotionalism which swept Italy at the peak of the Counter Reformation."[99] Most critics would agree with Cope that "it reveals a nontheological mind by arguing the usual questions on the source of matter, or the plurality of worlds, by reference to the Schoolmen and the most orthodox patristic commentators." Even if there is a cryptic expression of the idea that the invoked light in Milton's proem is the second Person of the Trinity, as Cope believes, the difference in tone seems fundamental.

But between Tasso's exordium to the *Mondo creato* and the proem to *Paradise Lost,* III, there is the difference between a plain appeal to the three Persons of the Trinity and a salute to light which can be theologically hypostatized only if its meaning in the first line is identified with that of the expressly metaphorical "Celestial light" at the end. Acceptance of Hunter's secure identification of the Muse, addressed in all four of Milton's great proems

97. David Daiches, *Milton* (London, Hutchinson University Library, 1957), p. 178.

98. Allan H. Gilbert, *On the Composition of "Paradise Lost"* (Chapel Hill, University of North Carolina Press, 1947), pp. 155, 159.

99. Cope, *The Metaphoric Structure,* p. 162.

as always the same Person, is not in the least endangered
if "Light" in the first line of his proem is read "in the
physical sense" upon which Kelley insists. To read it so
"does not"—as he adds—"concern Arian or orthodox views
of the Son."[1] But to read it as a theological metaphor
implies its identity with the later "Celestial light" and—
for Hunter—also with the Son of God of orthodox Christian theology. To accept it simply in the physical sense in
which its first commentator[2] accepted it, is undeniably not
only most consonant both with the syntax of the opening
twenty-six lines (as Kelley asserts), but also with the final
emergence of the climactic metaphor of "Celestial light,"
as Professor Ferry[3] now traces the development of the entire proem.

To accept it in the physical sense is also in line with
the characteristic concern of the Florentine Neoplatonists
not to permit any pantheistic or theologically unorthodox
inversion of the text "God is light" (I John 1:5) which
might obscure its metaphorical nature, as implied by the
warning in the context against men who "walk in darkness
and do not do the truth." In a representative passage[4] in

1. *This Great Argument,* p. 92.
2. The actor Richard Leigh, writing in *The Transproser Rehearsed* (1673), p. 43,
in conjunction of some kind with Archbishop Sheldon's chaplain, the Reverend
Samuel Parker, is quoted by Masson in *The Life of Milton* (6 vols. Edinburgh,
1880), *6,* 705, as treating the words "Eternal Coeternal beam" as nothing but
"the absurdity of his inventive Divinity in making light contemporary with its
creator."
3. Anne Davidson Ferry, *Milton's Epic Voice* (Cambridge, Mass., Harvard
University Press, 1963), chap. 1.
4. In *Liber de Sole,* chap. 9, after reciting the seemingly divine blessings of the
sun upon earthly life and recalling Plato's doctrine of intelligible truth and
knowledge of it in men's minds, Ficino interpreted Plato thus: "Putat insuper
ipsum bonum, scilicet Deum, ita saltem haec omnia superare sicut Sol lumen &
oculos colores. Sed ubi Plato Solem inquit, omne visibile superare, proculdubio
supra corporeum Solem, incorporeum auguratus est Solem Divinum." Marsilio
Ficino, *Opera Omnia,* "Riproduzione in fototipia a cura di M. Sancipriano, con
presentazione di P. O. Kristeller" (Turin, Erasmo, 1959), p. 971.

the *Liber de Sole* Ficino unequivocally maintained the line
between the Divine Light and the created intelligential
and physical lights by which God is revealed. Milton was
never in danger of blurring the "distinction between physi-
cial light and spiritual, which turns [as Professor Woodhouse sees] on the Christian conception of the two orders
of nature and grace."[5] He had no thought of blurring it
when he unconsciously sparked the controversy which has
recently arisen over his questioning designation of "th'Eternal Coeternal beam" and over his figure of God as dwell-
ing "from eternity" in "unapproached light." There, indeed, he was simply echoing the Psalmist's address to God,
"Who coverest thyself with light as with a garment, who
stretchest out the heavens like a curtain."[6] Hunter's studies
have demonstrated that for Milton's contemporaries the
word *light* was loaded with theological metaphor drawn
from Biblical and Neoplatonic tradition. And we must be
glad that in an attempt to set aside Kelley's[7] "high Arian"
Son of God in favor of a Son who is the second and de-
rivative stage of a two-stage Logos stemming from Philo
and the Fathers, he has surveyed the recurrence in their
work of the metaphor of the rays of the sun and of water
flowing from a fountain as doctrinal illustrations estab-
lishing that orthodox conception of the Son. After some
memorable quotations from Justin Martyr, Hippolytus,
and Lactantius, he concludes by quoting from Tertullian's
Against Praxias a passage which beautifully uses both metaphors for that theological purpose. But the passage was
read by some of the orthodox theologians with a different
emphasis—an emphasis more in line with Milton's use of
the metaphor to signify the illumination for which he prays
and also that larger illumination "wherewith God en-

5. A. S. P. Woodhouse, "Pattern in *Paradise Lost*," *UTQ, 22* (1953), 113.
6. Psalm 104:2.
7. Maurice Kelley, "Milton's Arianism again Considered," *HTR, 54* (1961),
195–205.

lightens and leads his people,"[8] haply sometimes by poetry which is "doctrinal to a nation."[9] Richard Hooker,
for example, took a very different kind of interest in the
passage from *Against Praxias* which Hunter quotes for its
theological, rather than for what may be called its evan-
gelical, bearing. Assuming that his readers would be familiar with a passage which had had a history in theological
debate, Hooker began his long paragraph by referring to
Tertullian's image in *Against Praxias* (chapter 8), then proceeded to shift its stress from its illustration of the relation of the Son to the Father and expounded it in a way
which is eloquently harmonious with the tenor of Milton's
prayer for Divine guidance in the proem to Book III.
Paraphrasing Tertullian, Hooker reasoned that "The Sonne
of God being light of light, must needs be also light in
light. The persons of the Godhead, by reason of the unitie
of their substance, doe as necessarily remayne one within
another, as they are of necessitie to be distinguished from
one another." A little lower down he repeated the figure:
"The Sonne in the Father as light in that light, out of
which it flows without separation." Finally Hooker turned
Tertullian's image into a universal symbol of the creative
and purifying power of the Fountain of Light: "All things
are . . . partakers of God, they are his Offspring, his influence is in them, and the personall Wisedome of God is
for that very cause said to excell in nimblenesse and agili-
tie, to pierce into all intellectuall, pure and subtile spirits,
to goe through all, and to reach unto everything which
is. . . ."[10]

Hooker must have known of several occurrences of the
sun and its inseparable rays in Scholastic discussions of
the relation of the Son to the Father—sometimes with ref-

8. *Christian Doctrine*, I.6 (CE, *14*, 360).
9. *Reason of Church Government*, Book II, preface (CE, *3*, 237).
10. Richard Hooker, *Of the Laws of Ecclesiastical Polity*, Book V.
    56 (6th ed. London, 1632, pp. 304–05).

erences to the Arian or Sabellian employment of the metaphor. Its abuse, to illustrate Arius' modal Trinity, was
mentioned by St. Thomas (*Summa Th.* l.q.42, art. 2): *Secun-
dus modus est juxta emissionem radiorum a sole; ubi deest aequali-
tas naturae.* Both Hooker and Milton surely knew that the
paired figures of the radiant sun and the streaming fountain were popularly very well known. To the question
"What be those resemblances that are commonly brought
to shadow out unto us the mystery of the Trinity?" in
Archbishop Usher's *A Body of Divinity, or the Summe and
Substance of Christian Religion, Catechistically propounded,*[11] the
answer is that as from the sunbeams proceed both light
and heat "and yet is none of them below another, otherwise than in consideration of order and relation," and that
as "from one flame of fire proceed both light and heat,
and yet but one fire: [so] in waters there is a well-head and
the spring boyling out of it, and the stream flowing from
both, and all these are but one water; and so there are
there [sic] persons in one Godhead." Both Usher and Milton knew that the companion images stemmed from many
sources, and neither the archbishop nor the poet was concerned about the possibility that they implied a Logos of
two, three, or four emanative stages, or might be exclu-
sively derived from any particular Patristic source.[12]

   Many people in Milton's first "fit audience" must have
known enough about the debate in the early Church over
the mystery of the Trinity to understand that it hinged
upon the orthodox rejection of Arianism on the theory

   11. London, 1649 (p. 76).
   12. In *If This Be Heresy* (Urbana, University of Illinois Press, 1963), p. 24,
Harry F. Robins quotes a passage of Hippolytus of Rome (*ANCL, 9,* 60–62),
which presents the evolution of the Logos in three stages: immanence in the
Father as an attribute, production by the Father as an invisible agent, and
visible emergence in the Son. "A fourth phase comes into being at the incarnation." On p. 55, after an analysis of the concept of a three-stage Logos "derived
from the substance but not the essence of God," Robins undertakes to demon-
strate that Milton conceived of the Logos strictly as Origen did.

that within the Trinity the Son and the Holy Spirit were subordinate to the Father, though outwardly the Godhead was indivisible. The debate had revolved around the ambivalent images of the radiant sun, the flowing fountain, and the branching vine. Reviewing the record in 1678, Ralph Cudworth[13] quoted Dionysius of Alexandria as following a well-trodden path when he described the second Person of the Trinity by comparing him to "the Splendour of the Light" of the sun and to "the Vapour of the Water" of a fountain. In Cudworth's historical perspective the images were interesting theologically because they "seem plainly to imply somme *Dependence* and *Subordination*" of the Son to the Father. In Hooker's broader view it was the intrinsic, esthetic power of the metaphors that counted. If they are seen in both perspectives as they emerge in Milton's proem to Book III, the passage takes its proper place in the tradition of light and dark imagery which Professor Williams[14] traces mainly from Dionysius into the poetry of Crashaw, and which is everywhere in Traherne's poems. Certainly, to come close to the immediate source of the proem to Book III in Milton's own mind, it sprang from a way of thinking like that behind the images of light in his prose—particularly in *Areopagitica*—and from the habit of mind which Professor Arthos traces to his life-long fondness for the praise of light which led his imagination constantly toward images clustering around that subject, "from Saint John and Plato and the Platonists, leading into the most complex metaphysics"[15] and to a passage like the opening lines of the third book of *Paradise Lost.*

13. Ralph Cudworth, *The True Intellectual System of the Universe* (London, 1678), p. 600.

14. George Walton Williams, *Image and Symbol in the Sacred Poetry of Richard Crashaw* (Chapel Hill, University of North Carolina Press, 1963), chap. 4.

15. John Arthos, *Dante, Michelangelo, and Milton* (London, Routledge and Kegan Paul, 1963), p. 104.

5

The Filiations of Milton's Celestial Dialogue

(*Paradise Lost,* III.80–343)

> It would not have occurred to Milton that poetry was a suitable medium for theological dispute. By an exercise of tact which, whether successful or not, is bold, he sets out the theological rules of the poem in Book III as coming from God himself.
>
> Kermode, *The Living Milton,* p. 91

Milton's prayer for "Celestial light . . . that I may see and tell / Of things invisible"[1] is not only the climax of the invocation to *Paradise Lost,* III. In what he called the "oeconomy or disposition of the fable"[2] the prayer is a stroke of literary economy in the modern sense of swift development of plot. It prepares for what would otherwise be a too abrupt transition from Hell and Chaos in Book II to the Empyrean heaven. In immediate response to it the poet is enabled to take his action into "the happy Realms of Light,"[3] the scene of a beatific vision comparable with Dante's in Paradise.

1. *PL,* III.54–55.
2. In the preface to *Samson Agonistes* (CE, *1,* 333).
3. *PL,* I.85.

There Milton takes the risk of putting the theology of his epic into a dialogue between God, the anthropomorphic, omnipotent Father, and his Son. Though Milton gave it no name, the scene is often called "the council in Heaven." Milton himself used the word "council" only for the caucuses of Satan's followers.[4] God's audience is not a council, conclave, or parliament. It consists of all angels and its theater resembles the heaven of St. John's Apocalypse. The "almighty Father" and the "radiant image of his Glory . . . / His onely Son"[5] sit environed by "all the Sanctities of Heaven," as Raphael saw them earlier standing "in Orbs / Of circuit inexpressible . . . / Orb within Orb." This dialogue must first be seen as part of "the continuity of the poetic fabric in its obvious contrasts with Hell [which] indicate how we are to regard Heaven."[6] The significance of the contrasts has been stressed by Maurice Kelley in *This Great Argument*,[7] and by B. Rajan in *'Paradise Lost' and the Seventeenth Century Reader*:[8] the counterbalance of the plot against Man in Pandemonium and the announcement of the design for his salvation in Heaven, on which depend the action and the theodicy of the whole poem; the contrasted motives for Satan's assumption of the perilous journey through Chaos to seduce Man and for the Son's assumption of the penalty of death itself for Man's redemption; and the contrast of the "deafening shout"[9] of the dispersing devils after their silence at the climax of the council in Pandemonium with the shout of the angels, "Loud as from numbers without num-

4. In *PL*, I.755; II.506; VI.416; and X.428.
5. *PL*, III.56–64; V.594–97.
6. In "The Dialogue in Heaven: A Reconsideration of *Paradise Lost* 3.1–417," *PMLA*, 72 (1947), 601–11. The point is made by Irene Samuel.
7. Princeton University Press, 1941.
8. London, Chatto and Windus, 1947 (pp. 47–50). Cf. Ernest Schanzer in "Milton's Hell Revisited," *UTQ*, 24 (1955), 136–45, and J. B. Broadbent in *Some Graver Subject* (London, Chatto and Windus, 1960), p. 111.
9. *PL*, II.520.

ber, sweet / As from blest voices, uttering joy"[10] when
they hear the Son's response to the Father's question:
"Which of ye will be mortal to redeem / Mans mortal
crime?"[11]

No scene of architecturally limited magnitude like Pandemonium could serve as a setting for the dialogue which
ends with the offer of God's "dear and onely Son" to "die
for mans offence."[12] Only a heaven like that of Revelation
can contain that apocalyptic ending. "Paraeus," said Milton in his preface to *Samson Agonistes,*[13] "commenting on
the *Revelation,* divides the whole Book as a Tragedy, into
Acts distinguisht each by a Chorus of Heavenly Harpings
and Song between." With such a song the angels in Milton's heavenly theater in the round praise the speakers in
his tragic dialogue which, like the scene in Revelation,
has a solemnly happy ending. Though God is "invisible /
Amidst the glorious brightness,"[14] the angels later say that
all the way along they have been listening to the Son's
moving report of "the strife / Of Mercy and Justice" in
his face.[15]

The dramatic situation in Milton's dialogue is of a kind
which he had sketched at some length, probably earlier
than 1640, in the third of his four "outlines for tragedies"
on the theme of *Paradise Lost* in the Trinity College Manuscript. The scene following the prologue was to be a debate between Justice and Mercy on the question "what
should become of man if he fall."[16] It was doubtless solved
by the third person in the allegorical dialogue, Wisdom.
The sketch does not hint at all that Wisdom is to be identified with the Logos, the divine Word and Son of God by
whom all things are to be made and fallen man redeemed;

10. *PL,* III.346–47.
11. *PL,* III.214–15.
12. *PL,* III.404–10.
13. CE, *1,* 331.
14. *PL,* III.375–76.

but that probability lurks in the fact that the scene closes with an angelic "hymne of creation." In the next act the only persons are "Heavenly love" and "Evening starre" contemplating Paradise in a way that makes the scene close naturally with a "marriage song" by the angelic chorus, and also makes it a foil for the third act, where Lucifer is heard in a monologue "contriving Adams ruine." All we know of Act 4 is that its persons are Adam and Eve "fallen," but in Act 5, with the appearance of Conscience citing "them to Gods Examination" in a role seemingly not much like Michael's in the last books of *Paradise Lost*, the impression is obviously intended to be tragic in Milton's sense when, after the dialogue between Raphael and Adam, he warns that he "now must change / Those Notes to Tragic."[17] The end of the projected tragedy does not seem to correspond to the note struck by Wisdom or by the chorus that hymned creation. In the Outline the last chorus "bewails and tells the good Adam hath lost."

Before criticism can go beyond superficial impressions of the conversation between the Father and Son in *Paradise Lost*, III, it must reckon with its filiation from his outlines of possible tragedies on the Fall. A. H. Gilbert regards them as more or less conflated in a fifth plan with an opening scene beginning with ten verses[18] which Edward Phillips quoted as surviving from it in *Paradise Lost*. However willing or reluctant we may be to follow Gilbert in his postulate of Milton's early composition of an unknown tragedy built upon a conflation of five or more

15. *PL*, III.406–07.
16. CE, *18*, 228–32.
17. *PL*, IX.5–6.
18. *PL*, IV.32–41. In Phillips' version "glorious" stands instead of "matchless" in line 41. See *The Early Lives of Milton*, ed. Helen Darbishire (London, Constable, 1932), p. 73.

early plans,[19] we cannot ignore the dramatic element
which J. H. Hanford first recognized in what often seemed
to him to be the Shakespearean quality of the dialogues
in "the economy of *Paradise Lost*."[20] In the style of the
dialogue in Heaven, however, there is nothing like the
language of Shakespeare's judges and advocates, and in
the design of the epic there is nothing very like the cases
which his dukes of Athens, Venice, and Vienna adjudicate.

The case which God prejudges in Heaven had been
pleaded over and over in the morality plays by the four
daughters of God, Justice and Truth for the prosecution,
Mercy and Peace for the defense. The survival of those
personified abstractions was observed by Robert L. Ramsay[21] in several Miltonic passages, such as the descent of
the "meek-ey'd Peace"[22] at Christ's birth, the warning to
the corrupt clergy of their impending exposure by "Truth,
the daughter not of Time, but of Heaven,"[23] the pleas of
Truth and Justice against King Charles in the last chapter
of *Eikon.* In the sonnet to Cromwell, plower of the nation's
way "To peace and truth," there is an echo of the verse
from which the traditional debate of the four daughters
of God stemmed: "Mercy and truth are met together;
righteousness and peace have kissed each other."[24] Ramsay
did not overstate the resemblance of Milton's apocalyptic
scene to St. Bernard's version of the dramatized debate of
the psalmist's figures as actors in moralities supposed to
take place in heaven at the time of the Fall or of the Nativity. Like St. Bernard, Milton must present God as insisting upon man's condemnation unless an innocent sub-

19. Allan H. Gilbert, *On the Composition of "Paradise Lost"* (Chapel Hill, University of North Carolina Press, 1947), p. 17.

20. James Holly Hanford, "The Dramatic Element in 'Paradise Lost,'" *SP,
14* (1917), 192.

21. "Morality Themes in Milton's Poetry," *SP, 16* (1919), 123–58.

22. *On the Morning of Christ's Nativity,* v.46.

23. *Of Prelatical Episcopacy,* CE, *3,* 91.

24. Psalms 85:10.

stitute will assume his guilt. In *Paradise Lost* Mercy cannot leave God's judgment seat to search through the world for that substitute before it is found in Heaven. The allegory of the daughters of God is only momentary in Milton's scene, but it emerges clearly when the "Father of Mercie and Grace"[25] declares that Mercy and Justice shall both prevail "Through Heav'n and Earth . . . / But Mercy first and last shall brightest shine."[26]

Tension between justice and mercy was so much a part of the tradition to which *Paradise Lost* belongs that it could not fail to figure in its action. There may have been several reasons for the decision to put it after the scenes in Hell, rather than to put it first as it was in the most elaborate outline for a tragedy on the theme of the Fall in the Cambridge MS. Besides the obvious advantage of plunging *in medias res* with the awakening of the fallen devils in Book I, their plot against man in Book II directly advances the epic plot by challenging the reply which is so spectacularly given in Book III. In the moralities the Son's chivalrous response to that challenge had always been the climax of the action. It must always have been felt as intensely moving, and especially so—as Hope Travers pointed out[27]—in *The Court of Sapience*. Though the debate of the Four Daughters might begin, as it does in *The Castle of Perseverance*, with sharp contention among Mercy and Peace, Justice and Truth over the soul of Mankind as he lies on his deathbed, it regularly ended in the triumphant appeal of Mercy and Peace to God the Father in Heaven. God

25. *PL*, III.401.

26. *PL*, III.133–34. Cf. the "Eternal Father" fulfilling "All Justice" (V.246–47) and Michael's half explicit personification of Justice in XII.99. But in the symbolism of the whole poem, as Jackson I. Cope writes in *The Metaphoric Structure of 'PL'* (Baltimore, 1962), p. 169, since "God is the generative 'eye' from which emanates the totality of being . . . shine is no metaphor but the essence of mercy, as of all good qualities flowing from their source, for 'God is light.'"

27. In *The Four Daughters of God*, Bryn Mawr College Monographs, 6 (1907), 155–57.

is merciful and seats Mankind at his right hand, where
his Saviour also sits. But when the Father widens the
scene into the "Great Judgment," Justice is not slighted.
Then, as Arnold Williams reminds us,[28] "King and Kaiser,
knight and champion, pope and patriarch will render their
accounts." In the moralities Mercy always prevailed with
God for the repentant sinner, but "in the streyt argument,"
as she warns in *Mankind,*[29] "Iustice & Equite xall be forty-
fyid," and the sinner must "beware of *the* continuance."

For readers who know the background of Milton's dialogue in Heaven it is most impressive because it trans-
cends the courtroom situation, with God's daughters acting as defenders and prosecutors. In such a scene Milton
might have produced something like the strident diatribes
by Mercy, Justice, and Piety in William Drummond of
Hawthornden's "The Shadow of Justice," or like Giles
Fletcher's debate between Mercy and Justice in *Christs
Victorie in Heaven.* The result would have been floods of
rhetoric, with Justice speaking in "the thunder that mount
Sinai heard"[30] and Mercy's "heav'nly Eloquence" flower-
ing into "golden phrases" that "shed forth streames of
choycest rhetoric, / Welling celestiall torrents out of poesie."[31] Because the Son of God does not participate in
Fletcher's debate, and because Mercy's plea for man is
mainly an indictment of the Devil for tempting him and
an extenuation of his sin on the ground that "He was but
dust,"[32] the judge seems guilty of the partiality for man
which Justice has anticipated by foreseeing Mercy's ploy of
shifting man's responsibility for his sin upon his tempter.[33]
In the dialogue in *Paradise Lost* that excuse is voluntarily

28. In "The English Moral Play before 1500," *Annuale Mediaevale, 4* (1963), 9.
29. *Specimens of Pre-Shakespearian Drama,* ed. John Matthews Manly (2 vols.
Boston, Ginn, 1897), *1,* 348–49.
30. *The Poetical Works of Giles Fletcher and Phineas Fletcher,* ed. Frederick S. Boas
(2 vols. Cambridge, the University Press, 1908), *1,* 22.
31. Ibid., p. 30, stanza 48.
32. Ibid., p. 36, stanza 73.
33. Ibid., p. 24, stanza 27.

admitted for what it is worth by the Father when he says in his first speech that, because Satan was "Self-tempted, self-deprav'd," whereas "Man falls deceiv'd / By th'other first: Man therefore shall find grace, / the other none."[34]

By abandoning the debate between Justice and Mercy over fallen Man in favor of a dialogue between the Almighty Father and the Son, Milton found the way to a dialogue of distinct persons. Though "all his Father shon / Substantially express'd"[35] in the Son, modern criticism is rather inclined to contrast him with the Father as much the cleverer as well as the wiser and kinder of the two. A. H. Gilbert sees him as "a prudent courtier, beginning with deference his speech to the monarch (III.144), then endeavoring to persuade him not to go too far in his punishment of disloyal man."[36] John Peter contrasts our "strangely unfavorable first impressions of God" with our "unqualifiedly approving first impressions of the Son."[37] He praises the Son's flattering tact in coaxing the Father not to renege his decree that "Man shall find grace." Peter naively assumes that the Son shares his own impression that the Father has been "playing to the gallery of his auditors," i.e. to all the Sanctities of Heaven in the apocalyptic scene. On such an assumption the Father is stripped of the moral and intellectual honesty of Justice in the moralities and is on the way to exposure as the "nakedly bad" sadist of William Empson's theology,[38] while the Son

34. *PL*, III.130–32.

35. *PL*, III.139–40. The expression is best understood, as it is by Maurice Kelley in *This Great Argument*, p. 30, in the light of several passages in the *Christian Doctrine* as capable of meaning not that "the essence of the Father shines in the substance of the Son," but rather that "the Son was generated from the substance of the Father but is not therefore co-essential with Him."

36. In "Form and Matter in *Paradise Lost*," *Milton Studies in Honor of Harris Francis Fletcher* (Urbana, University of Illinois Press, 1961), p. 52.

37. In *A Critique of "Paradise Lost"* (New York, Columbia University Press, 1960), p. 12.

38. William Empson, *Milton's God* (London, Chatto and Windus, 1961), p. 246.

becomes a humane and sophisticated twentieth-century lawyer pleading against the stupid brutality of the judge and the law.

But such criticism ignores the prime background of the Son's plea in the speech of Beelzebub preparing the way for Satan's outpouring of "Monarchal pride"[39] in his open play to the gallery of his auditors in Pandemonium. In the far-reaching economy of the epic, as Joseph H. Summers points out,[40] Satan's egotism is a foil for the Son's sacrifice of the ego in the speech beginning "Behold mee then, mee for him, life for life / I offer,"[41] which is later to be echoed when Eve begs that God's sentence upon Adam "may light / On me, sole cause to thee of all this woe, / Mee mee onely just object of his ire."[42]

Modern critical recognition of the Son's wisdom and humanity at the Father's expense has pivoted mainly upon the speech which seems so tactful to John Peter, the speech beginning: "Father, thy word is past, man shall find grace."[43] In analyzing its opening lines as "largely, if inadvertently, at his Father's expense" Peter was anticipated by Grierson, who quoted the first fourteen lines as counterbalancing the Father's failure to understand that not only "Mercy of which God speaks, but simple Justice would seem to require some consideration of the human nature given to Adam and Eve, its limitations, before such sweeping judgements were endorsed."[44] And the same fourteen lines are quoted by Arnold Stein as evidence that the scene of the Son's choice of "sacrifice to fulfill all justice is one of Milton's great triumphs of style."[45] None

39. *PL*, II.428.

40. In *The Muse's Method* (Cambridge, Harvard University Press, 1962), p. 179.

41. *PL*, III.236 ff.

42. *PL*, X.934–36.

43. *PL*, III.227 ff.

44. Sir Herbert J.C. Grierson, *Milton and Wordsworth* (New York, Macmillan, 1937), p. 112.

45. Stein, *Answerable Style*, p. 128.

of the three essays, of course, rests its case for the Son's gracious humanity simply upon this speech. Peter and Stein find those attributes no less clearly expressed in most of his later appearances. But there is less and less agreement with Grierson that "We remember less Christ the promised redeemer than Christ who goes forth in all the panoply of Ezekiel's vision to overthrow the rebellious angels."[46] Among modern critics only J. B. Broadbent recoils from the Son's character definitely enough to condemn his "flexible rhetoric" in the speech which "picks up the Father's decree 'Man therefore shall find grace,' and weaves lyrical patterns with it as if to beautify brutality."[47]

For several reasons modern criticism has tended to polarize the Son and the Father. The tendency has been encouraged by Maurice Kelley's reaffirmation[48] of Milton's "Arianism" and by his crushing criticism[49] of M. A. Larson's theory that he accepted what was essentially Servetus' view of a modal Trinity. Since for Larson the Son was "simply the Word of God communicating himself into sense," he could so far misunderstand the dialogue in Book III as to say that, though "In heaven the Word and the Father are represented as speaking to one another, God is always invisible and *inaudible*"![50]

An absolute modal interpretation of the Son in *Paradise Lost* drains his speeches in the dialogue in Heaven of their interest as acts of faith in the Father's mercy. If the Son is literally nothing more than God's "word, . . . wisdom, and effectual might," as the Father calls him,[51] he is not in any proper sense of the word the "numerically distinct" person which Milton so insists upon making him in the

46. *Milton and Wordsworth,* p. 105.

47. J. B. Broadbent, *Some Graver Subject,* p. 148.

48. *This Great Argument,* p. 119.

49. In "Milton's Arianism Reconsidered," *Harvard Theological Review, 54* (1961), 195–205.

50. M. A. Larson, *The Modernity of Milton* (Chicago, University of Chicago Press, 1927), p. 123.

51. *PL,* III.170.

Christian Doctrine I.5. If his will is not so free as that of the spirits of whom God says, "Freely they stood who stood, and fell who fell,"[52] what virtue is there in his self-sacrifice to deserve God's praise in the long speech ending with the command to the angels to "Adore the Son, and honour him as mee"?

The Father's praise and the choral response of the angels leave us in the realm of apocalyptic vision. A truth has been revealed which synthesizes the thesis of justice and the antithesis of mercy. But has it been taught to a bigoted father by the diplomatic eloquence of his son, speaking with a plausible mixture of sentimentality and worldly wisdom? Has God been softened by reasoning like Adam's when—as Christopher Ricks puts it[53]—we find him "presumptuously thinking that God will look silly if now that they [himself and Eve] have fallen he destroys them:"

> least the Adversary
> Triumph and say; Fickle their State whom God
> Most Favors, who can please him long; Mee first
> He ruind, now Mankind: whom will be next?
> Matter of scorne, not to be given the Foe . . .[54]

The answer lies in the direction of Bishop Newton's note on *Paradise Lost* III.153: "An imitation of Gen. 18.25: 'That be far from thee to slay the righteous with the wicked: and that the righteous should be as the wicked, that be far from thee: Shall not the judge of all the earth do right?' " With this situation in Genesis J. E. Parish[55] also compares Moses' struggle with the Almighty when, "with infinite patience and shrewd understanding of Jehovah's

52. *PL,* III.102.

53. In *Milton's Grand Style* (Oxford, Clarendon Press, 1963), p. 32.

54. *PL,* IX.947–51.

55. John E. Parish, "Milton and an Anthropomorphic God," *SP, 56* (1959), 619–25.

vanity," he prevails upon him to forget his threat to smite the battle-shy Israelites "with a pestilence." In the pleas of Abraham and Moses to a stern deity there is more than the germ of the Son's response to the Father's promise that "Man . . . shall find grace" with the plea:

> For should Man finally be lost, should Man
> Thy creature late so lov'd, thy youngest Son
> Fall circumvented thus by fraud, though joynd
> With his own folly, that be from thee farr,
> That farr be from thee, Father, who art Judg
> Of all things made, and judgest onely right.[56]

If our interest in Milton's development of the dialogue can stand the shock of the exposure of God's vulnerability to the Son's suasion by means of his image in the eyes of the angels, we can suspend contempt for his deity and consider what the Son says in the light of Moses' plea for his panicky people:

> "Now if thou dost kill this people as one man, then the nations who have heard thy name will say, Because the Lord was not able to bring this people into the land which he swore to give them, therefore he has slain them in the wilderness."[57]

It may help understanding of Milton's management of his dialogue if we put ourselves in the place of the lawyers of Lincoln's Inn when they heard John Donne conclude a meditation on God's patience in listening to Abraham's plea for mercy on Sodom and Gomorrah with the rhetorical question: "Shall not the judge of all the earth do right?" And Donne added the example of God's patience with Moses when he pleaded for mercy on the timid Israelites by suggesting what Donne euphemistically called

56. *PL,* III.150–55.
57. Numbers 14:15–16.

"the inconveniences that might follow" their punishment by a divinely sent plague.[58]

The conversations of Abraham and Moses with God are relevant to Milton's dialogue, but still more relevant are the reproachfully intimate appeals to him in the Psalms to which the Moralities were indebted for his four daughters. After the vision of the reconciliation of mercy and truth, righteousness and peace in Psalms 85:10, in Psalms 86 "David strengthens his prayer" for divine mercy in a public calamity by reminding God of his vaunted pre-eminence among all gods. Later, in the same tone of reverence and intimacy, he praises God because justice, mercy, and truth share his throne. But he also warns God that Israel's reverses destroy confidence in his will and power to keep his covenant to preserve it as a kingdom forever, and that the sneers of its enemies threaten his prestige in the world. In the heavenly dialogue the Son translates David's plea from earth to Heaven.

Milton had a sense of humor, and he may have been aware of a different kind of celestial translation of the pleas of Moses and David. It occurs in the picaresque setting of Matheo Aleman's *The Rogue: or the Life of Guzman de Alfarache,* which he may have known in the Mabbe translation of 1622.[59] So Francis Peck suggested in 1740, and Ants Oras concurs[60] in thinking that his parallels from it to *Paradise Lost* are "close." The closest of them occurs in Guzman's wayside entertainment of some companions with "A morall Fable of the gods of old-time, and the Councel that was held in heaven against Mankind."[61] The

58. *Sermons of John Donne,* ed. George R. Potter and Evelyn Simpson (10 vols. Berkeley, University of California Press, 1957), *3,* 146.

59. *The Rogue, or the Life of Guzman de Alfarache,* written in Spanish by Matheo Aleman and done into English by James Mabbe. Anno 1623 [o.s.] With an Introduction by James Fitsmaurice-Kelly. Ed. Charles Whibley (10 vols. London, Tudor Translations, 2d ser. 1924), *1,* 147.

60. In *Milton's Editors, and Commentators from Patrick Hume to Henry John Todd* (Tartu, University of Tartu Press, 1931), p. 171.

61. *The Rogue,* p. 147.

scene resembles those in the Moralities where Justice and
Mercy debate man's fate. Jove is dissatisfied with men's
crass worship of the god Content, for whom they have forgotten him. Momus, who is a kind of travesty of Justice
in the Moralities, demands the extermination of the un-
grateful race; but Apollo wins the unanimous support of
the rest of the assembly for its questionably more merciful
subjection to the god Discontent. Addressing Jove, he reasons coolly:

> If thou destroy the world, in vaine then are those
> things, which thou hast herein created; and it were
> imperfection in thee, to un-make that, which thou
> hast already made; only for to mend that which thou
> now findest amisse: Much lesse, would I have thee
> repent thy selfe that thou hast made Man; for that
> will be but discredit thy selfe and thine owne worke.
> Besides, how can it stand with the power and good-
> nesse of a Creator, to take too strict a course against
> his Creature, and to exceed, by extraordinary meanes,
> in his chastisements?[62]

Peck's faith in a link of any kind between the speech
of Guzman's Apollo and Milton's Son of God is hardly
convincing, though Milton might not have been annoyed
by the comparison. If Milton knew Guzman's fable, he
would have regarded Apollo less as an advocate of mercy
than of a tempered and grimly appropriate kind of justice for mankind.

In Ariosto's *Orlando Furioso,* XIV.70–71 Milton had certainly encountered a very different but more distinct analogue to the Son's plea to the Father. It, too, is touched
with humor—humor of the kind that is always latent in
Ariosto's solemn scenes. The Saracens are at the gates of
Paris in overwhelming force, and in its largest church
Charlemagne prays God for mercy on the French, though

they deserve it all too little. "Let not the punishment come
from thy enemies," he begs, "for if they destroy thy friends
they will say that thou art powerless to protect the defenders of thy church and sepulchre." If Milton paused
for a moment's reflection on the scene, he must have been
struck by the resemblance of Charlemagne's warning to
God and the warnings of Moses and David about the
danger to the divine prestige among the nations if God's
people are destroyed. In drawing attention to Charlemagne's prayer A. H. Gilbert observes[63] that it is more
"extreme" than the Son's warning to the Father. Charlemagne is speaking for the benefit of a terrified crowd to a
God more anthropopathetic than Milton's. The scene is a
crisis in human destiny where emotions are tense to the
point of pitiful absurdity. In Milton's scene the level is
above fear or any passion except love of mankind, of truth,
and of God's self. The difference would not be lost on
Milton. It was one of the many reasons why he preferred
the "higher argument" of *Paradise Lost* to that of Ariosto's
romantic epic.

The control of emotion in Milton's dialogue—its limitation to the joy of the Father and the angels in the Son's
offer of sacrifice for mankind—is of course due to epic
decorum. But it is also due to the example of scriptural
style and still more to the weight of the doctrine of the
Atonement with which he is dealing, and to the imagery
traditionally clustering around it. One of the most important early forms of the doctrine which still to some extent
affected the imagination of the seventeenth century has
been recognized by C. A. Patrides[64] in St. Anselm's theory
of the atonement against God's sensitive royal honor as
universal king requiring the punishment of mankind unless
a divine-human being will make "satisfaction" for it. Most

---

63. In *Milton Studies in Honor of Harris Fletcher,* p. 52.
64. In "Milton and the Protestant Theory of the Atonement," *PMLA, 74*
(1959), 8–10.

important was the forensic theory of the Atonement of most Protestant Reformers, who "tended to distinguish between the Father, pictured as the stern guardian of Divine Law, and the Son, who offered Himself freely out of love to pacify the wrath of God." The wrath of the infallible Judge of all the earth is as dispassionate as Law itself. His justice is the traditionally fundamental divine attribute which St. Thomas Aquinas declared it to be when he wrote that it implies the perfection of God's nature, and identified it with truth (*Justitia Dei est veritas*).[65] Or, in the Anglican terms of Archbishop Usher: Justice "is an essential property of God whereby he is infinitely just in himself, for, from, by himself alone, and none other (Psalm 11.7)." The corollary is that by the anger of God we should understand "Not any passion, perturbation, or trouble of the mind as it is in us."[66]

The passionless justice and wrath of God in Protestant and Catholic theology were traditionally contrasted with the sacrificial love of his Son, but the contrast was limited by orthodox trinitarian faith. It involved no clash of wills or personalities. In the celestial debates of the Moralities Father and Son are not for a moment alienated from each other as representatives or auditors of the conflicts between Justice and Mercy. The speakers in Milton's celestial dialogue are, of course, far from being personifications of those virtues, though as persons they are no less distinct. To modern readers more sensitive to their distinct personal differences than to the final union of their wills the Son seems to be the Father's superior in love, wisdom and even in diplomatic shrewdness. Latent in this nascent theory is a crude distortion of the kind of heroism which we are told makes Christ the hero of *Paradise Regained* by virtue of the "firm obedience to the Law of God" which

---

65. *Summa Theologica*, 1.q.21, 1 ad 4; and 1.q.22.20.

66. James Usher. *A Body of Divinity, or the Summe and Substance of Christian Religion, Catechistically Propounded and explained . . .* (London, 1649), p. 70.

is prophesied of him in his earthly ministry in *Paradise Lost.*[67] In the dialogue in Heaven anything like emotional stress upon the differences between the interlocutors is impossible.

But it is interesting to note that Milton went as far as he did in developing the ambivalence of the suppliant figure of the Son. His Italian studies had introduced him to the compound of severity and mercy which T. M. Greene recognizes[68] as characteristic of the poetry and painting of the age which produced Vida's *Christiad* (1535) and Marino's *Gerusalemme Distrutta* (1632), with its painful portrayal of the Virgin pleading for God's mercy on the city. The compound motif, "frequent in Baroque poetry," seems to him to "recur in not so very different form at the close of a very different poem—*Paradise Lost.*" Greene does not overstate the fondness for fusion of severity with mercy when he says that it "pierced to the heart of the age" because its "quasi-sadistic taste" revelled in their "dialectic."

As an extreme example of fondness for that dialectic Greene points to the crucial scene in *La Strage degl'Innocenti.* There, with what seems like utter lack of tact, Marino introduces Pietà (Pity) urging God to prevent the slaughter of the Hebrew children in Bethlehem by Herod's soldiers. But God's reply is that Justice rightly insists upon their massacre so that Satan's wickedness may be demonstrated, and so that the Church may glory in their martyrdom. By modern standards this divine interpretation of justice seems monstrous, but to scholastically trained minds it might seem defensible in the light of St. Thomas's observation that without tyrannical persecutions there could be no such thing as the patience of martyrs. Marino, of course, was not alluding to St. Thomas's passage, and was not at

67. See *PR,* I.3 and *PL,* XII.397.
68. In *The Descent from Heaven* (New Haven, Yale University Press, 1963), pp. 250–51.

all interested in its context in a discussion of the universal application of Aristotle's axiom in the *De Generatione et
corruptione* that the death of one individual is the price
both of the birth of another and of the preservation of
the species.[69] His portrayal of God as defending the slaughter of the innocents on grounds of pure justice is rightly
treated by Greene as a clumsy attempt to invest an un-
heroic incident with epic glory.

In contrast with Marino's glorification of the justice of
the slaughter of the innocents Milton's resolution of the
conflict of justice with mercy is a victory of poetic tact.
Their absolute claims are kept inviolate while they are
transcended by the Son's reply to the Father's question to
the "Heav'nly Powers":[70]

> Which of ye will be mortal to redeem
> Man's mortal crime, and just th' unjust to save,
> Dwells in all Heaven charity so dear?

But by the time when Pope accused Milton of turning
God into a "School-Divine,"[71] his judgment in allowing
his divine persons to speak at all was being questioned
on both aesthetic and theological grounds. Already his
Heaven was beginning to seem like "an echoing gallery
of pure theological reason," as Tucker Brooke called it.[72]
Though modern opinion regards the divine speeches as
spun out with grim satisfaction, Milton certainly used all

69. Nam corruptio unius est generatio alterius [*De generatione et corruptione,* 17]
per quam species conservatur. Cum igitur Deus sit universalis provisor totius
entis, ac ipsius providentiam pertinet ut permittat quosdam defectus esse in
aliquibus particularibus rebus, ne impediatur bonum universi perfectum. Si
enim omnia mala impedirentur, multa bona deessent universo. Non enim esset
vita leonis, si non esset occisio animalium; nec esset patientia martyrum, si non
esset persecutio tyrannorum. *Summa Theologica,* 1.q.22, art. 2.

70. *PL,* III.214–16.

71. The context of Pope's charge in *Imitations of Horace, Epodes* 2.1, implies that
the objection was already common among sophisticated readers.

72. In *A Literary History of England,* ed. A. C. Baugh (4 vols. New York,
Appleton-Century-Crofts, 1948), *2,* 691.

his rhetorical skill to secure them against seeming cruel, arbitrary, or tedious. To Addison[73] it seemed that in them he obviously "proceeds with a kind of fear and trembling, whilst he describes the sentiments of the Almighty." Was his primary motive creative and dramatic? Or was it to clarify the "theological rules of the poem . . . as coming straight from the Almighty"? Rather more the latter than the former, for a theological reason which had aesthetic implications for a public convinced, as he was, that "God, who at sundry times and in divers manners . . . spoke to the fathers by the prophets, hath . . . spoken to us by his Son,"[74] Milton could write his divine dialogues boldly. If all Scripture had been dictated to God's mouthpieces, and if the style of the Hebrew of the Old Testament and the Greek of the New Testament was the plainest and noblest ever written, the Scriptural substrate of the speeches vindicated both their theology and their style. And actually by the most recent count[75] of the unmistakable Scriptural echoes, there are no fewer than eighty-seven in 329 lines— enough to give every line the semblance of authentic divine utterance.

In daring to write the divine speeches Milton felt no presumption—any more than Cowley did when, in one of the rare divine interventions in his *Davideis,* he presented God as speaking directly out of a cloud of heavenly glory to the Israelites, who were violating his wishes by asking to be governed by a human King. "In wondrous sounds his *Voice* was heard" protesting that "This stubborn land sins still":

> Five hundred rolling Years, hath this stiff
> Nation strove,

73. *Spectator,* No. 315.
74. Hebrews 1:1.
75. James H. Sims in *The Bible in Milton's Epics* (Gainesville, University of Florida Press, 1962), p. 262.

To' exhaust the boundless Stores, of our
    unfathom'd *Love*.
Be't so then; yet, once more, are we resolv'd
    to try
T'outweary them through all their *Sins Variety*.[76]

For readers familiar with the Scriptural account of the
lapses of Israel from the golden age of the charismatic
judges to the monarchy of Saul, the sound of God's own
warning voice was clear in Cowley's paraphrase of his protest to Samuel (I Samuel 8:6–8) that ever since their exodus from Egypt the Israelites "have rejected me, that I
should not reign over them."

    In the few and short divine speeches in the *Davideis* we
hear the very tone of self-justification and "plaintiveness"
to which J. B. Broadbent objects[77] in Milton's representation of God as asking "Whose fault" were the falls of angels and men. The emergence of that tone in God's speeches
in the *Davideis* and its many occurrences in words attributed to God in Scripture may not make it acceptable to
our taste. Still less does the appeal to biblical examples
justify what Broadbent calls in condescending Arnoldian
terms the "Hebraic mannerisms"[78] of Milton's God, or
reconcile sensitive modern readers to what William Empson calls "God's appalling jokes."[79] But such off-hand
condemnation of Milton ignores the fact that he, too, understood the difficulty of reconciling the passions of the
anthropomorphic God of the Old Testament to the standards of human decency. In the opening chapter of the
Christian Doctrine he faced the problem in the historical

  76. *Davideis*, 4.24.
  77. In *Graver Subject*, p. 144. More politely described, this weakness is what
Walter Bagehot called (in *Literary Studies*, London, 1905—approvingly quoted
by Christopher Ricks in *Milton's Grand Style*, p. 20) the "curiously fatal error of
making God 'argue.'"
  78. Ibid., p. 152.
  79. In *The Listener*, 64 (1960), 111.

perspective which reaches back to Homer and the earliest
books of the Bible. The anthropomorphism of many Scriptural representations of God was disturbing, he felt, for
literal readers. And fundamentally he regarded himself as
obliged to read literally.

The way out of the difficulty was through a firm distinction between what Milton recognized as the consistently frank anthropomorphism of God's representation in
Scripture and the anthropopathetic representations of the
angry, jealous, and lustful Homeric gods to whose una-
shamed passions Plato and other pagan philosophers had
objected. The distinction rested upon the theological doctrine of God's absolute transcendence. Its literary implication explained Scripture itself. As C. A. Patrides has shown
in "*Paradise Lost* and the Theory of Accommodation,"[80] it
was declared in theological works like Richard Bernard's
The Bibles Abstract and Epitomee (1642) and was undoubtedly
familiar to many seventeenth-century readers in St. Augustine's statement of it in *The City of God* (15.25):

> God's anger is no disturbance of mind in Him, but
> His judgment assigning sin the deserved punishment;
> and His revolving of thought is an unchanged order-
> ing of changeable things. For God repents not of any-
> thing He does, as man does: but His knowledge of a
> thing ere it be done, and His thought of it when it
> is done, are both alike firm and fixed. But the scrip-
> ture without these phrases cannot instil into our un-
> derstandings the meaning of God's works, nor terrify
> the proud, nor stir up the idle, nor exercise the in-
> quirers, nor delight the understanders. This it cannot
> do without declining to our low capacities.[81]

80. *University of Texas Studies in Language and Literature*, 5 (1963), 58–63.
81. Healey's translation (2d ed. 1620; Everyman, 2 vols. 1945), 2, 93. Milton
was aware that for his less critical readers there would be no difficulty in
accepting the popular, dogmatic form of the belief in the *Summa Totalis* of
John Davies of Hereford that, though to God

For the theology of the *Christian Doctrine* and for the poetry of *Paradise Lost* alike Milton accepted Augustine's principle as confirmed by Genesis 1:26. "If," he reasoned, "God be said 'to have made man in his own image, after his likeness,' and that too not only as to his soul but also as to his outward form," then it followed that we should not be "afraid to attribute to him what he attributes to himself."[82] Never should we think that in acting or speaking in terms of the passions which Scripture attributes to him God could say anything unworthy of himself. Believing securely that God could not be scandalized by any of his "accommodations" of himself to human understanding in Scripture, Milton did not apologize for the divine acts and attributes to be found there.

Paradise Lost itself, then, must be a work of "accommodation" in the way that Raphael explained when he told Adam that

> ". . . what surmounts the reach
> Of human sense, I shall delineate so,
> By lik'ning spiritual to corporal forms,
> As may express them best."[83]

If in the dialogue in Heaven God seems to speak passionately, it is the reader, and not God, who feels, the passion.

. . . often, *Hate* ascribed be
Yet that in him, is simply, good, and iust,
For, hee thereby impugns Impiety:
And, in his wrath, he doth (what Iustice must)
Scowre, *Ill* from *Good;* sith *Euill, Good* doth rust;
Yet hee to *Wrath* still goes with *Leaden feet,*
Sith his *Wrathes* hands are yron that bray to dust:
But he, in mercy, flies the Meeke to meet,
On feet that wingèd are to make them fleet.

The Complete Works of John Davies of Hereford, ed. Alexander B. Grosart (2 vols. Chertsey Worthies Club, 1878), *1,* 6.

82. CE, *14,* 30–34.

83. *PL,* V.570–73.

Milton believed as firmly as St. Thomas Aquinas[84] did that, except for the unitive love of God for himself and his creatures, *nulla passio est in Deo.* Coleridge thought[85] that for an obvious theological reason Milton rightly confined "the language of excitement" and "poetic passion" in God's speeches "to the language of Scripture," and that only once in all *Paradise Lost* did he allow "the *passio vera,* or *quasi humana* to appear." Rather oddly, it seems, Coleridge's exception to prove his rule was that in VI.710–18, where "the Father contemplates his own likeness in the Son before the battle." Of course, Coleridge was not implying that the Father took more pleasure in contemplating his image in the Son as that of a god of battles than he took in contemplating it in the Son in whom "Love hath abounded more than Glory abounds."[86] But he left that perhaps unconscious hint to be pounced upon by the psychological critics who have followed Raleigh[87] in finding "the author of *A Defence of the People of England*" in "the proud, voluble candour" and "uneasy boastfulness" of some of God's speeches in *Paradise Lost.* When in 1819 Coleridge wrote his lecture on the poem, he was not even unconsciously preparing the way for Shelley's assault on its God in *A Defense of Poetry* as one who "in the cold security of undoubted triumph inflicts the most horrible revenge upon his enemy."[88]

For theological reasons Coleridge found it natural to approve of the exclusion of human passion from God's speeches. Contempt for those reasons and for Milton's God prompts the dictum of a modern disciple of Shelley that,

84. *Summa Theologica,* 1.q.20.1 ad 3.
85. *Coleridge on the Seventeenth Century,* ed. Roberta F. Brinkley (Durham, Duke University Press, 1955), p. 577.
86. *PL,* III.312.
87. Walter Raleigh, *Milton* (London, Edward Arnold, 1900), p. 131.
88. *Essays and Letters by Percy Bysshe Shelley,* ed. Ernest Rhys (London, 1886, p. 27. Empson quotes the passage at length in *Milton's God,* pp. 20–21.

"the utterance of God is good in proportion as it is drained of personality: the less we *feel* God in what he says, the better the effect. The majestic language describing the 'dread tribunal' of the Son (3.326) is an instance. We listen to a full-toned Voice from the void."[89] The clash of views on God's speeches in the dialogue is beautifully exemplified by the contrast between Waldock's irony in praising the Voice from the void and Arnold Stein's cordial acceptance of the God of *Paradise Lost* as a being "outside the universe of action" who is not and should not be "presented as a dramatic character." For both metaphysical and esthetic reasons Stein regards it as right that his "Language and cadence are as unsensuous as if Milton were writing a model for the Royal Society, and attempting to speak only to the understanding."[90] That is just what "the omniscient voice of the omnipotent moral law" is doing in the speeches which Miss Samuel observes need no "rhetoric to persuade" because they simply represent "the nature of things expounding itself."[91]

It is a little too easy for defenders of the character and style of the Father in the dialogue in Heaven to build upon his avoidance of senuous metaphor and emotional tone. His most specious psychological analyst, Broadbent, builds upon his legal metaphors. They are, he says, part of "a legalism indigenous to Judeo-Christianity."[92] Certainly they were the natural inheritance of the legalistic conceptions of the Fall and Atonement which Patrides has traced from Patristic theories of Christ serving as the ransom of all souls fallen into Satan's possession or—later—of all souls that have offended God's honor, or—later still—his justice. Their outgrowth was the Reformers' forensic theory of the Atonement which Patrides regards as "a

---

89. A. J. A. Waldock in *"Paradise Lost" and its Critics*, p. 104.
90. Arnold Stein, *Answerable Style*, pp. 127–28.
91. Irene Samuel in "The Dialogue in Heaven," *PMLA*, 72 (1957), 603.
92. *Graver Subject*, p. 144.

commentary on Milton's epic."[93] His illustrations of it are
drawn from the whole spectrum of English theology in the
seventeenth century, extending from *The Exaltation of Christ*
(1646) of the Baptist Thomas Collier to the *Sermons* (fourth
edition, 1641) of Bishop Lancelot Andrewes, who asked:[94]
"Cannot GOD *forgive* offences to Him made, of His free
goodnesse, of His meere *mercy,* without putting His SONNE to
all this pain?" His answer was: "Fond men! If He would
quit His *Iustice,* or wave His *truth,* He could: But, His
Iustice and *truth* are to Him as *essentiall,* as *intrinsically essentiall,* as His *mercy. Iustice* other wise remains unsatisfied:
and satisfied it must be, either on Him or on us." The
fact is that the counterpoise of justice and mercy in the
debate which Milton inherited from the theologians as
well as from the morality plays was itself a forensic metaphor. In it justice and truth set the example of pleading
in terms of legal principles. As lawyer for the defense
Mercy can be made to look like an honest woman only
with the help of theology.

The emergence of that help is of course the crowning
element in the entire dialogue. It is prepared for by an
accumulation of rhetorical schemes which Broadbent has
discussed in his assertion of the inadequacy of Milton's
divine rhetoric for the support of the main theme of the
dialogue. To him, they seem to be mere jugglings "with
a limited number of . . . syntactical shapes."[95] Their only
effect is to dehumanize the Father whose "querulousness"
Broadbent sees as his most obvious human trait. To Gilbert[96] the energy of those tight schemes seems Longinian.
Looking at them more narrowly, Cope has challenged the
traditional denial of all sensuous imagery in the Father's

93. C. A. Patrides, "Milton and the Protestant Theory of the Atonement,"
p. 10.
94. P. 100.
95. *Graver Subject,* p. 146.
96. *Studies in Honor of Harris Francis Fletcher,* p. 50.

speeches by pointing out five light/dark metaphors which concur in serving the all-containing rhetorical figure of the irony of God's merciful providence both in the dialogue and in the entire epic action. Then, turning to the "reiterative schemes of alliteration, anaphora ('Should man . . . should man'), antimetabole ('be from thee far, / That far be from thee'), and epanalepsis ('unmake / For him, what for thy glory thou hast made')," Cope treats them as the necessary rhetorical elements in a ritualistic statement of the unity of purpose and understanding between the Father and the Son in the entire dialogue.[97]

An odd superficial concurrence between Broadbent and Cope is their agreement upon the common character of the Father and Son which serves to point up their radically different ideas of that character. For Broadbent "The Son's rhetorical modulations of the theme of grace"[98] are less impressive than his echoes of the paternal "eschatological crunchings" which betray their common vengeful spirit. Closely related to this view of deity is Broadbent's feeling that plaintiveness is the least offensive of the Father's traits in a court where he must be judge, counsel, and plaintiff in one."[99] But the really great problem of that judge, as Milton well understood, was to exonerate himself of the charge of responsibility for all evil and its penalties, which has always been brought against omniscience. In the first movement of the dialogue God counters that charge with the answer that Broadbent traces back through Hooker in the *Laws of Ecclesiastical Polity* to Boethius in *The Consolation of Philosophy:*

> As if Predestination over-rul'd
> Thir will, dispos'd by absolute Decree
> Or high foreknowledge; they themselves decreed

97. Jackson I. Cope, *The Metaphoric Structure of Paradise Lost,* pp. 169–74.
98. *Graver Subject,* p. 153.
99. *Ibid.* p. 144.

> Thir own revolt, not I: if I foreknew,
> Foreknowledge had no influence on their
>   fault . . . .[1]

The answer may not satisfy all minds. To Milton it did because, like Adam, he had learned in the hard way that evil is something that cannot be prevented by human "foreknowing"[2] in a world where he believed that men had full freedom of will.

The crux is the freedom of the will which Milton asserted in full consciousness of its denial by many of the thinkers of the Renaissance. It is that assertion which critics like Grierson,[3] Peter,[4] and Empson[5] cannot forgive him. Nor can they forgive John Diekhoff for seriously defending Milton's position.[6] Here Milton must be judged mainly in the light of his own time. For Erasmus, as for Spenser, all evil was caused by the human will. For all theologians in Milton's time it was still as true as it was when Tertullian said it, that "there would be no reward of good or evil if men were good or evil by necessity, and not by choice."[7] In this matter Milton spoke from passionate conviction. He spoke also with the fervent agreement of most of his Arminian contemporaries. "For infinit Reasons," said Traherne, "it was best that He [man] should be in a Changeable Estate, and have power to chuse what himself listed. for he may so chuse as to becom One Spirit with GOD Almighty."[8]

In the structure of *Paradise Lost* Raphael's account of

---

1. *PL*, III.114–18.

2. *PL*, XI.773.

3. *Milton and Wordsworth*, pp. 112–17.

4. *A Critique of "Paradise Lost,"* p. 12.

5. In *The Listener*, p. 111.

6. In *"Milton's 'Paradise Lost' "* (New York, Columbia University Press, 1946), pp. 76, 82–85, 108.

7. In *Contra Marcion*, as quoted by Henry Hammond in *Of Fundamentals* (1654), chap. 16.

the revolt in Heaven and of Abdiel's resistance to it in Book V is obviously designed to give Adam and Eve a distinct understanding of their own capacity for obedience to God, and to convince the reader that "Of their free will they are disobedient." The first point has been brilliantly made by Gilbert in "The Theological Basis of Satan's Rebellion and the Function of Abdiel in *Paradise Lost*."[9] The second is necessarily the point of departure for Diekhoff's chapter defending the concept of "Man's Guilt"[10] to a society where

> Our laboratories sabotage free will
> And we are leased certificates to lust
> With no taskmaster now to bear us ill.[11]

A no less distinct structural element in Milton's assertion of free will is his treatment of the devils in their partially psychological hell in Books I and II and Satan's soliloquy confessing that he is his own hell because his self-will "Chose freely"[12] to rebel and now disdains pardon at the price of repentance. The willful obduracy of the rebel angels is expressly a main element in Milton's treatment of the steps in their fall. Until the third day of the battle in Heaven it is implied that they might have made peace if they had not "stood obdur'd . . . hope conceiving from despair."[13] They are like the Pharaoh of Exodus to whom Milton compares them in *Paradise Lost* I.306–15, whom he recalls in the *Christian Doctrine* I.7[14] as "becoming ever

8. *Centuries, Poems and Meditations,* ed. Margoliouth (2 vols. Oxford, Clarendon Press, 1958), *1*, 212.

9. *MP, 40* (1942), 19–42.

10. In *Milton's "Paradise Lost,"* pp. 49–75.

11. John Malcolm Brinnin in "A Devotion for John Milton" in *No Arch, No Triumph* (New York, Knopf, 1945), p. 66.

12. *PL,* IV.72.

13. *PL,* VI.785–87.

14. CE, *15,* 80.

more angry and obdurate in his resistance to the commands of God."

In the main structuring of *Paradise Lost* the dialogue in Heaven itself exemplifies its own principle that finite wills are free only when they obey the will of God. On aesthetic rather than theological ground that suggestion is made by Roy Daniells in a chapter on "Unity, Power, and Will"[15] as main factors in the imaginative creation of the poem. He does not make the comparison with Abdiel, but he sees the dialogue as culminating in the demonstration of God's mercy "as an act of will and unity of purpose between Father and Son." Human salvation is the object of the act. It is treated in a way which Daniells regards as distinctly characteristic of Milton's peculiarly personal and Puritan variety of Baroque sensibility. A Bernini might have treated the subject evangelically or mystically; Milton keeps it "firmly controlled within a concept of filial obedience and subject to the primacy of will." Though Daniells does not call the dialogue a drama or give it that name, as Miss Samuel does, he thinks of it as the surrender of the Son's will to the Father's and quotes the lines which expressly subordinate the Son's love for man to his "Filial obedience" as he "attends the will / Of his great Father."[16] For such submission Daniells does not hesitate to assume that throughout *Paradise Lost* "all motivation" is thrown "back into the will of the Father. This can be done," he declares, "because the Son's status is less than that of the Father." And to make his assumption uncompromisingly plain, he adds that here we see "Milton's Arianism becoming explicit."[17]

At this moment it is hazardous to assume that Milton wrote the dialogue in Heaven from a consciously Arian

15. Roy Daniells, *Milton, Mannerism and the Baroque* (Toronto, University of Toronto Press, 1963), p. 68.

16. *PL,* III.269–71.

17. *Milton, Mannerism and Baroque,* p. 101.

point of view. As Patrides[18] has shown, he repudiated far too many of Arius' principles in the *Christian Doctrine* ever to have been willing to accept that label. But at the same time Patrides casts no doubt upon the "subordinationist" view of the Son which Milton so elaborately affirms in the treatise. Yet in *Paradise Lost* Patrides finds a deliberate affirmation of "co-equality between the Father and Son," which perhaps "represents an effort to 'correct' the treatise's denial of that co-equality." In this surmise he is hardly likely to be followed by sympathizers with Broadbent's feeling that in the dialogue in Heaven itself Milton fails in a not very tactful attempt to disguise his "Arianism," and betrays it when in "the angels' final paean to the Son . . . subordinationism is confirmed: 'the strife of Mercy and Justice' is resolved outside the Father in him who, 'sat / Second to thee.' "[19]

Though, as Broadbent notes, Milton identifies himself with the angels' paean, that fact should be weighed against the instances of affirmed or implied co-equality between Father and Son throughout the epic. Their preponderance weighs against Broadbent's assumption together with Daniells' that as a whole *Paradise Lost* is "Arian." Within the limits of the dialogue in Heaven, if with Parish we relate it to God's Scriptural conversations with Moses and Abraham, the situation seems to develop into a paradoxical inversion of Peter's view of the Son as the Father's tactful tutor. But as the Father's pupil, he becomes a subordinate being. Only in Cope's very different idea of the situation as a kind of "ritualistic dialogue" does the scene in Heaven imply the co-equality of the actors. In their almost antiphonal exchanges of interlocking rhetorical "schemes" or plays on words that spiral up to the solution of the paradox of the Fall by the irony of the Re-

18. C. A. Patrides, "Milton and Arianism," *JHI, 25* (1964), 421–29.
19. *Graver Subject,* p. 155.

demption it is hard not to imagine them as playing two perfectly balanced parts on a stage. Cope does not—like Daniells—make an explicit theological inference, but he unmistakably implies it when he writes that, "As the dialogue in Heaven unfolds . . . God develops the paradox of the fall in his divided persons as Father and Son, Judge and Redeemer."[20]

Anything like drama in the development of the scene— anything like the different kinds of conflict or even the differentiation of persons such as Miss Samuel, Peter, and Daniells have variously recognized in it, is alien to Cope's view. Indeed he explicitly objects to Miss Samuel's treatment of it as "a dramatic encounter universalizing the freedom of will through the act of a Son ignorant of the ultimate structure of the eternal myth."[21] But even when the Son is imagined as a pure hypostatization of one of God's divided parts, it is hard not to think of him as speaking out of his imperfect knowledge of the secret mysteries which Milton quotes Christ, in the *Christian Doctrine* I.5,[22] as saying were known only to the Father.

Perhaps in the end, if the conflicting views of the best interpreters cannot be reconciled, the gap between them can be bridged or narrowed if the conversation between the Father and Son is given the name which they all casually use to refer to it—a dialogue. The question whether it is a dialogue of two persons or a dialogue within one divided person may then be subordinated to its proper function as dialogue in a more or less Platonic sense: the quest of truth. It is the voice of that divine daughter that its style has consistently tried to echo even in the passages where Miss Samuel and Parish differ from Coleridge in thinking that God's words are touched with emotion because the Son has deserved his exaltation by recognizing

20. *Metaphoric Structure,* p. 175.
21. Ibid., p. 167.
22. CE *14,* 316.

the full meaning of the Father's love for him and for man. Of course the method of its search for truth in the dialogue is not conspicuously dialectical, though Parish might regard it as pedagogical. But implicit in it is the dialectic of Plato and his successors, pagan and Christian. Justice cannot consist in the enforcement of any mere legal claims of Satan or of God upon the souls of men. The justice of the ruler of the universe must excel that of the human rulers who—by Socrates' reasoning[23]—are bound, like a true physician or pilot, to seek no personal profit in doing their work. In making justice a divine virtue Christianity had from the first united it with mercy. In St. Thomas's dialectic mercy could be mingled with justice only after divine mercy had been cleared of resemblance to human emotion and defined in terms of effective action, especially in the tempering of God's just punishments.[24] Though Milton was no student of St. Thomas, he was the heir of the literature which stemmed from St. Thomas's reckoning[25] of the many advantages accruing to man from God's decision not to remit sin by a mere act of merciful absolution, but to accomplish it by the Crucifixion. That decision was reached by divine justice meditating on itself. Its later dialectic took the form of the many debates between mercy and justice which contributed to the inspiration, substance, style, and structural importance of Milton's dialogue in Heaven.

23. *Republic* 1.15; 341.c–d.
24. *Summa Theologica,* 1.q.21, art. 4.c, and ad 1.
25. Ibid., 3.q.46, arts. 1–3.

❦ 6 ❧

"Myself am Hell"

> For him Hell is still a place of torment; the earth, a place of struggle and trial.
>
> E. E. Stoll

Thirty years ago Denis Saurat[1] declared that, as far as Satan is concerned, the drama of *Paradise Lost* is wrapped up in the words of our title and their context:

> Me miserable! which way shall I fly
> Infinite wrath, and infinite despair?
> Which way I fly is Hell; myself am Hell;
> And in the lowest deep a lower deep
> Still threatn'ing to devour me opens wide,
> To which the Hell I suffer seems a Heav'n.
>
> [IV.73–78]

At the same time Lascelles Abercrombie hung Milton's characterization of Satan upon his pivotally important "symbolic behaviour" in his soliloquy in Book IV. Rather incoherently the symbolism was explained in terms of "the depths of the personality" as entangled in "the absolute antinomy—fixt fate, free will" emerging in the devil's "transparent character."[2] More clearly, by relating the

---

1. Saurat, *Milton: Man and Thinker,* p. 179.
2. Lascelles Abercrombie, *The Idea of Great Poetry* (London, Secker, 1925), pp. 200–01.

soliloquy (Book IV) to Satan's profession (I.106–08), of an

> unconquerable Will
> And study of revenge, immortal hate,
> And courage never to submit or yield,

and to our last view of him (Book X) as a serpent chewing the apples of Sodom, Abercrombie indicated the structural importance of Satan's discovery of the hell within him to the design of the entire poem. More recently, in "Milton's Hell Revisited,"[3] Ernest Schanzer has made the soliloquy in Book IV the focus of a study of Milton's hell as a macrocosm of which Satan and his followers are the microcosm. The hell which they have created within themselves is a parody of heaven. Its jarring hinges, its raucous noise, its "Vain wisdom . . . and false philosophy," its spurious hierarchy, and its infernal trinity of Satan, Sin, and Death are all parodies of their heavenly counterparts. The key to them all is Satan's confession that his "spiritual fall is a process continuous throughout the poem:

> 'myself am Hell;
> And in the lowest deep a lower deep
> Still threat'ning to devour me opens wide,
> To which the Hell I suffer seems a Heav'n.' "

In Schanzer's illuminating report on Milton's hell its most difficult ontological problem is—perhaps unintentionally—solved without examination and almost in an aside when he says that "Satan is the creator of the microcosm of Hell, just as God is the creator of the Macrocosm." This assertion is imperiled by Milton's firm statement in the *Christian Doctrine* (I.33),[4] that hell is a place outside our universe which God has created for the punishment of bad angels and bad men. He adds that hell is too

3. *UTQ* 24 (1955), 144.
4. CE, *16*, 372.

138 CHAPTER SIX

remote from our world for its inhabitants to entertain any
hope of its destruction in the final conflagration that Revelation promises will result in "a new Heaven and a new
earth." As usual, Milton is categorical in stating a belief
and obviously serious in declaring it. In this case he is
certainly no less serious than Antonio Rusca was in pro-
claiming the traditional faith in a subterranean hell when,
in 1621, in an essentially Scholastic handling of the subject, he asserted that hell is "a subterranean place of torment prepared by God for wicked spirits and souls."[5]
Rusca's work is dogmatic and literal about hell's geogra-
phy. The imaginatively barren result, if Milton knew the
work, must have been as antipathetic to him as was Rusca's
theology, yet both men concurred in conceiving hell as the

> place Eternal Justice had prepar'd
> For those rebellious   [I.70–71]

It is not difficult to collect passages from *Paradise Lost*
of which Rusca would have approved for their traditional
representation of hell as

> a fiery Deluge, fed
> With ever-burning Sulphur unconsum'd,

flaming as "one great Furnace," from whose

> flames
> No light, but rather darkness visible
> Serv'd only to discover sights of woe,
> Regions of sorrow, doleful shades, where peace
> And rest can never dwell, hope never comes . . .
>   [I.62–69]

Indeed, it is only too easy to read more into the allusion
to the inscription over the gate of Dante's hell in Milton's

5. Antonio Rusca, *De inferno et statu daemonum ante mundi exitium, libri quinque.
In quibus Tartarea cavitas, parata ibi cruciamentorum genera. Ethnicorum de his opin-
iones, daemonumque conditio, usque ad magnum Iudicij diem, varia eruditione, describun-
tur* (Milan, 1621).

words, "hope never comes," and to treat them as ground
for regarding the Miltonic hell as fundamentally medieval.
And, in truth, it is medieval and Dantesque in the sense
that "the Difference between Heaven and Hell is absolute."
That, says C. M. Bowra, is what Satan "admits to himself" when he says, "Myself am Hell."[6] The difference is
absolute, and it is a matter of justice that it should be so.
Quite as definitely as Dante's, Milton's hell is an ines-
capable absolute which divine justice and love have created. Milton's conception, Sister Miriam Joseph assures
us, is orthodox. "Through rebellion Satan experiences a
'Hell within him,' " and so divine justice is satisfied, just
as it is when, "through obedience Adam is assured of a
'Paradise within him.' "[7] But can we be sure that the
two hells, Dante's and Milton's, are ontologically alike?
Is Milton's hell truly local and, in the ordinary sense of
the word, physical?

In trying to answer that question, it will help if we first
remember that Dante has been pronounced unorthodox by
Thomas Aquinas' standards because he dared to write
"the *Paradiso* to show that heaven is on earth, as in the
Inferno he showed that hell is on earth."[8] It will help also
if we remember that the phrase "Myself am Hell" has a
theological taproot which Grant McColley traced back to
the doctrine of the anonymous author of the *Discourse of
Devils:* "all the fiends are in darkness wherever they go because darkness is the essence of their being."[9] In a com-
plementary image, Bonaventura expressed the same idea
when he said that the devils "carry the fire of hell with
them wherever they go." In a rather indiscriminate way

6. C. M. Bowra, *From Virgil to Milton* (London, Macmillan, 1948), pp. 221–22.
7. Sister Miriam Joseph, "Orthodoxy in *Paradise Lost*," in *Laval théologique et
philosophique, 8* (1954), 180.
8. Allan H. Gilbert, *Dante's Conception of Justice* (Durham, Duke University
Press, 1925), p. 143.
9. Grant McColley, *Paradise Lost: An Account of Its Growth and Major Origins,
with a Discussion of Milton's Use of Sources and Literary Patterns* (Chicago, Packard,
1940), pp. 140–41.

McColley found a parallel for the idea in Thomas Aquinas' statement that the demons are "bound by the fire of hell even while they are in the dark atmosphere of this world," where God uses them in the natural order to procure man's welfare without in the least diminishing their anguish, "because they know that confinement in hell is their due." For Thomas we know that hell and its pains were physical no less than they were spiritual; but we know just as definitely that, in Medicean Florence, Bonaventura's words were repeated in contexts implying that both for the demons (such as there might be) and for the human damned, the pains of hell were entirely spiritual or psychological. In a commentary on the *Divine Comedy* a once famous Florentine Neoplatonist, Cristoforo Landino, declared that the devils "forever carry their inferno about with them,"[10] but the hell within them was reflected by no outward macrocosm.

Landino's conception of hell was a major part of an epic theory that might easily relate him to Milton and perhaps did contribute directly to the first two books of *Paradise Lost.* The theory had been expounded by Landino's master, Marsilio Ficino, for whom all epic poetry dealt with the single theme of the struggle of the soul toward divine illumination. The result was a conviction that the *Divine Comedy* and the *Aeneid* could be read as developments of a common theme. The heart of the *Aeneid* was the hero's visit to the realms of the dead in the sixth book, and the revelations of the Sibyl to Aeneas were to be understood simply as variations on the words of Milton's Satan as applicable to any damned spirit: "Myself am Hell." But in the unlocated places where Ficino taught that "the Souls, according to the habits assumed [in this life], are led by an inner and secret inclination to the punishments and rewards appropriate to their habits,"

10. *Dante con l'espositione di Cristofero Landino* (Venice, 1564), p. 159 (*Inferno,* 34).

there was no need or room for Satan. For Ficino, as Oskar
Kristeller observes, the Furies became "simply bad passions to which the impure Soul is subject; the tortures
of Tantalus, Sisyphus, and others indicate the painful images of the sick imagination persecuted by its own products. Tartarus itself is the place where the Soul sleeps and
is persecuted by its dreams."[11]

Another recent interpreter of Ficino, André Chastel,[12]
has pointed out that his allegorical interpretation of the
classic myths about Hades—particularly the revelations
about it in the sixth book of the *Aeneid*—became a vital
part of the theory of the epic and, indeed, of the poetic experience itself in the Quattrocento in Italy and so remained
there, and in France, far into the following century. The
key to the *Aeneid* and the *Divine Comedy* alike, said Landino
in his commentary on Virgil in the *Discussions at Camal-
dula*, was to be found in Socrates' myth of the descent of
souls into our universe as it is found in the *Phaedo*. From
that famous passage Landino drew the first article of his
creed: "nihil aliud inferorum locum animis nostris esse . . .
quam corpus ipsum quo veluti carcere includuntur."[13]
This is not the place to survey Landino's enthusiastic summary of the myth of pre-existing souls descending through
the spheres of the planets to immerse themselves in the
Lethean streams of matter and the active life. What is
important here is the clearly stated corollary: "Nam quae
de tartaris fabulantur poetae ea omnia animam in corpore
pati manifestum est." Landino was anxious to honor the
Christian doctrines of the creation of all souls at the birth
of their bodies and of the existence of a local hell for the

11. Quoted from Ficino by Kristeller in *The Philosophy of Marsilio Ficino*, p.
361.

12. André Chastel, *Marsile Ficin et l'art* (Geneva, Droz, 1954), p. 144.

13. Cristoforo Landino, *Libri quattuor* (Strassbourg, 1508), p. 57 . The following quotations come from fols. 58ʳ–58ᵛ, and all are from the fourth book of
the *Disputationes Camaldulenses*, which is the second part of Landino's interpretation of the *Aeneid*.

punishment of the wicked in the bowels of the earth, but he was still more anxious to defend the precious Platonic truth that "viventes homines cum in vitia labuntur, ad inferos ruere." It is strictly in the light of the Platonic myth that Landino interprets the story of Aeneas' descent to the underworld and the Sibyl's admonition: *Facilis descensus Averno.*

In *Paradise Lost* the uncompromisingly moral and psychological hell of the Neoplatonists is imaginatively realized in full and conscious conjunction with Milton's belief that hell is a place outside our universe which God has prepared for the reception of evil spirits and wicked men. As we shall see in the second part of this essay, that belief was essential both to his demonology and to his plot. It may be true, as J. B. Broadbent thinks, that Milton regarded his "ever-burning Sulplur unconsum'd" as a mere "symbol of internal misery," but it is hardly accurate to regard him as "irritated at having to support the more sophisticated and Christian notion of an inner hell with classico-medieval flames and sulphur."[14] Of course, there never was any doubt in his mind as to his preference for the sophisticated notion of hell, which he knew was no less pagan than Christian. In *The Doctrine and Discipline of Divorce* (II.3),[15] he approved that notion and in the same sentence attributed it to the pagans:

> To banish forever into a local hell, whether in the air or in the centre, or in that uttermost and bottomless gulf of chaos, deeper from the holy bliss than the world's diameter multiplied; they thought not a punishment so proper and proportionate for God to inflict as to punish sin with sin.

Both Milton and his audience were familiar with the sophisticated notion of hell in both pagan and Christian

14. J. B. Broadbent, "Milton's Hell," *ELH, 21* (1954), 170.
15. CE, *13,* 442.

tradition. They knew that it went back beyond Lucretius'
assertion in *De rerum natura* (3.908–1023), that the only hell
is the superstitious fears and passions of men in this world.
They knew that Seneca's assertion of the immortality of
noble spirits was coupled with a denial of the physical
tortures of Tartarus at the close of his letter *To Marcia,
On Consolation*. In spite of the protests of Catholic and
Protestant theologians against the encroachments of the
sophisticated conception of hell, it had the growing prestige of the great pagans behind it and also the force of a
current of humanist speculation which was older than the
Florentine Neoplatonists. Such speculation had been
boldly turned into dogma by Coluccio Salutati, when he
said: "Quod infernus intelligitur a poetis humanum corpus aut sensualitas et infimum baratrum vitiorum aut
ignorantiae cecitas."[16] Salutati's view matches well
with Spenser's allegory of Guyon's visit to an underworld,
the Delve of Mammon, which is clearly psychological, although its landscape is like Virgil's hell, or perhaps more
like Dante's or like that in *The Mirror for Magistrates*. In
Spenser's inferno Pontius Pilate shares the pains with Tantalus to serve as an

> Ensample . . . of mind intemperate
> . . . to all that live in high degree . . .
> To teach them how to vse their present state
> [*Faerie Queene*, II.7.60.3–5]

In the double time of *The Faerie Queene* Guyon is in both
the here and the hereafter. Because he is temperate, he is
immune from the torments of Tartarus, which, Landino
explains, have no power over temperate men. But around

16. Coluccio Salutati, *De laboribus Herculis*, ed. B. L. Ullman in *Thesaurus
mundi* (Zurich, 1951), p. 227. In a similar vein the young Milton spoke in the
First Prolusion of the pangs of guilty consciences as the onslaughts of Sphinxes,
Harpies, Gorgons, and Chimaeras, who hunt their victims down with flaming
torches in their hands.

him flow the rivers of the classical hell whose waters will
never assuage the thirst of Tantalus—for the same reason
that, in an earlier canto, the flames in the "secret bowelles"
of Pyrochles cannot be quenched by any earthly lake or
river. Spenser's allegories illustrate Ficino's doctrine of the
natural gravitation of all souls to the rewards and punishments, alike in this world and in the next, which correspond to their characters and finally segregate them by
what Kristeller calls a kind of "ontological principle."

As we have seen, it was possible to believe in Ficino's
kind of segregation and at the same time to be skeptical
or even negative about a local hell in the life to come.
On narrowly moral grounds, as well as on those of a criti-
cally humanistic study of the Bible and the classics, the
sophisticated and purely psychological idea of hell had
the strong appeal to Milton that appears so clearly in the
passage that has been quoted from the *Doctrine and Discipline of Divorce.* And in favor of his unqualified preference
for that idea, it is possible to cite several passages from the
second book of *Paradise Lost,* the most striking of which is
his treatment of the rivers of hell in very much the way
that Spenser treated them in his purely allegorical inferno
of the Delve of Mammon. For Milton the rivers are actual
enough to be main landmarks in the topography of his
hell—just as the four rivers of his paradise are as actual
as the Tigris, which

> at the foot of Paradise
> Into a Gulf shot under ground, till part
> Rose up a Fountain by the Tree of Life.
> [IX.71–73]

Yet the four rivers of Milton's paradise seem to be tinged
with the mass of fluctuating allegory about them that was
part of Christian tradition, and—quite definitely—the
rivers of his hell are allegorical:

Abhorred Styx, the flood of deadly hate,
Sad Acheron of sorrow, black and deep;
Cocytus, nam'd of lamentation loud
Heard on the rueful stream; fierce Phlegeton
Whose waves of torrent fire inflame with rage.
Far off from these a slow and silent stream,
Lethe, the river of oblivion, rolls
Her wat'ry Labyrinth, whereof who drinks
Forthwith his former state and being forgets,
Forgets both joy and grief, pleasure and pain.
                                          [II.577–86]

Unlike the first three rivers in the list, Lethe fits awk-
wardly into the allegory that would make them all symbols of various passions. The flaw is soon corrected, however, when we learn that all the efforts of the roving
fiends to drink the Lethean stream are opposed by Medusa "with Gorgonian terror" and that

            of itself the water flies
     All taste of living wight, as once it fled
     The lip of Tantalus.   [II.612–14]

The sophisticated idea of hell is implicit in the names
of the four rivers themselves, as Milton implies by his
explanations of them in the text. As he well knew, he was
on ground familiar to his readers. Many of them would
remember that the greatest of the Renaissance mythographers, Natale Conti, had put the essence of the Neoplatonic allegories of the four infernal rivers and the moral
to be drawn from them into two brief sentences: "Neque
potuit quispiam ad inferos accedere, nisi per haec flumina,
vel (ut verius dicam) per turbulentissimas has animi cogi-
tationes, quas antiqui per suas fabulas significarunt. Qui
quidem ita vivendum esse per haec figmenta ostendebant,

vt intrepidi essemus ad omnem post mortem fortunam."[17]

The easy descent to hell was by way of the passions, and by their control a man might fearlessly look forward to any fortune that could befall him beyond the grave. Conti's tone is pagan and Stoic. It is a far cry from Paul's faith that death has no sting. But it is perfectly consistent with a faith in future reward and punishment like Plato's confidence in the future relative happiness of the good and his acceptance—in the *Phaedo* (113e)—of Tartarus as an eternal place of punishment for those who have committed many great acts of sacrilege or wicked and abominable murders. Though it is a sophisticated and psychological hell that emerges from Conti's allegorization of the myths, of its rivers and its sufferers—Tantalus, Sisyphus, and Ixion—in the end he leaves us with an impression less of many microcosmic, private hells than of a macrocosm which resembles Milton's hell:

> A Universe of death, which God by curse
> Created evil, for evil only good,
> Where all life dies, death lives, and Nature
>   breeds,
> Perverse, all monstrous, all prodigious things,
> Abominable, inutterable, and worse
> Than Fables yet have feigned, or fear conceived,
> Gorgons and Hydras, and Chimaeras dire.
>   [*PL,* II.622–28]

The negative conception of evil in these lines is clearly Augustinian, and no less Augustinian is the allegorical conception of hell whose irreducible core is something actual, a universe "worse than fables yet have feigned." Milton knew that his readers could find Augustine's well-known assertion that both hell and the Earthly Paradise

17. Natalis Comes, *Mythologiae libri X* (Frankfurt, 1596), Book III, chap. 3, p. 199.

are to be conceived actually, as well as allegorically, quoted in popular works like John Salkeld's *A Treatise of Paradise*[18] and Thomas Milles's ΑΡΧΑΙΟΠΛΟΥΤΟΣ.[19] Augustine's saying that "every disordered spirit shall be a punishment to itself" is quoted by Milles, together with his statement in the *City of God* (13.21), that every possible edifying allegory should be extracted from the biblical account of the Earthly Paradise, but only as long as no shadow of doubt is cast on the literal scriptural record of "the true and local one." And Milles noted that Augustine's doctrine about hell was analogous. The allegorists should be encouraged to extract all available values from their interpretations of the true and local hell, but they must never endanger the faith in it that Scripture literally justifies. Milles recalled that the sophisticated, allegorical theory of hell was entertained by Jerome and Ambrose, by Proculeius and Hierocles, and by "the prophets generally," but he took his stand with Origen and Augustine in accepting a hell that is local.

In this matter Milton also stood with Augustine, though he localized his hell outside our universe, remote in Chaos, where he reasoned, in the *Christian Doctrine*, that it must certainly lie. All the traditional fables about it fell far wide, as well as short, of the truth; yet, without entirely disdaining their help, in the first two books of *Paradise Lost* he felt himself to be representing an actual hell not untruthfully somewhat in the way that Raphael tried to "delineate" heaven to Adam in Books V and VI, "By

18. John Salkeld, *A Treatise of Paradise* (London, N. Butler, 1620), pp. 56–57.

19. Thomas Milles, ΑΡΧΑΙΟΠΛΟΥΤΟΣ *Containing, Ten Following Bookes to the Former* TREASURIE *of Auncient and Moderne Times. Being the Learned Collections, Iudicious Readings, and Memorable Observations: Not onely Divine, Morall, and Philosophicall; But also Poeticall, Martiall, Politicall, Historicall, Astrologicall, &c. Translated out of that worthy Spanish Gentleman, Pedro Mexia, and M. Francesco Sansovino, that Famous Italian, As also, of those Honourable Frenchmen, Anthony du Verdier, Lord of Vauprivez; Loys Guyon, Sieur de la Nauche, Counsellor vnto the King; Claudius Gruget, Parisian, &c.* (2 vols. London, 1619), 2, 13.

lik'ning spiritual to corporal forms" with the suggestion
that hell is in many ways a shadow of earth, as Raphael
told Adam that earth is

> but the shadow of Heav'n, and things therein
> Each to other like, more than on Earth is thought.
>
> [V.572,575–76]

In the preceding lines Raphael pairs hell with heaven as
the subjects of his talk to Adam. Later on he is explicit
and sardonic in making hell local when he recalls Abdiel's
warning to Satan to leave heaven and take his evil followers with him "to the place of evil, hell." If this line
stood alone, it might not seem to imply anything more
than metaphorical, but its literal force becomes unmistakable sixteen lines farther on, when Satan replies that
he and his hosts mean to win the impending battle

> Or turn this Heav'n itself into the Hell
> Thou fablest   [VI.291–92]

No less definite are the words of the Son of God later in
the account of the battle in heaven, when he undertakes to

> rid Heav'n of these rebell'd,
> To their prepar'd ill Mansion driven down,
> To chains of darkness, and th'undying Worm.
>
> [VI.737–39]

Darkness and the worm may be allegorical, but the "ill
Mansion" is not.

If Milton seems naïve, unscientific, or poetically or
philosophically inconsistent in consistently treating hell as
both a psychological microcosm and a local macrocosm
or actual "place outside our universe which God has created for the punishment of bad angels and bad men," we
should compare the doctrinal reticence and imaginative
power of his treatment of hell with the barren dogmatism

of a contemporary effort to make somewhat similar ideas
seem seductively esoteric and, at the same time, easily
comprehensible to simple readers. The effort in question is
the now forgotten *Mundorum explicatio* which Samuel Pordage had published in London in 1663. Though it is little
better than doggerel, it was an honest attempt by a man
perhaps "deep-versed in books" but certainly "shallow in
himself" to explain a sophisticated idea of hell. On page
110 of his hyperdidactic book he hits on the treacherous
device of having a devil explain hell to a visitor who is
curious about the fire that he sees all around him but
which the devil explains is powerless to hurt the evil spirits
because they, "though sensible, cannot feel Material Fire."
In a queer, non-physical way, however, it appears that the
visible fire that surrounds the visitor does torture the
demons because—as his guide informs him—it

> from ourselves proceeds, and . . . is made
> By that strong enmity which doth invade
> Us, 'gainst the adverse Orb of Light: and know
> This Fire doth from bitter harshnesse grow;
> As when you rub your flint upon a wheel
> Which turneth round, and is composed of Steel,
> You see some bitter grating Fires proceed.
> So our harsh grating Spirits Fire breed,
> Which is the same you see; This is the pain
> That we, and all the damned in remain.

Enough has been quoted to show what pitfalls beset a
theological rhymster who, four years before the publication of *Paradise Lost,* undertook to inspire his contemporaries with a belief in the eternal coexistence of hell and
heaven in the universe of which this world is a part. The
only justification of *Mundorum explicatio* is the fact that it
was a not entirely unhealthy reaction against such horrific
works of popular theology as Henry Greenwood's *Torment-*

150CHAPTER SIX

ing Tophet, or, A Terrible Description of Hell, Able to Break the Hardest Heart, and Cause It Quake and Tremble.[20] Yet even this frightful little book had enough value for the sophisticated hell to declare that "Hell follows men as near as the shadow doth the body."[21]

But the psychological and local hells were combined in more learned and influential works than Greenwood's *Tophet.* They confront us abruptly in one of the most influential Neo-stoic books of the seventeenth century, the *Heaven upon Earth* of Milton's early adversary, Bishop Hall. As a classicist and as a Stoic, the bishop had a more enlightened faith than many of his contemporaries in the pains of private hells, and as a Christian he had an unquestioning, matter-of-course belief in the local hell that he regarded as scriptural. Enlarging on the "bitternesse of the pangs of sinne," he warned his readers not to be "like unto those fondly impatient fishes, that leap out of the pan into the flame"—not to leap "out of this private hell that is in themselves, into the common pit, chusing to adventure upon the future paines that they have feared, rather than to endure the present horrors they have felt: wherein what have they gained, but to that hell which was within them, a second hell without?"[22] These words throw an interesting light on "the hot hell" that Milton's Satan carries with him wherever he goes.[23] They may seem to reverse the emphasis on the words of Mephistophilis in Marlowe's *Faustus* which have been quoted by various editors to illustrate Satan's confession that he himself is hell:

> Why this is hell, nor am I out of it:
> Think'st thou that I, that saw the face of God,

20. London, 1614.

21. The passage is quoted by G. W. Whiting in *NQ, 192* (1947), 227.

22. Joseph Hall, *Heaven upon Earth and Characters of Vertues and Vices,* ed. Rudolf Kirk, Rutgers Studies in English, 6 (New Brunswick, Rutgers University Press, 1948), 92.

23. *PL,* IV.20, IX.467.

And tasted the eternal joys of heaven,
Am not tormented with ten thousand hells,
In being depriv'd of everlasting bliss?

[I.3.78–82]

Actually, Marlowe's passage is not so good an illustration of Milton's as are Bishop Hall's homely words. The speech of Mephistophilis rather invites the inference that the devil's only punishment is the loss of the beatific vision. Bishop Hall left no room for that illegitimate inference. His passage is a perfect parallel to the assumption in *Paradise Lost* that, while Satan himself *is* hell, his "evil mansion" is at the same time truly and unmetaphorically extant somewhere in the remote fastnesses of Chaos.

The sophisticated hell of remorse or hardness of heart in sin obtained equally well either with demons or men. Sir Thomas Browne stated an experience which many of his contemporaries shared when he wrote: "I feel sometimes a hell within myself: Lucifer keeps his court in my breast . . . for every devil is a hell unto himself."[24] In writing so, Browne was not exposing a covert agreement with "the Pironicks, whose position and opinion" it was— as Thomas Nashe recalled in *Christ's Teares over Jerusalem,* "that there is no Hel or misery but opinion."[25] Nor should Browne's testimony be confused with Omar Khayyam's story:

I sent my Soul into the invisible
Some letter of the After-Life to spell;
And by and by my Soul returned to me,
And answered, 'I myself am Heaven and Hell.'

24. *Religio medici,* Book I, ¶ 51, in *The Works of Sir Thomas Browne,* ed. Geoffrey Keynes (4 vols. London, Faber and Faber, 1964), *1,* 62.
25. *The Works of Thomas Nashe,* ed. R. B. McKerrow (5 vols. London, Bullen, 1904–10), *2,* 116.

We are comfortably sure that on its short excursion into
the invisible the soul of Omar met no terrors resembling
those that confronted Odysseus and Aeneas in Hades, and
that it saw nothing like Dante's inferno or the orthodox
hell of Antonio Rusca. Browne's thinking may not have
been untinged by heresy, but its tone is no more that of
Edward Fitzgerald than it is that of Lionel Trilling when he
reduces Freudianism to a view of man caught in an "inex-
tricable tangle of culture and biology . . . having a kind of
hell within him from which rise everlastingly the impulses
which threaten our civilization."[26]

To find the true direction of Sir Thomas Browne's
thought, we should go to the philosophical theologians
and mystics of his time and most obviously to the Cambridge Platonists, whose thinking on the subject was put
into a popular aphorism by Benjamin Whichcote when
he declared in a sermon that "the Fewel of *Tophet* burning
is the guiltiness of man's conscience, malignity, and
naughty disposition towards goodness and holiness."[27] It
is also well known that Browne had something in common with the German mystics, whose religious experience
was dominated by a conviction of the soul's power to
create both heaven and hell for itself. Their master was
Jakob Boehme, but their poet was the "Cherubic Wanderer," Angelus Silesianus, Boehme's pupil, whose *Geistreich Sinn- und Schlussreime* abounds in spiritual epigrams
declaring that

Der Himmel is in dir und auch der Höllen Qual.
Was du erkiest und willest, das hast du überall.[28]

Literally, the words of Angelus are equivalent to Omar's,

26. Lionel Trilling, *The Liberal Imagination* (New York, Viking Press, 1950),
p. 64.
27. Benjamin Whichcote, *Select Sermons* ed. Lord Shaftesbury (London, 1698),
p. 96.
28. Angelus Silesianus, *Geistreich Sinn- und Schlussreime,* ed. and trans. Willard
Trask, *The Cherubic Wanderer* (New York, Pantheon Books, 1953), p. 145.

but actually they are a mystic surcharge of the saying of Christ to his disciples that "The kingdom of God is within you."[29] From that element in Christian teaching, Boehme extracted the not un-Miltonic principle that "We are of God's substance and have heaven and hell in ourselves," with the corollary that "Heaven and hell are everywhere all over this world."[30] An obvious, though perhaps somewhat overstressed, parallel has been drawn between such utterances of Boehme and the boast of Milton's Satan that he is

> One who brings
> A mind not to be chang'd by Place or Time.
> The mind is its own place, and in itself
> Can make a Heav'n of Hell, a Hell of Heav'n.
> [I.252–55]

Just how great and direct the influence of "Boehmanism" may have been in Milton's development of Satan's character there is no sure way to tell. We can only say that it was one among the many bracing winds of doctrine which inspired the Protean faith of the Renaissance in the Erasmian epigram, *Faber est suae quisque fortunae.* To that iron string the heart of the man of the Renaissance could vibrate sympathetically, regardless whether he was a mystic or a buccaneer; but its main charm lay in its suggestion that eternity as well as time was the slave of human virtue. It might be interpreted in a Machiavellian sense, which turned virtue into *virtù* and looked only to worldly prosperity; but most humanists interpreted it in the light of the debate in the last book of Cicero's *Tusculan Disputations* on the question whether virtue can secure happiness

29. Luke 17:21.
30. The first quotation is from Boehme's *The Threefold Life of Man* (chap. 14, V. 72) and the second from his *A Description of the Three Principles of the Divine Essence,* trans. John Sparrow (London, 1648), chap. 21, V. 62. Their influence on Milton's passage was suggested by Margaret L. Bailey, *Milton and Jakob Boehme* (New York, 1914), p. 158.

in all situations in life, even the most dreadful. Cicero's dialectical test of the contempt of the Stoics for physical health and worldly success retained its power to convince men of the Stoic faith in virtue as the only key to happiness. Even for modern readers there is still power in Cicero's portrayal of the virtue that despises all secondary goods and rises to immortal hopes in the contemplation of the stars. But as Cicero revolves the doctrine in his long discussion of the unfailing virtuous self-control and consequent happiness of the wise man, it becomes too dialectical and dogmatic. It is in danger of becoming one of Bacon's idols of the theater, a shining, stereotyped doctrine of the philosophic schools. If taken too seriously as a guide in life—as it was by many idealistic Christian Stoics—it too easily came to deserve the criticism that Milton expressed in *Paradise Regained* of the Stoic's

> philosophic pride
> By him call'd virtue; and his virtuous man,
> Wise, perfect in himself, and all possessing
> Equal to God, oft shames not to prefer,
> As fearing God nor man, contemning all
> Wealth, pleasure, pain or torment, death and
>   life,
> Which when he lists, he leaves, or boasts he
>   can,
> For all his tedious talk is but vain boast,
> Or subtle shifts conviction to evade.
>
> [IV.300–08]

It was perhaps from this passage in *Paradise Regained* that Thyer took a hint for his comment on Satan's boast that

> The mind is its own place, and in itself
> Can make a Heav'n of Hell.

"These," Thyer said in a note which was part of the editorial tradition as far down as Todd's Variorum, "are some of the extravagances of the Stoicks, and could not be better ridiculed than they are here, by being put in the mouth of Satan." Thyer could trust his eighteenth-century readers to understand his meaning. He did not need to remind them of the history of a fading idol of the theater any more than he needed to instruct them that "the punishment of Satan or his *fate* is not so much a judgment imposed upon him by the divine will as it is the very nature of the character that he has created for himself."[31] The originality and value of Thyer's suggestion lay in its parallel of the experience of Christian humanists with the fading Stoic idol and Satan's dramatic development in *Paradise Lost*. At the revival of Stoicism in the sixteenth century the idol had worn the guise of the virtue of constancy, to which the greatest of the Neo-stoics, Justus Lipsius, had devoted his most famous book. Without attempting a survey of the Neo-stoic movement, we may accept Rudolf Kirk's judgment that, by the time of the publication of Lipsius' *De constantia* on the Continent in 1584 and of Guillaume du Vair's *La Philosophie morale des Stoiques* in 1586 (?), "Neostoicism was firmly established as a philosophy."[32] It was, of course, a carefully Christianized Stoicism that Lipsius had to present, but his stress on the submissive Christian virtue of patience could assume a prouder form when it emerged as the Stoic virtue of constancy. The calmness that Lipsius recommended to his countrymen at the height of the Spanish tyranny in the Low Countries might easily glide into arrogance of the kind that Joost van den Vondel studied with real psychological insight in his *Lucifer*. In a political situation like

31. P. F. Fisher's summary of the matter in "Milton's Theodicy," *JHI, 17* (1956), 46.

32. *Two Bookes of Constancie. Written in Latine by Iustus Lipsius. Englished by Sir John Stradling,* ed. with introduction by Rudolf Kirk, notes by Morris Hall (New Brunswick, Rutgers University Press, 1939), p. 15.

Satan's, at the head of his rebel legions in Book V of *Para-dise Lost* and later, after their defeat, in Books I and II, constancy in both leader and followers becomes the mood of

> A mind not to be chang'd by Place or Time,

tragically confident that it can "make a Heav'n of Hell, a Hell of Heav'n."

In all Stoic speculation, both in ancient times and in the Renaissance, there was a tendency to think vaguely, some-times sentimentally, and sometimes proudly, about the central Stoic virtue of perfect self-control as the key to happiness. It is latent in Jerome Cardan's comfortable saying: "A man is nothinge but his mynde: if the mynde be discontented, the man is all disquiet though all the rest be well, and if the minde be contented though all the rest misdoe it forceth little."[33] The dogma permeates Du Vair's ethic. When it was combined with a confident Christian faith that "the kingdom of God is within you," it became a fortress of confidence in the soul's captaincy of its fate. It might even be glorified with a kind of mystical insight by a thinker like Lipsius, who reasoned that the Stoic conception of the *summum bonum* had risen to levels of something like Christian illumination in the writings of Seneca and Cicero. If, as he believed, the ancient Stoics had held that the highest good is to be seen only in God,[34] then no Christian could question Cicero's attainment of a kind of beatific vision that was sufficient both for the courageously pious and for the happy life.[35] The parable of the Pearl of Great Price might then become a counter-part of the Stoic fable of the balance of Critolaus, which

---

33. *Cardanus Comforte. Translated into Englishe. By Thomas Marsh* (London, 1576), p. A8ᵛ.

34. Iustus Lipsius, *Manuductionis ad Stoicam philosophiam*, II.22, in *Opera Omnia* (Antwerp, 1637).

35. *Tusculan Disputations*, v. 18; fable of Critolaus, v. 17.

showed the goods of the soul on one scale as far outweigh-
ing the goods of the body and all external things, even
when the earth and the seas were thrown onto the other
scale for good measure. Such high thinking had inspired
an emperor to warn his subjects against unphilosophical
whining because they did not possess retreats in the moun-
tains, by the sea, or in the country, when it was within
the power of every one of them to retreat into the secure
asylum of his own soul.[36] Such thinking had consoled a
philosopher-statesman, under an unjust sentence of banishment in the darkest days of the empire, to reflect that
"every lot is blessed to the man who accepts it with equa-
nimity," for "nothing is miserable unless you think it so."[37]
Even on the most mundane level, Montaigne was convinced of the truth of the ancient maxim of which Hamlet made a fair paraphrase when he said: "Nothing is
either good or bad but thinking makes it so." Montaigne
tested the doctrine by a score of anecdotes of human reactions to the jests of fortune, and he emerged convinced
of man's power to master his woes with the help of Philosophy, who is always at hand to whisper: "Though it is
bad to live in necessity, at least there is no necessity to
live in necessity."[38]

In Montaigne's essay the idealism of Stoic contempt for
everything except the wealth of the spirit has cooled a
bit. It seems like mere worldly wisdom with perhaps a
touch of something like humor in it. There is no trace left

36. Marcus Aurelius, *Meditations* 4.1.
37. Boethius, *Consolation of Philosophy,* 2, prose 4.
38. *The Essayes of Michael Lord of Montaigne,* trans. John Florio (2 vols. London, Dent, 1910), Book I, Essay 40, "That the Taste of Goods or Evils doth
greatly depend on the Opinion we have of them." Vol. 1, p. 291. In *PQ, 6*
(1927), M. A. Larson treated Milton's character as a noble product of Marcus
Aurelius' doctrine of moral self-sufficiency, but his actual dissatisfaction with
Stoicism as blind to human weakness and to divine grace is established by
Jacques Blondel in his edition of *PR* (Paris, Aubier, 1955), p. 82. Cf. F. Kermode in *RES,* n.s. *4* (1955), 317–30.

of the *O Altitudo* of the ancient Stoic teaching in the *Fable of Critolaus,* which is the sort of thing that Thyer had in mind when he said that there was satire of "the extravagances of the Stoics" in Satan's boast of his power to make "a Heav'n of Hell, a Hell of Heav'n." If we should try to push Thyer's suggestion beyond the point where he wisely dropped it, a case of sorts might be made for regarding the degeneration of Satan's character in *Paradise Lost* as a dramatic exhibition of the Stoic's "philosophic pride." Such an exegesis might plausibly argue that the psychology of Satan's ruin in those ever opening depths of evil within himself is really a criticism of Stoicism rather than the simple Augustinian conception of Satan that many scholars assume that it is. It might be argued that Milton was reacting against the actual Stoic extravagance of George Chapman's plays, with their confidence that "As we are men, we death and hell controule," as Peter Ure has pointed out that Fulke Greville reacted against Chapman by dramatizing the sad truth that "flesh and blood may itself become hell."[39] Earlier drama, as Miss Helen Gardner has brilliantly shown,[40] dealt with "the theme of damnation" in *Doctor Faustus* and in Middleton's *Changeling* in a way that naturally threw off verbal parallels to Satan's discovery when he said, "Myself am Hell." But it would be unfair both to Milton and to Miss Gardner to reduce Satan to a dramatic satire of outgrown Stoicism. He has too much in common with Faustus and Beatrice Joanna and even with Macbeth. And he has too much of the tradition of Christian thought about the psychology of evil, and of the Evil One in him, to be understood apart from that tradition, especially from the contemporary Christian mysticism, which blended so easily with Stoic

39. Peter Ure, "Fulke Greville's Dramatic Characters," *RES,* n.s. *1* (1950), 312.

40. Helen Gardner, "Milton's Satan and the Theme of Damnation in Elizabethan Tragedy," *ES,* n.s. *1* (1948), 46–66.

doctrine and also with the demonology of the Florentine Neoplatonists.

Up to this point the discussion has reached no further than the last of Satan's soliloquies, his reflection before tempting Eve for the second time, when he acknowledges that all good has become "bane" to him and that his state would be much worse in heaven (IX.123–24). But at least two of the strands of tradition that have been examined have some light to throw on his final appearance in *Paradise Lost* in what A. J. A. Waldock called the "cartoon scene":[41] the moment when the roar of welcome on his return to hell and to Pandaemonium turns to a hiss in the throats of his followers:

> for now were all transform'd
> Alike, to serpents all, as accessories
> To his bold riot: dreadful was the din
> Of hissing through the hall, thick swarming now
> With complicated monsters, head and tail,
> Scorpion and asp, and amphisbaena dire,
> Cerastes horn'd, Hydrus, and Ellops drear
> And Dipsas (not so thick swarm'd once the soil
> Bedropt with blood of Gorgon, or the isle
> Ophiusa). . . .   [X.519–28]

It may surprise modern readers to find that the scene has had many defenders, not only in the time when Addison defended this "beautiful passage in the tenth book" in *Spectator* 297, on the ground that it softened the reader's natural disappointment over Satan's victory in Eden, but even today, when poets like Lascelles Abercrombie and Edith Sitwell can declare that "we need never expect words and metre to do more than they do here,"[42] and rhap-

---

41. A. J. A. Waldock, *"Paradise Lost" and Its Critics* (Cambridge, the University Press, 1947), p. 91.

42. *The Idea of Great Poetry*, p. 80.

sodize over "the splendour of this passage" in terms of its
supreme mastery of the sibilants and the "light and dark
vowels."[43] The technical perfection of the lines as a purple
patch of poetry, however, is not what is at stake. The
question is whether the passage is open to Waldock's objection that it is a mere piece of extraneous cartooning
with no real connection with the plot, which—as far as
Satan is concerned—has long since fallen to the level of
crude allegory. The best reply to this objection is perhaps
that of Arnold Stein, who regards the scene as a possible
"psychological climax" and defends "the mass metamorphosis into serpents" as "also a physical climax, an external confirmation (necessary in the drama) of the internal
failure."[44]

If we look at this question purely in terms of the tradition behind it, there is much to be said for Waldock's objection to the scene as simply allegorical. It is not likely
that Milton named the amphisbaena in ignorance of the
fact that it was hieroglyphically regarded as a symbol of
inconstancy and adultery, or that he mentioned the ceras-
tes without expecting some of his readers to recall that in
the systematic notation of the symbolism of serpents in
Aldovrandus' famous work[45] it was a hieroglyph for the
lust for power. Probably few well-read men in the seventeenth century thought of the dipsas without recalling that
in Lucan's account of it in *The Civil War* (9.737–50), the
"thirst-snake" was treated as a moral allegory akin to that
of thirsty Tantalus, whose torments in the classical underworld had long been rationalized as a fable of character
determining destiny here and perhaps also hereafter.[46]

43. Edith Sitwell, *The Pleasures of Poetry* (London, Duckworth, 1938), p. 25.
44. Arnold Stein, "Satan and the Dramatic Role of Evil," *PMLA, 45* (1950),
226.
45. Ulisse Aldovrandus, *Serpentum et draconum historiae libri II* (Bologna, 1640).
46. Edward Topsell (in *Historie of Serpents,* London, 1608), refers to Lucan's
account of the dipsas and allegorizes it as vaguely related to the story of Tantalus.

But there are other sides to the tradition behind the metamorphosis of the devils into serpents and its sequel in Milton's account of their deception by a

> Fruitage fair to sight, like that which grew
> Near that bituminous Lake where Sodom
>   flam'd;
> This more delusive, not the touch, but taste
> Deceiv'd; they fondly thinking to allay
> Thir appetite with gust, instead of Fruit
> Chew'd bitter Ashes.   [X.561–66]

The tale is allegory, but imbedded in it are bits of historical tradition and cosmic myth which Milton's editors have not done much to explain by appealing to Josephus' description of the apples of Sodom in the *Wars* (4.8.4). Josephus may explain the myth of which we catch a glimpse in Joseph Beaumont's *Psyche* (I.8), in his explicitly allegorical and yet medieval picture of hell as

> High wall'd with strong *Damnation,* moted
>   round
> With flaming Brimstone; right against the Hall
> Burns a black bridge of brass; the yards
>   abound
> With all invenom'd Herbs and Trees, more
>   rank
> And fruitlesse than on *Asphaltite's* bank.

Here Beaumont is trying to say what Milton says in a more general way about the realm where the only living things are more "prodigious

> Than fables yet have feign'd, or fear con-
>   ceiv'd."

But this idea and its illustration in the apples of Sodom are only incidental to Milton's metamorphosis of the devils. The metamorphosis itself has no known parallel in English poetry, although—as E. C. Baldwin pointed out[47]—there is a hint of it in Fletcher's *Purple Island* (stanza 11), where a part of the preliminaries is the statement that the dragon prince of the devils

Tempts them to lust and pride, prevails by slight:
  To make them wise, and gods he undertakes.
Thus while the snake they heare, they turn to snakes;
To make them gods he boasts, but beasts and devils
      makes.

Fletcher's lines were rooted in a tradition which was later to suggest Milton's metamorphosis of the devils into serpents and was also to suggest their much more elaborate metamorphosis in Vondel's *Lucifer*. From the beginning to the end of that drama the fall of the angels is treated in terms of a theory which was known in England in the writings of Henry More, but which may have been familiar to Vondel in Boehme's teaching that, when "the divine light went out of the Devils, they lost their beauteous forme and Image, and became like Serpents, Dragons, Wormes, and evill Beasts: as may be seen by *Adam's* Serpent."[48] The result of the defeat of the rebel angels in a battle which Vondel presents on a scale equal to the war in heaven in the sixth book of *Paradise Lost,* we are told, is simply that they are changed into various animal shapes.

In a bare summary Vondel's treatment of the rebel angels seems like sheer allegory, but the quotation from Boehme implies by its allusion to Adam's serpent that, if he is dealing in allegory, it is of the apocalyptic kind that Milton used when he followed up his metamorphosis of the devils with his strange and expressly factual reference to Adam's serpent—the serpent about which the demons later tried to deceive mankind by calling it

47. E. C. Baldwin, "Milton and Phineas Fletcher," *JEGP, 33* (1934), 544–46.
48. *Three Principles,* chap. 4, v. 64.

Ophion with Eurynome the wide-
Encroaching Eve perhaps'   [X.581–82]

who they "fabl'd

had first the rule
Of high Olympus, thence by Saturn driv'n
And Ops, ere yet Dictaean Jove was born.
[X.582–84]

The secret of these cryptic lines may never be fully un-
riddled, but they are probably to be traced to the influence
of a passage in Origen's *Contra Celsum* (6.43), which identifies Ophioneus, the serpent deity, who—according to the
sixth-century (B.C.) philosopher Pherecydes—led the Titans
in an unsuccessful attack on Olympus, with "the serpent
which was the cause of man's expulsion from the divine
paradise, and deceived the female race with a promise of
divine power of attaining to greater things."

The secret of the punishment of the devils by their
metamorphosis into serpents in Satan's last scene in *Paradise Lost* is involved in the larger mystery of Milton's
theory of

Th'infernal Serpent, . . . whose guile,
Stirr'd up with Envy and Revenge, deceiv'd
The Mother of Mankind.   [I.34–36]

A short way to deal with this theory would be to accept
Miss Maud Bodkin's view of it as conforming to her doctrine of the tragic archetype. In its light she sees Milton's
"tragic" conception as explaining the "power of his language in this strange passage of the punishment of Satan."[49]
To this Robert Adams objects that, even if her diagram-
matic view of tragic character were acceptable, it is un-
profitable to invoke archetypes "to explain effects too com-

49. Maud Bodkin, *Archetypal Patterns in Poetry* (London, Oxford University Press, 1934), pp. 234–35.

plex or profound for a merely aesthetic accounting."[50]
The objection is sound, though it slights the service done
by Miss Bodkin and her Jungian sympathizers who see the
supreme ectype of the archetypal serpent-adversary of God
and man in the Satan of *Paradise Lost.*

The truth in Miss Bodkin's theory is easily overstressed.
Its devotees are likely to miss the fact that, as a key to
Milton's serpentine conception of Satan, it falls short of
philological investigation of myths, like that of the serpent-
demon Ophion leading the Titans against Olympus.[51] The
reference to that obscure story in *Paradise Lost* (X.581–84),
is perhaps our most striking evidence of the fact which is
everywhere apparent in his assumption of ultimate historical truth in the Christian interpretation of the Fall of
Man in Genesis and of the Fall of the Angels as he understood it to be recorded in the second Psalm and in the
Apocalypse. Out of that mysterious cosmic history he created a Satan whose career ended in punishment by metamorphosis into serpent form and banishment to a realm
where all things are monstrous reflections of the evil in the
hearts of his followers. There the truths of history and allegory are hardly distinguishable. There the demons would
naturally assume bestial forms after the similitude of their
natures, as Plato said in the *Timaeus* (42 *b–c*), that the souls
of inveterately wicked men do, in their successive rebirths.
And without fading into an abstraction of pure allegory in
that world of evil, Satan would find that he himself was
hell.

50. Robert M. Adams, IKON: *John Milton and Modern Critics* (Ithaca, Cornell
University Press, 1955), p. 42.

51. In *Classical Mythology of Milton's English Poems* (New York, Holt, 1900),
p. 34, Charles Grosvenor Osgood noted the glancing allusions to Eurynome by
Ovid (*Metamorphoses* 4.210, 219) as probably glancing back at the sketch of
the story by Apollonius of Rhodes in the *Argonautica* (1.503–11), where Orpheus
is represented as singing "how once Ophion and Eurynome, daughter of Ocean,
held the rule of snowy Olympus, and how he, struggling with mighty arms,
yielded honor to Cronus, and she to Rhea, and they fell into the waves of
Ocean . . . while Zeus was still a boy . . . living within the Dictaean cave."

7

Satan and the "Myth" of the Tyrant

In this essay the word *myth* is not used in Jung's sense, or in the sense in which it is used by Mrs. MacCaffrey in *Paradise Lost as "Myth,"* or in R. J. Z. Werblowsky's *Lucifer and Prometheus,* or in Wayne Shumaker's *"Paradise Lost:* The Mythological Dimension." Nor is the word used as it is by Northrop Frye in his discussions of tragic and comic myth in *Anatomy of Criticism.*[1] Without, it is hoped, undue emphasis upon the Platonism in Milton's political thought, the word *myth* is here applied to the Miltonic conception of the political process as it is stated to Adam by Michael in the last book of *Paradise Lost* when Adam is overwhelmed by the vision of the harm to be done to his descendants by Nimrod and the builders of the tower of Babel:

> To whom thus *Michael.* Justly thou abhorr'st
> That Son, who on the quiet state of men
> Such trouble brought, affecting to subdue
> Rational Liberty; yet know withal,

---

1. MacCaffrey, *"Paradise Lost" as Myth;* R. J. Z. Werblowsky, *Lucifer and Prometheus* (London, Routledge and Kegan Paul, 1952); Wayne Shumaker, *"Paradise Lost:* The Mythological Dimension," *Bucknell Review, 10* (1961), 75–86; Northrop Frye, *Anatomy of Criticism* (Princeton, 1957).

Since thy original lapse, true Liberty
Is lost, which always with right Reason dwells
Twinn'd, and from her hath no dividual being:
Reason in man obscur'd, or not obey'd,
Immediately inordinate desires
And upstart Passions catch the Government
From Reason, and to servitude reduce
Man till then free. Therefore since hee permits
Within himself unworthy Powers to reign
Over free Reason, God in Judgment just
Subjects him from without to violent Lords;
Who oft as undeservedly enthral
His outward freedom: Tyranny must be,
Though to the Tyrant thereby no excuse.

[XII.79–96]

In the world of the poem the archetypal tyrant is Satan. For the present purpose it is not necessary to consider him as hero or fool, or to meditate on the mystery of evil of which he has been a traditional solution. It is enough to accept him simply as the spirit which Gilbert Murray has called "Satanism, the spirit which hates the World Order wherever it exists." Though our thinking about the problem of evil may be more or less theological, and more or less hopeful than Murray's, we may accept his definition of Satanism as a mysteriously wanton adversary of man in "the great pilgrimage of the spirit [which] from the beginnings of history onward has been on the whole not only a movement from ignorance to knowledge, from collective impotence to collective power, from poverty of life to richness of life, but also in some profound sense a pilgrimage from lower to higher."[2]

If this definition in terms of Satanism seems too abstract to represent Milton's thought about the prince of the devils

2. Gilbert Murray, *Satanism and the World Order* (London, Allen and Unwin, 1920).

in the ninth chapter of the first book of his *Christian Doctrine*, it should not be forgotten that in closing that chapter Milton remembered the great tempter's many names: Beelzebub (as Christ called "the prince of the devils," Matthew 12:24), "Satan," or the enemy or adversary of Job (1:6); and several more, one of which is "Abaddon, Apollyon," or the "destroyer" of Revelation (9:11). Though the names suggest an identity as elusive as the multiple forms of evil itself, they cannot make the prince of the devils less of a personal evil spirit than his followers, the fallen angels whom Milton describes as reserved for final punishment in hell and yet sometimes permitted to wander throughout the whole earth, the air, and heaven itself. All definitions of Satan concur in making him the destroyer. Rajan, though he observes that Milton's contemporaries held Calvin's view of Satan as a personal "enemie that is in courage most hardie, in strength most mightie, in policies most subtle," yet thinks that for Milton he was most characteristically "the creature who finds ease 'onely in destroying.' "[3] For the historian, Denis de Rougemont says candidly that the Devil can hardly be more than the "phantom" of human invention which has tormented mankind through "centuries of ignorance." But for de Rougemont, Satan is one of "the figures of myth [which] guide us more surely than modern experiment and the analysis of reason." Yet in the end he can define Satan only by opposing him to "the inner order of saintliness, the cosmic order and its immense discourse, the order of the laws sworn to in the commonwealth, the order of language and the order of virtues."[4] De Rougemont's authentication of Satan as a fundamental "myth" of human experience comes close to Mrs. MacCaffrey's recognition

3. B. Rajan, *"Paradise Lost" and the Seventeenth Century Reader* (London, Chatto and Windus, 1947), pp. 94, 104.

4. Denis de Rougemont, *The Devil's Share* (New York, Pantheon Books, 1944), pp. 26–28, 220.

that the "aptest epithet" for Milton's Satan "is the Destroyer" (p. 147). But in the destroyer opposed to the
cosmic order and the laws sworn in the commonwealth
we recognize the "Satanism" which Gilbert Murray opposed to the principles of order and human law which
were enunciated by Plato and Cicero. And so in a modest
way the ancient myth of man's rational cosmos and its
enemies may stand beside the modern myth of the primordial destroyer in de Rougemont's "anthromorphic"
world where "reason finds itself disarmed before the brutal
eruptions of an evil organized by obscure forces, according
to the mysterious logic and the irresistible efficacy of the
unconscious."

No demonstration of the Platonic character of Michael's
words is needed for readers who are familiar with Plato's
theory of the correspondence between the forms of the state
and the variety of characters among men, between the
tyrannous character of the spirit of entire communities
and the vulnerability of their governments to usurpation
by tyrants. This doctrine is laid down in the eighth book
of the *Republic,* it is analysed in the *Gorgias* (468b ff.), and
in the *Laws* (272e–273b), it is crystallized in the myth of
the retreat of the gods of order from the world with the
ensuing great earthquake and the destruction of all living
beings.

The link with the passage in the *Gorgias* (483d–e) is not
the most important, but it is obvious and interesting. In a
shrewd exposure of the violence of absolute monarchs for
whom right is simply their own might, Socrates traps Callicles into approving Darius' conquest of Scythia and
Xerxes' invasion of Greece as supreme examples of might
making right. Socrates, of course, was taking advantage of
an established feeling among his countrymen that—as
Aristotle explained in the *Politics* (3.9.3)—the barbarians
were naturally more servile than the Greeks, and the Asi-

atics than the Europeans, and so they submitted easily to despotism. In the ideal, universal form which Plato gave to his theory of the moral foundation of the State in the *Republic* and in its typically Greek use to explain the prevalence of tyranny in Asia, the theory came to Milton directly; indirectly it came also through many literary channels. In the form of prejudice against the Asiatic tyrants it lay ready to his hand for associative effect in one of the most strikingly placed of his portraits of Satan in the opening lines of the second book of *Paradise Lost*, where the curtain rises on Satan sitting

> High on a Throne of Royal State, which far
> Outshone the wealth of *Ormus* and of *Ind*,
> Or where the gorgeous East with richest hand
> Show'rs on her Kings *barbaric* Pearl and Gold.

Editorial comment on these lines has not stressed their ultimate origin in the *Gorgias* and the *Politics*. Editors have rightly focused attention on Ormus and India as symbols of the contemporary drive of the trading companies, English and Dutch particularly, for control of the trade in jewels and spices which was funnelled through the fabulous port of Ormus on the Persian gulf. So Milton wished his readers to feel about the passage, and that obvious fact is worth consideration by the German critics who have condemned him as a moral accomplice of British imperialism in its early phase. Actually, as B. A. Wright has just observed, the effect of the passage is to throw light both upon Milton's attitude toward Satan as a claimant for heroic honors in the poem and upon the rapacity of the merchant adventurers in the East. Their motives in sending their armed ships to the Spice Islands are like his on his perilous voyage from Hell to Eden. "And so," says Wright, "as Satan starts on his flight towards the gates of Hell and his hazardous quest for the new world of man,

Milton calls up this vision of a voyage from India to the Cape"[5]

> As when far off at Sea a Fleet descri'd
> Hangs in the Clouds, by *Equinoctial* Winds
> Close sailing from *Bengala,* or the Isles
> Of *Ternate* and *Tidore,* whence Merchants bring
> Thir spicy Drugs: they on the Trading Flood
> Through the wide Ethiopian to the Cape
> Ply stemming nightly toward the Pole.   [II.636–42]

Wright's interest is mainly in the hazards, not in the prizes, of the eastern voyages which he compared with Satan's; but he is aware that in the tableau (in I.347–49), where the devils rally to "th'uplifted Spear / Of thir great Sultan waving to direct / Thir course," the moral association of Satan with the traditional tyrants of the East is anticipated. In a note in 1958, Manfred Weidhorn made an elaborate comparison of Milton's Satan with the Xerxes of Herodotus,[6] but did not bring out the full political potential of the implicit image in Milton's text. A year later Jacques Blondel pointed to the comparison in *Paradise Lost* (X.306–11), of Satan's involvement in the bridge-building of Sin and Death as the final mark of Milton's conception of him as a kind of archetypal tyrant trampling everything sacred under his feet. His act, said the ancients, was a "sacrilège, nefas; de même, les puissances infernales profanent elles aussi la matière, en la pliant a leur volonté perverse pour enchaîner l'homme, comme le roi antique voulut asservir la Grèce."[7]

By making the modern Turkish sultans illustrations or symbols of the tyranny of the arch-tyrant Satan, Milton

5. Bernard A. Wright, *Milton's "Paradise Lost"* (London, Methuen, 1962), p. 109.

6. Manfred Weidhorn, *NQ,* n.s. *9* (1958), 389–92.

7. Jacques Blondel, "Milton: Poète de la Bible dans le *Paradis Perdu,*" *Archives des Lettres Modernes, 3* (1959), 33.

encouraged his identification with figures on his immediate political scene, and E. M. W. Tillyard was undoubtedly right in saying that his Satan "is partly a Renaissance tyrant."[8] The two concepts were closely linked in the minds of his contemporaries and in *Eikonoklastes* Milton himself made Turkish tyranny the thrice-applied measuring rod for England under the unchallenged unconstitutional rule of King Charles.[9] In his *Observations on the Articles of the Peace* he repeated a familiar story of an attempt to set up "the Turkish Tyranny" "with best expedition, and least noyse in France."[10] In these references to recent events there is, of course, no exposition of the Platonic political moral implicit in them; but in the entries under "Tyrannus" in the Commonplace Book, where Milton was writing with no controversial motive, he recalls the incident in France and many instances of tyrannous usurpation and abuse of authority in Anglo-Saxon England. In the cool atmosphere of his study at Horton the relation between the evils of tyranny and the vices of society seemed perfectly clear.

It would, of course, be inaccurate to treat Milton's attitude in the entries in the Commonplace Book as simply and consciously Platonic—as it may seem to be in Michael's advice to Adam in the twelfth book of *Paradise Lost*. In the passages which have been quoted from the prose works the pattern of thought is clearly as much religious as it is philosophical; nor would Milton have admitted the distinction. His thinking is always Christian, with all that the Christian world-view implies about the role of human character and divine providence in the affairs of nations. Milton would never have disagreed with the

8. E. M. W. Tillyard, *The English Epic and Its Background* (New York, Oxford University Press, 1954), p. 433.

9. Chaps. 10, 27 (CE, *5*, 170, 282–83); *Complete Prose Works of John Milton* (New Haven, 1953–), *3*, 453.

10. CE, *6*, 253; *Complete Prose*, *3*, 313.

opinion of St. Thomas Aquinas in the *De Regimine Princi-pum* (I.6.52) that

> . . . it is by divine permission that wicked men re-
> ceive power to rule as punishment for sin, as the Lord
> says by the prophet Osee: "I will give thee a king in
> wrath," and it is said in Job that he "maketh a man
> that is an hypocrite to reign for the sins of the peo-
> ple." Sin therefore must be done away with in order
> that the scourge of tyrants may cease.

Since in *Eikonoklastes* Charles I was so definitely compared with the proverbial Turkish tyrant, and since in
Paradise Lost that comparison is implicit in several of the
descriptions of Satan, it is easy to conclude that Charles
and the sultans were alike ectypes of the Satanic archetype
in Milton's mythology. And from such loose application
of the principle that things equal to the same thing are
equal or identical with each other, it is easy to follow
G. Wilson Knight in equating Hitler and Charles as ectypes in the series which Milton began with Nimrod—
easy, that is, if we agree with Knight that, "as for Charles,
he was to Milton precisely what Hitler seems to us."[11] In
support of the statement Knight quotes a rhetorical question from the first *Defence of the English People*[12] where Milton asks whether, when the king raves (*quoties delirare libet
regi*), the best citizens should not open their mouths in
protest.

Chronology prevents Knight from finding Miltonic authority for his inclusion of Hitler among the Satanic ectypes, but his thinking is as sound as was Coleridge's when
he wrote in the lecture on *Paradise Lost:*

11. G. Wilson Knight, *Chariot of Wrath* (London, Faber and Faber, 1942), p.
170.

12. CE, *7*, 82.

The character of Satan is pride and sensual indulgence, finding in self the sole motive of action. It is the character so often seen *in little* on the political stage. It exhibits all the restlessness, temerity, and cunning which have marked the mighty hunters of mankind from Nimrod to Napoleon.[13]

Discussion of Hitler as a Satanic ectype must wait while the one-to-one topical identification of Charles with Milton's Satan is examined. An objection to it is unconsciously indicated by Knight when he generalizes about "the Satanic party" as representing "mankind in its fruitless struggles; in them," he adds, "Puritan revolution and Episcopal idolatry, Cromwellian force and Stuart finery (clearly suggested at I.497–502) are all contained."[14] Topical historical allegory gives way altogether when Charles and the Cromwellian force which destroyed him are both seen as ectypes of Milton's Satan. Nor is the situation helped when Knight declares "the equivalence of Satan to the Puritan party extremely close."

The fact is, attribution of any topical political intention to Milton's epic plan involves irreconcilable hypotheses. The first would entangle the royalism in his aristocratic nature so definitely with the Stuart crown that Charles and his partisans could not possibly be identified with Satan and his followers. But Ross, the analyst of Milton's royalism, avoids suggesting anything of that kind when he says that, though traces of "the kingly ideal, the royal 'type,'" are found in Milton's epic plans "well after the

13. Quoted from *Coleridge on the Seventeenth Century*, ed. Roberta Florence Brinkley (Duke University Press, 1955), p. 578. In *PQ, 41* (1962), 307–08, Benjamin T. Sankey, Jr., quotes the longer passage in *The Statesman's Manual*, appendix B, where Coleridge gave his reasons for regarding the character of Napoleon as essentially that which "Milton has so philosophically as well as sublimely embodied in the Satan of *Paradise Lost*."

14. *Chariot of Wrath*, p. 137.

last moment in which he might possibly have had respect for the Stuarts," his "epic royalism" was derived "from a sense of the past, from Plato, from Spenser, from Christian tradition—never from Charles."[15]

The second hypothesis, Knight's surmised close equivalence of Satan to the Puritan party, necessarily involves the assumption that one of the leaders of the Long Parliament or of the New Model Army or of both, should be recognizable in some of the features of Milton's Satan. And in the "mighty chief" whose "Heart/Distends with pride" as he "Darts his experienced eye" through "the armed files" of the devils rallying around him in hell (I.566–71), Knight recognizes "indeed, a Cromwell casting an experienced eye over his ironside warriors." But the essence of the scenes in Hell is Satan's enjoyment of a control of his "Synod of Gods" such as Cromwell never enjoyed over his parliaments. And the eulogy of Cromwell in the *Second Defence* leaves no doubt that at least for a very long time he represented the anti-tyrant which George Williamson demonstrates that he always remained for Milton.[16] Ross also recognizes Cromwell as having long been the embodiment of the Platonic ideal of philosopher king, though in the end his image may have been supplanted for Milton by that of Jan Sobiesky, the savior of Vienna from the Turks, who was elected king of Poland in the year of Milton's death.

If Milton had intended to make Cromwell and his supporters in the Long Parliament and in the Army recognizable in the persons of Satan and the devils in Books I, II, V, and VI of *Paradise Lost,* he would have had to revise the entire plan of the poem on the general lines of Joost van den Vondel's *Lucifer.* In that play, written in 1654, the action begins with and until the end of the third act con-

15. M. M. Ross, *Milton's Royalism* (Ithaca, Cornell University Press, 1943), p. 72.

16. George Williamson, "Milton the Anti-Romantic," *MP, 40* (1962), 151.

sists in maneuvering among the archfiends Apollyon, Beelzebub, and Belial, to whip up a revolt against God and
persuade Lucifer to accept the command of the rebel
angels. Lucifer's seeming reluctance even to countenance
the revolt is perfectly carried through. Vondel has been
understood to have Cromwell's rise to power in England
as a kind of objective correlative for the action of those
first three acts. The once-serious suspicion that *Paradise
Lost* was influenced by *Lucifer* cannot be confirmed. If
Milton read the play, as he probably did, he learned from
it not to make the conspiratorial scene between Satan and
Beelzebub in his fifth book the opening scene in his epic,
and not to present Satan first as a politician calculatingly
and somewhat hesitantly accepting command in a crisis.
If he had followed Vondel's pattern, he would have had
to make Satan abject in defeat and might have omitted
all infernal scenes, as Vondel did. In Vondel's pattern, if
Milton had used it, Satan might seem to be identifiable
with Cromwell, but he would have been even more readily
identifiable with the far less heroic figure of Shaftesbury,
Dryden's Achitophel. In actual life as he participated in
the machinations of Cromwell's parliaments, Shaftesbury
seems to Morris Freedman to have created an image that
would have served Milton as an ideal "'answer' to Vondel's depiction of Cromwell."[17] Indeed, as "an arch opponent of Cromwell," Shaftesbury is skilfully presented in
Freedman's study as a figure from which Milton may have
drawn his Satan.

It is, of course, possible that the debate in Pandaemonium would not be quite what it is if Milton had not felt
as bitterly about the venal factionalism in Cromwell's
parliaments as he did when he indicted them openly in
his digression in the *History of Britain.* But the dangers of
such an assumption are shown by its history in the criti-

17. Morris Freedman, "Satan and Shaftesbury," *PMLA, 74* (1959), 545.

cism of *Paradise Lost*. George Whiting has traced a debate
on the subject which began in the *London Chronicle* on No-
vember 15, 1763, with a bold assertion that in the second
book of the poem Milton repudiated his old sympathies
by representing the Whigs as the devils. In the series of
replies to the suggestion the poem was reduced to a *roman
à clef,* and its diabolic figures were consciously or unconsciously turned into actors on the contemporary political
scene.[18]

In Walter Bagehot's very different view of *Paradise Lost*
we have an example of the dangers of naïve identification
of Milton with his rebellious angels. Only by radical mis-
reading of the poem could Bagehot have supposed that
Milton's "real sympathy—the impetus and energy of his
nature— . . . [slipped] back to the Puritan rebels whom
he loved"[19] presumably more heartily when he wrote his
epic than he did when he had shared in their counsels
under the Commonwealth. By identifying Milton with his
rebel angels Bagehot was drifting with the still strong
Romantic tendency to identify him with their prince. That
way lies the aesthetic, if not the moral, idolatry of Satan
which was at its height in 1850 when George Gilfillan
proclaimed Satan to be "the most *tremendous conception* in
the compass of poetry—the *sublimest* creation of the mind
of man."[20] Today we are not sure that we are all of the
Devil's party without knowing it, even though Miss Bodkin, speaking in *Archetypal Patterns in Poetry* of Blake's dictum and of the modern feeling of hopelessness against the
odds of destiny, does tell us that when a reader is "caught
into the theme of *Paradise Lost,* he—like the poet himself—

18. George Whiting, "The Politics of Milton's Apostate Angels," *NQ, 163*
(1932), 384–86.

19. Walter Bagehot, "Wordsworth, Tennyson, and Browning," *Literary Studies, 2* (London, 1910), 345–46.

20. George Gilfillan, *A Second Gallery of Literary Portraits* (Edinburgh, Hogg,
1850), p. 20.

becomes—knowing it or not—'of the Devil's party.'"[21] We hear Northrop Frye saying that "Blake's point is not that Satan is the hero of *Paradise Lost,* but that there is no hero to *Paradise Lost.*"[22] We feel A. J. A. Waldock and John Peter plucking at our sleeves to denigrate the mind and the whole artistic integrity of Milton's Satan. On the other hand, anything like romantic admiration of Milton's Satan has now been rendered impossible by the criticism that admires the virtuosity which adumbrates his decay in the early similes describing him and consummates it in the false rhetoric of his temptation of Eve.

Though we may not accept the belittling of Satan for artistic reasons by Waldock's followers or quite like his belittling for moral reasons by the followers of C. S. Lewis, we know that interpretation of Milton's treatment of his myth in *Paradise Lost* must now be cleared of all romantic sentimentality and of the modern psychologism which makes him a reflection of the irrational elements in Milton's own nature. Milton created him as an example of the self-deception and the deception of others which are incident to the surrender of reason to passion. His creation was a deliberate attempt to represent the demon who fell through pride and became the father of lies in the prosecution of his war against God at the expense of mankind. Traditional theology and traditional mythology, the deepest involvement of Renaissance thought in the problems of the contemplative versus the active life, are all mingled in the myth of Satan in Milton's poem. But the thinking is contemporary as well as traditional. The ceaseless activity of the devils in Hell and Satan's unresting drive through Chaos and the spheres of the newly created universe to the regions of earth and back again to Pandaemonium, are examples of the evils of what Bacon had called the "Ac-

21. Bodkin, *Archetypal Patterns in Poetry,* p. 234.
22. Northrop Frye, *Fearful Symmetry* (Princeton, 1947), p. 219.

tive Good" in a passage of the *De Augmentis*. Without any thought of direct influence upon Milton in the following passage it is possible to find some light in it upon Milton's feeling that a battle in Heaven with echoes of Hesiod's war of the Titans against the Olympian gods should figure largely in *Paradise Lost*. But the passage also illuminates more fundamental things in Milton's myth of Satan:

> But here it must be more carefully observed, that this active individual good has no identity with the good of society, though in some case it has an incidence into it: for although it many times produces and brings forth acts of beneficence (which is a virtue of communion), yet there is this difference, that these acts are mostly done not with a view to the benefit and happiness of others, but to a man's own power and greatness; as plainly appears when this kind of active good strikes on a subject contrary to the good of society. For that gigantean state of mind, which possesses the troublers of the world (such as was Lucius Sylla, and infinite others in smaller model, who are bent on having all men happy or unhappy as they are their friends or enemies, and would shape the world according to their own humours, which is the true Theomachy), this I say aspires to the active good of the individual (apparent good at least), though it recedes farthest of all from the good of society.[23]

In this passage Bacon wrote for the behoof of men who were intelligent enough to think in terms of the illusions of the active life and the "Active Good." He was extending his favourite doctrine of the idols—especially those of the Market Place and of the Theatre—which are the enemies of the advancement of science. Here they reach

23. *De Augmentis Scientiarum*, VII.2. The translation is from *The Works of Francis Bacon, 9*, 203–04.

to the illusions which darken men's discernment of spirits. Unstatesmanlike politicians delude themselves and their followers with images which are triply false. As representations of the character of the aspirants to office they are deceptive. As substitutes for critical reflection upon public problems they are superstitious. As idealized symbols of popular prejudices and passions they are immoral idols. Essentially Platonic thinking of this kind is involved in an aspect of Milton's "myth" of Satan which J. M. Steadman discusses in "Image and Idol: Satan and the Element of Illusion in *Paradise Lost.*"[24] Steadman sees Satan the aspirant to divine honors as "Th'Apostate" whom Milton calls an "Idol of Majesty Divine" as he sits in his "sun-bright Chariot . . . enclos'd/With Flaming Cherubim, and golden Shields" (VI.100–02). The word *Idol,* Steadman observes, is technical: "In affecting divine honors Satan represented the sort of heroic *eidolon* which Favorinus and Suidas had defined as a fictitious likeness, which Bacon described as a false appearance, and which Plato had classified as a *phantasma* distinguished from a true *eikon* or likeness." Steadman traces the term and the distinction which it represents to several Italian critics—especially to Mazzoni in his *Difesa della Commedia di Dante*—and to a passage in Bacon's *Advancement* which distinguishes fallacious *idola* from true images of virtue of all kinds. The source of the distinction is Plato's *Sophist* and its warning to those who would not give up truth to beware of the *phantasmata* which usurp the recognition due only to true *eikones*. As the admired leader of the fallen angels Satan is an idol in both the Platonic and the Baconian senses. And Steadman aptly adds that "Hell was thronged with such *phantasmata* or *eidola*. The fallen angels, subsequently known by 'various Names, / And various Idols through the Heathen World,' would seduce the greater part of mankind."

24. J. M. Steadman, in *JEGP*, 59 (1960), 648.

It is characteristic of Steadman that, instead of following Coleridge's impulse to recognize a contemporary ectype
of Milton's Satan, he should look for literary prototypes.
Three types of such prototypes occur to him: the Achilles
type, to which Ajax, Turnus, and Rinaldo belong; the
shrewdly diplomatic type, of which his only example is
Odysseus; and the type of the leader who must have the
mixed virtues necessary to preserve order among his followers. His examples are Agamemnon, Aeneas, and God-
fredo in the *Jerusalem Delivered*. Other examples of the three
prototypes might easily be found in Italian and French
epic and romance. Tasso's Saracen challenger of Godfrey's
crusaders, the frenetic warrior Argantes, has been suggested[25] as a better example of the first of the three prototypes than the rebellious and proud Achilles himself. In
contrast with all his warrior prototypes, says Lawrence
Sasek, Satan's absolute fearlessness magnifies him into a
superhuman incarnation of human violence and passion.
But violence is the least impressive of Satan's character-
istics, vital to Milton's conception of him though it may
be. It is the tragic element in him which makes him most
impressive to us, and of all his literary prototypes the most
tragic is undoubtedly Virgil's Turnus, the noble but violent
opponent of Aeneas and of his divine destiny in Italy.

In the most recent and most searching of the scholarly
comparisons of Milton's Satan with Turnus we are reminded that Turnus was "the specific means Virgil adopts
to criticize the standard of Achilles"[26] and that similarly
in several situations in *Paradise Lost* Satan is conversely
measured against the tragic Turnus of the *Aeneid*. The two
are linked by Milton's introduction of Satan towering over
his followers "In shape and gesture proudly eminent"

25. By Lawrence Sasek in his unpublished Harvard dissertation, "Satan and
the Epic Hero: Classical and Christian Tradition" (1953), p. 352.

26. Davis P. Harding, *The Club of Hercules* (Urbana, University of Illinois
Press, 1962), pp. 45–52.

(I.590) as Turnus towers[27] over the forces rallying to his support in troops which are catalogued in Virgil's following lines only less impressively than Satan's legions are catalogued by Milton. Harding is the first commentator to make the link between the two towering figures and the solemn rosters of their followers. But the resemblances between Satan and Turnus continue also in the famous simile describing the scene where Satan

> Stood like a Towr; his form had yet not lost
> All her Original brightness, nor appear'd
> Less then Arch Angel ruind, and th'excess
> Of Glory obscur'd; As when the Sun new ris'n
> Looks through the Horizontal misty Air
> Shorn of his Beams, or from behind the Moon
> In dim Eclips disastrous twilight sheds
> On half the Nations, and with fear of change
> Perplexes Monarchs.   [I.591–99]

Much though the commentators have praised this passage, to which a censor is traditionally supposed to have objected on the ground that it might encourage the superstitious hopes of Charles II's enemies, it was left for Harding to develop its importance as "part of Milton's grand strategy for the covert discrediting of Satan." Through the first four books of *Paradise Lost* he points out a number of embedded, implied comparisons of Satan with various Homeric heroes—all of them to his discredit. At the end of Book IV they come thickest where, confronted by Gabriel,

> *Satan* allarm'd
> Collecting all his might dilated stood,
> Like *Teneriff*, or *Atlas* unremov'd:

---

27. ". . . inter primos praestanti corpore Turnus / Vertitur arma tenens et toto vertice supra est" *Aeneid* 7.783–84.

> His stature reacht the Skie, and on his Crest
> Sat horror Plum'd.   [IV.985-89]

The skyscraping figure of Satan gigantizes Virgil's comparison of Aeneas to an Appennine peak as he confronts
Turnus for their decisive struggle. But Harding notes that
the final detail of Milton's description of Satan—". . . and
on his Crest / Sat horror Plum'd"—is not drawn from the
description of Aeneas, but "distils the essence of Virgil's
striking image of the horrible snake-like Chimaera, 'breath-
ing from her throat Aetnean flames,' which adorned the
crest of Turnus' helmet." The implied association of Satan
and the serpent here and elsewhere has also its latent
threat of the doom of the serpent to be bruised by the
"seed of the woman" as the serpents Tityos and Typhon
were slain by the arrows of Apollo or the thunderbolts of
Zeus. But in the scene between Satan and Gabriel the
former's fate is openly declared at the climax of Book IV,
when it is weighed in God's "golden Scales yet seen / Be-
twixt *Astraea* and the *Scorpion* sign" in the zodiac. The
image of God's scales weighing an individual's fate carried
no moral overtone when Hector's death at Achilles' hands
or even the defeat of Troy by the Greeks was foretold by
it in the *Iliad*, but for Milton's readers it had that quality
as definitely as the same figure has it when in Daniel 5:27
Belshazzar is warned, "Thou art weighed in the balance
and found wanting." It was no accident, says Harding,
that Milton "saw fit to end the Fourth Book with a final
allusion to Turnus. For the last verse of the book is a skillful reworking of the last line of the *Aeneid* which, briefly,
poignantly, and unforgettably, records the death of Turnus
and the passage of his soul to the eternal shades: "vitaque
cum gemitu fugit indignata sub umbras."
   Virgilian criticism has never made the mistake of regarding Turnus as the hero of the *Aeneid*, but it has more and
more come to regard him as a tragic figure which its cre-

ator fully intended should command pity. In his struggle to hold Lavinia and the Latin kingdom against Aeneas he is magnificent. His disappointments are almost great enough to win the reader's sympathy in spite of his violence. But when all is told, sympathy for him does not extend to approval of his relentless feud with Aeneas and with the destiny of which Aeneas is the symbol. The "rage / Of *Turnus* for *Lavinia* disespous'd" might make him a tragic hero in Milton's eyes (IX.16–17), but his passion is expressly listed with the traditional epic themes which are described in the prologue to Book IX as less heroic than that of *Paradise Lost*. In the end Turnus' rage cuts him off from all possibility of reconciliation with the Trojans and from all hope of being more than an object of pity and terror to the readers of his story.

In the prologue to Book IX Milton says that he must now change the "Notes" or theme of his story to "tragic." The tragedy to be narrated is the sin in Eden, not the sin of Satan or the sins of any of his ectypes in history. It is not necessary to inquire in just what sense Milton used the word "tragedy" here, but it may be extensible from the sin of Adam to the greater sin of Satan, the self-tempted, for whom God declared that grace could not be found (III.131–32). It is obvious that, as B. A. Wright has most recently reminded us, the fact of Satan's wickedness and impenitence to the end "makes him a great tragic figure"; but he adds the immediate warning that, "although Milton first planned *Paradise Lost* as a tragedy, it is not, as we have it, a tragedy but an epic. The neo-classical theory of the 'forms' is not just pedantry; a writer ignores it at his peril. To regard Satan as the hero of Milton's epic is to stultify the poet's whole intention."[28]

The question may, however, arise as to whether a tragic figure may not play a great and essential, though sub-

28. *Milton's "Paradise Lost,"* p. 54.

ordinate, role in an epic. Victory of some kind—hard-won, perhaps hardly worth winning, but indefeasible—is the proper theme of epic. A defeated epic hero is a contradiction, but defeated opponents or anti-types of the hero are indispensable in an epic where cosmic and absolute actors are the principals. Of such opponents or anti-types of the truly heroic or good, Satan must be the supreme example. In an essay to which Wright refers on the page which is in part quoted above, Helen Gardner traces the emergence of the Satanic tragic hero from Marlowe's Faustus, Middleton's Beatrice-Joanna, and Shakespeare's Macbeth to Milton's Satan.[29] All four tragedies involve the progressive isolation of the hero by his own deeds and resolutions. The most striking parallel with Satan is Macbeth, with his self-revealing soliloquies and his painfully conscious approach to the point of no return. To some extent he is also like Satan because he is a public figure, a usurper as well as an abuser of power and therefore by classical definition doubly a tyrant. Pride or ambition is the passion which motivates the first crime of both figures, but their accumulating wickedness with progressive hardening of the heart is due to the almost inevitable consequence of their public stations.

As the romantic myth of Satan has yielded to the criticism of historical scholarship and to modern psychological approaches to *Paradise Lost,* a new myth of a peculiarly political, tragic Satan is emerging. The basic conception may be less Miltonic than we suppose, but it is certainly to be found in Vondel's *Lucifer,* which was deliberately planned to expose the interplay of snowballing popular resentment over an act of authority as it is exploited by astute leaders to accumulate the mass support and passion necessary for open revolt. But it is essentially the

29. Gardner, "Milton's 'Satan' and the Theme of Damnation in Elizabethan Tragedy," *ES, 1* (1948), 46–66.

same kind of process of conspiracy interworking with mob psychology that Raphael reports Satan as sparking first in the mind of Beelzebub on the night following the presentation of the Son as God's vice-gerent in Heaven. "New Laws," says Satan

> thou see'st impos'd;
> New Laws from him who reigns, new minds may raise
> In us who serve, new Counsels, to debate
> What doubtful may ensue, more in this place
> To utter is not safe. Assemble thou
> Of all those Myriads which we lead the chief;
> Tell them that by command, ere yet dim Night
> Her shadowie Cloud withdraws, I am to haste,
> And all who under me thir Banners wave,
> Homeward with flying march where we possess
> The Quarters of the North, there to prepare
> Fit entertainment to receive our King
> The great *Messiah,* and his new commands. . . .
>
> [V.679–91]

Moving swiftly among Satan's myriad hierarchies, Beelzebub scatters "Ambiguous words and jealousies." Loyalties are confused by his intimation everywhere

> That the most High commanding, now ere Night,
> Now ere dim Night had disincumberd Heav'n,
> The great Hierarchal Standard was to move.
>
> [V.699–701]

When the signal is given, the habit of unquestioning obedience to "thir great Potentate" blinds the mass of his hierarchies to his "lies," and instantly they become a revolting army on the march. By a trick of semantics their leader has been transformed into their idol; their divinely commissioned potentate has become "the most High." When we meet them again later in their experience though earlier in Milton's narrative, more powerful semantic drugs prove capable of blinding them to the meaning of their defeat. While still in Heaven on the eve of battle they have heard Satan declare that their being was not owing to God, that they were "self-begot, self-rais'd" by a "quick'ning power" of their own "when fatal course / Had circl'd his full Orb" (V.860–62). Defeat in Heaven has not purged their minds of the illusion that they are the spontaneously generated "Ethereal sons" of the celestial soil, and in Hell they are ready to listen with Beelzebub to Satan's doctrine that "by Fate the strength of Gods / And this Empyreal substance cannot fail" (I.116–17). Since God solemnly addresses the loyal angels in Heaven as "all ye Gods" (III.341), Beelzebub may well feel secure against any suspicion of flattery when he addresses the council of devils in Pandaemonium as "Synod of Gods" (II.391). In the *Christian Doctrine* (I.5), Milton observed that "the name of God is not infrequently ascribed, by the will and concession of God the Father, even unto angels and to men."[30] But, as J. C. Maxwell observes, an ambiguous play with the title "gods" is central in Satan's temptations of his followers and later of Eve, for they are both structured around the central text of the story of the temptation in Eden, "Ye shall be as gods."[31] In the abuse of that one word is all the lure and logic of Satan's flattery of his legions.

Before his hosts in Pandaemonium Satan is the archetypal demagogue. Comparison with "Hitler addressing one of his monster rallies, with all the trappings of banners, uniforms, and insignia," seems to justify Daiches' assertion that "The whole debate as it develops in Book II is a classic presentation of the abuses of democratic assembly."[32] The archetype includes both demagogue and audience.

30. CE, *14*, 245.
31. J. C. Maxwell, in *NQ, 193* (1948), 242.
32. Daiches, *Milton*, p. 166.

"Hell's totalitarianism," Broadbent rightly says, "is most obvious in the devils; Satan, though in the created world he occasionaly turns humane, in Hell is predominantly a *führer.*"[33] But it is questionable whether Milton was as much concerned as we are today about mob-psychology and its part in the evolution of dictatorships. Yet that view of the debate in Hell is clearly much closer to Milton's thought than is Chateaubriand's notion that "Cromwell and his associates served as Milton's models for his portraits of the infernal crew"—a notion which Kenneth Muir calls "absurd."[34] Milton, of course, had no more respect for the univocal horde of devils than he had for the members who might be elected to a popular assembly which a member of the revived Rump Parliament proposed in the political crisis in September 1659. Such an unwieldy body, said Milton, could convene "only now and then to hold up a forrest of fingers, or to convey each man his bean or ballot into the box."[35] The mere numbers of Satan's inner council of a "thousand Demi-Gods on golden seats" (I.796) would have seemed to Milton to be a travesty of a responsible governing body.

If to the end of his life Milton continued to regard Cromwell as an anti-tyrant (as he certainly did in the *Second Defence of the English People*), then certainly it was not to represent Cromwell that he conceived his figure of Satan. Nor do the four main participants in the infernal debate, Moloch, Belial, Mammon, and Beelzebub, readily match any of Milton's contemporaries. Their function is to provide a foil and a setting for Satan's original proposal of an assault by a single champion, himself, upon the world which rumor said was to be created, and upon its inhabitants. His strategy and his courage are to stand out against the evasive policy of essential surrender to defeat

33. Broadbent, *Some Graver Subject,* p. 78.
34. Kenneth Muir, *John Milton* (London, Longmans, 1955), p. 129.
35. *A Readie and Easie Way* (CE, 6, 131).

of Belial and Mammon, and Moloch's rash demand for a direct assault upon Heaven. Their speeches and Beelzebub's following preparation for the gesture which is to make Satan forever Hell's unchallengeable ruler are magnificent in themselves—so magnificent that Gilbert has said that Milton developed the situation "for its own sake with great pleasure and with little thought of its connection with other parts of the poem, except in the character of Satan."[36] But the value of the debate in Hell is more than vindicated if it adds anything of value to his characterization.

As characterization it is indispensable, for it dramatizes Satan as an idol set in contrast not only with God but with Milton's life-long ideal of the true orator of the breed that was once

> renound
> In *Athens* or free *Rome*, where Eloquence
> Flourishd, since mute. . . .   [IX.670–72]

When Satan approaches Eve in the garden his assumed stance is the false image of such an orator, but the comparison fits him equally well as he stands "with Monarchal pride / Conscious of highest worth" (II.428–29), ready to make his final pitch for power in Pandaemonium. When he returns from earth triumphant in Book X, it is to receive the absolute homage of the "consulting Peers / Rais'd from thir dark *Divan*" (X.456–57). Again there is the implied comparison with a Turkish sultan as a type of absolute ruler. And, as Zera Fink has observed, the authority which Satan has gained in *Paradise Lost* is reaffirmed by acclamation of the devils in council in *Paradise Regained* when

---

36. Gilbert, *On the Composition of Paradise Lost*, p. 104.

> Unanimous they all commit the care
> And management of this main enterprize
> To him their great Dictator.   [I.111–13]

Indeed, Fink regards the entire poem as "an expression of Milton's lack of faith in dictatorship as it was conceived in seventeenth century political thought."[37]

To shift the suggestion to *Paradise Lost* and regard Satan there as in any sense the archetype of ectypes like Napoleon, Hitler, or Lenin clearly involves the risk of over-weighting the political potential of the poem and also of thinking uncritically in terms of Paris, Nuremberg, or Moscow. The ectypes are sure to be chosen on grounds personal to the reader even though he may think that Milton, if he could be with us at this hour, would surely concur in the identification. In the poem Milton names only one ectype, Nimrod. But in the way he refers to some of the passionate heroes of the classical epics, he implies that others are to be found in history as well as literature. Links with actual life are to be inferred from Satan's distinct though fleeting resemblances to Achilles, Turnus, and others. But besides Nimrod another historical ectype of Milton's dictator-Satan has been confidently identified in the pattern of *Paradise Lost:* William Blissett points out that Milton's Satan seems to reflect the "Satanic in Lucan's Caesar"[38] which had left its print upon Ben Jonson's *Catiline* and several other Jacobean plays. Blissett's parallel between the *Pharsalia* and *Paradise Lost* is a rather shadowy one between Satan's voyage through Chaos and Caesar's effort to cross the storm-tossed Adriatic to get reinforcements before the battle of Pharsalia. Both passages, that in Book II of *Paradise Lost* and that in Book V

---

37. Zera S. Fink, *The Classical Republicans* (Evanston, Northwestern University Press, 1943), pp. 195–96. Reprint 1962.

38. William Blissett, "Caesar and Satan," *JHI, 18* (1957), 222–32.

of Lucan's *Civil War,* are very long, and the parallels are acknowledged to be "in general conception rather than in details of execution." The most convincing evidence adduced is a final group of four short passages from *Paradise Lost* which reveal "the Caesarian in Milton's Satan." None of them has a verbal parallel in the *Civil War,* but a definite link of one of them with the Caesar of recorded history is possible through Plutarch's *Life of Caesar* (11.2). It is the passage where Satan declares that in his

> choyce
> To reign is worth ambition though in Hell:
> Better to reign in Hell, then serve in Heav'n.
>
> [I.261–63]

Milton was certainly aware that to illustrate the point that Caesar's master passion was ambition Plutarch had recalled a story that when passing through a mountain village he had said that he would prefer the first place in such wretched surroundings to the second place in Rome. The transfer of those words from the supreme type of human ambition to Satan seems to have been traditional. In the *Adamo Caduto* of Serafino Salandra, Satan declares that he has deliberately preferred reigning in Hell to remaining in Heaven.[39] The verbal parallel is not exact, but no one familiar with Plutarch's anecdote could fail to make the link with it from Milton's passage or from Salandra's. Probably the link was also intended by Vondel when in the second act of *Lucifer* he made Lucifer exclaim:

> Better it were by far
> To be the first Prince in a lower Court
> Than second, or still less, in heaven's Light.[40]

But it is one thing to recognize ectypes of Milton's Satan

39. Serafino Salandra, *Adamo Caduto* (Cozenzo, 1647), II.1.
40. See the translation by Watson Kirkconnell in his *The Celestial Cycle* (Toronto, University of Toronto Press, 1952), p. 374.

in Nimrod and Julius Caesar, and perhaps another to link him with the political dictators who have involved their countries in wars against humanity in the twentieth century. The distinction is a fine one and it involves a difference between Milton's first readers and ourselves. Rajan indicates what it is when he warns against modern sympathy for Satan's "Promethean qualities" which to many of us cover the flaws in his moral and intellectual arguments, his appeal to "just right and the fixt laws of Heav'n" and his outcries against God's "tyranny." "Other politicians," Rajan concludes, "have made claims somewhat similar, and Satan's assertions as the champion of Liberty would amuse, rather than perplex, those who were brought up to think of him as the first Liar."[41]

For modern readers who approach *Paradise Lost* with Milton's basically Platonic conception of the government of the state and of the soul as matters of what Milton called "right reason," there is no mystery in the successful rebellion of the Father of Lies against the divine "tyranny" in the name of liberty. But for a reader who comes to the poem with Broadbent's ambivalent psychological view of its author, the repudiation of the traditional conception of epic heroism in the prologue to Book IX itself shares "a flickering remote beauty with Pandemonium, the *ignis fatuus* in which Satan glides to tempt Eve, the glister of the forbidden fruit itself."[42] At the climax of Satan's review of his troops when

his heart
Distends with pride, and hardning in his strength
Glories   [I.571–73]

at this "moment of deepest involvement in the grandeur of the devils," Broadbent thinks that "the reader finds himself thrown by the enormous weight of that 'Glories' into

41. *"Paradise Lost" and the Seventeenth Century Reader*, pp. 95-96.
42. *Some Graver Subject*, p. 97.

identity with a fascist Satan." This is all the likelier to
happen if the reader is imbued with Sir Herbert Grierson's
dissatisfaction with Milton's God as an absolute ruler and
with his concern lest Milton's confidence in the justice that
he preached in his regicide tracts should end in a dangerous doctrine, "one that might be used to justify Lenin or
Mussolini or Hitler alike."[43] If Milton's political tracts
are brought into the interpretation of his poem, anything
is possible unless the longest view is taken. That view, as
Barker so deliberately takes it, must recognize constant
conviction of "the harsh Puritan belief in the duty and
privilege of the righteous to impose the divine will on the
unregenerate mass," but it must also remember that the
"very centre of Milton's thought on liberty" was always
faith in "the Creator of natural freedom" and in "the
Redeemer of both spiritual and natural freedom" to whom
he appealed in the added final paragraph of the second
edition of *The Readie and Easie Way to Establish a Free Commonwealth.*[44]

The Milton who wrote the closing sentence of the *Way*
and had Michael teach Adam the lesson of the government of reason in the souls of citizens as the key to political freedom, was not speaking with irony. In *Paradise Lost*
as a whole he was a deliberate ironist in structure, characterization, and style. In his treatment of the devils of
Books I and II, what Broadbent calls a basis "for satire of
the underside of tyranny,"[45] he seems to the present writer
to be more of a satirist than an ironist, though the line
may be hard to draw. To Mrs. MacCaffrey, they seem, as
they do to G. Wilson Knight, to "represent mankind in
its fruitless struggles," and to be involved with Satan in
an irony, which, like all irony, "is fundamentally tragic:
it calls out simultaneously our sympathetic emotions and
our critical intellects. Hence," she says, "all arguments as

43. Grierson, *Milton and Wordsworth,* p. 63.
44. Barker, *Milton and the Puritan Dilemma,* pp. 273, 289.
45. *Some Graver Subject,* p. 87.

to where our sympathies lie in the early books of Milton's epic are vain; they lie *both* with the follies of the fallen, and with the rigor and discipline that are necessary to our salvation as reasonable beings."[46] In view of God's condemnation of all the rebel angels as "self-tempted" (III.130) and therefore beyond grace, Mrs. MacCaffrey seems to strain the *conscious* ambivalence of Milton's irony in drawing the "underside of tyranny." He would be less gracious to the horde of devils and, *a fortiori*, to Satan, although it seems from his soliloquies that Milton would approve all that Arnold Stein says in his brilliant study of the "trap of leadership" in which Satan finds himself caught. The private Satan who himself is Hell is the obverse of the public Satan who is admired in Pandaemonium.

But *Paradise Lost* cannot be read as a justification of Satan and his ways either to man or God. That conclusion unexpectedly emerges from Miss Ann Lodge's rigorously objective study of him as a classic case of paranoia in "Satan's Symbolic Syndrome." Her procedure is simply to observe the resemblances of Satan's self-portrayals in his soliloquies and in his speeches in Pandaemonium to Brickner's list of the "major symptoms of paranoid behaviour: megalomania, the need to dominate, persecution complex utilizing projection and exaggerated self-reference, retrospective falsification, and an absolutely logical, though delusional, character of thought." She ends with a prognosis which rests upon the basic assumption in *Paradise Lost* that angels and men enjoy an inviolable original freedom unless they "enthrall themselves" (III.125). The enthralment of the rebellious angels is paranoid because, rather than being a revolt against an arbitrary divine decree, it "is analogous to disobeying a law of gravity," and amounts simply to "defiance of their environment." "It is with this outlook," she says, "that Milton so stresses obedience. It

---

46. *"Paradise Lost" as Myth*, pp. 182–83; cf. *Chariot of Wrath*, p. 137.
47. Ann Lodge, *Psychoanalytic Review*, *43* (1956), 411–22.

represents not so much a becoming humility as the only deeply realistic approach to action."[47]

Miss Lodge is impartial between the psychiatric theories of therapy for paranoids which oppose the doctrine that "the physician's love heals the patient" to faith in a "realistic and merciless environment as sometimes the best treatment and the best physician." When a paranoid achieves power, however, and when he is institutionalized by society, she regards his case as all but hopeless. The records of her great historic paranoids—Ivan the Terrible, Napoleon, Marx, Stalin, and Captain Nemo[48]—offer no hope for the cases of men caught in the trap of leadership. There is nothing in *Paradise Lost* to encourage Origen's view that Satan will ultimately be saved. In its modern form, as proposed by Giovanni Papini, that view attracts Miss Lodge because it asserts the freedom of even the perverse will and implies the inexhaustible love of God. Milton, of course, would have included it among the heresies with which he said that Origen's works were "thick sown."[49] In the *Christian Doctrine* he expressly denied it.[50] The more symbolically the myth of Satan is understood in *Paradise Lost*, the more unequivocally final his ultimate exclusion from all society except his own must be, unless the poem is to end in pessimism. On Miss Lodge's showing, the paranoid character of Milton's Satan is not such as to encourage modern critics who fail to recognize in that "megalomaniac and destructive spirit" anything less than "a superlative prophetic picture of the world of conquerors of our time."[51]

48. The inclusion of Nemo seems as odd as the omission of Balzac's Vautrin, that embodiment of "l'archange déchu qui veut toujours la guerre" and possesses "tous les sentiments humains, moins un seul, celui de repentir." *Le Père Goriot* (Paris, La Renaissance du Livre, n.d.), p. 182.

49. *Of Reformation* (CE, *3*, 21).

50. CE, *16*, 363.

51. The words are from Douglas Bush's *"Paradise Lost" in Our Time* (Ithaca, Cornell University Press, 1945), p. 55.

In substance, if not in style, Miss Lodge's prognosis in the case of the archetypal paranoid is as prophetic as Michael's apocalyptic metaphor describing Satan as doomed to be finally dragged "in Chains / Through all his Realm: and there confounded" left (XII.454-55). And in substance the psychiatrical prognosis comes close to Satan's own analysis in his most revealing soliloquy when he confesses that "Where wounds of deadly hate have pierc'd so deep," only a "worse relapse" could follow any attempt at reconcilement (IV.98-100). That soliloquy reviewing his private experience on the way to the tyrant's fall into the trap of leadership is simply the obverse of the public experience of the society which Michael describes to Adam as doomed to servitude "When upstart Passions catch the Government / From Reason."[52] Though Michael's style in prophesying the end of the archetypal paranoid may be apocalyptic, his metaphor is no more lurid than the facts of Waterloo and of Hitler's death in Berlin. It is from the historical record of the careers of Satan's ectypes that Miss Lodge draws her unfavourable prognosis in his case. And actually, in her psychiatric prognosis of the probable end of the myth of Satan, her thinking is as Platonic as Michael's, for her fear that Satan is incurable corresponds with Plato's mathematically established demonstration of the supreme misery of the man of tyrannical nature who is so unfortunate as to become an actual tyrant.[53]

---

52. *Paradise Lost,* XII.88–89. For the context see above, p. 166.
53. *Republic* 9.578c ff., 587e.

❧ 8 ❧

Milton's Celestial Battle
and the Theogonies

Two recent studies of the sixth book of *Paradise Lost*—Arnold Stein's essay entitled "Milton's War in Heaven"[1] and Dick Taylor's monograph *The Battle in Heaven in Paradise Lost*[2]—begin by quoting Raphael's warning to Adam:

> . . . what surmounts the reach
> Of human sense, I shall delineate so,
> By lik'ning spiritual to corporal forms,
> As may express them best.   [V.571–74]

Then the studies go their different ways toward the common goal of refutation of Dr. Johnson's judgment that the "confusion of spirit and matter" weakens the narrative with "incongruity." Building on Arthur Barker's recognition of the sixth book as focal in the structure of the epic,[3] Taylor gives proper perspectives to its treatment of Obedience, Free Will, True Liberty, and the principle of Hierarchy in the emerging character of the Son of God and the degradation of Satan's character. In terms of struc-

1. Arnold Stein, "Milton's War in Heaven: An Extended Metaphor," in *ELH, 18* (1951), 201–20; reprinted in *Answerable Style,* pp. 17–37.
2. Dick Taylor in Tulane Studies in English, 3 (1952), 69–92.
3. Barker, "Structural Patterns in *Paradise Lost,*" *PQ, 28* (1949), 17–30.

196

tural logic, Milton could hardly hope for a better defense. In terms of poetic consistency Stein makes his case against the objection of "incongruity" and "confusion of spirit and matter" in Milton's celestial battle by reducing it to a single "complex metaphor."

Taylor and Stein face a severer critic of Milton than Johnson in Duncan Spaeth, who condemns him for even trying to handle the subject of war, which he said he was not "sedulous to indite" and formally repudiated as an epic theme in favor of

> the better fortitude
> Of Patience and Heroic Martyrdom.
>   [IX.31–32]

Echoing Johnson in Coleridge's language, Spaeth finds that "Milton's battle-scenes in heaven fail to induce that willing suspension of disbelief which constitutes poetic faith." He dislikes the "subtle disquisitions on the use of Force to make Reason prevail, which leave even Milton only half-convinced," and he is annoyed by divine meddling on battlefields either in heaven or on the windy plain of Troy. He is readier to excuse it in Homer's deities than to tolerate it in Milton's God. His objection is put in a way which nicely introduces the subject of the present study, when he declares that in Milton's choice of a myth for his narrative he blundered as Homer would have done if he had "made the τιτανομαχία the theme of his epic instead of the legendary but not mythical story of Troy."[4]

The thesis of the present study is that Milton definitely conceived his celestial battle as representing events which were none the less actual for surmounting the reach of human sense, and that he found evidence for their occurrence and models for their likening to corporal forms in

4. Duncan Spaeth, "Epic Conventions in *Paradise Lost*," in *Elizabethan Studies and Other Essays in Honor of George F. Reynolds* (Boulder, Colo., 1945), pp. 204–05.

the classical accounts of the assaults of the Titans and giants on the gods of Olympus, of which the best example is in Hesiod's *Theogony*.

To say that Milton found proof of the actual occurrence of his celestial war in the ancient titanomachies and gigantomachies amounts to saying that he regarded those accounts of war in heaven as substantially recording events which are less fully recorded in scriptural passages like the account of Michael leading the loyal angels against the legions of Satan (Revelation 12:7–9); the doom pronounced on the serpent (Genesis 3:15), that the seed of the woman should bruise its head; and the mysterious fall of Lucifer (Isaiah 14:12). Milton's acceptance of these passages as recording actual events is established by his opening statement in the chapter "On the Government of Angels" in the *Christian Doctrine* (I.9), that many of the angels revolted from God before the fall of man. As evidence he quoted Luke 9:26 and Luke 8:2, and among several passages from the epistles (II Peter 2:4): "God spared not the angels that sinned." Then, leaving no doubt of his adherence to the biblical record of the war in heaven, he went on to quote Revelation 12:7, and to explain that Michael, as leader of the embattled angels, must not be confused with Christ. The actual vanquisher of the devil, who singly tramples him under foot in the presence of the two exhausted armies of angels, is Christ.

In the *Christian Doctrine,* Satan's motives for revolting do not figure, yet Allan H. Gilbert[5] is clearly right in thinking that the exaltation of the Son over Satan and all other angels in Book V seemed to Milton to have the sanction of Psalms 2:6: "Yet have I set my king upon my holy hill

5. "The Theological Basis of Satan's Rebellion and the Function of Abdiel in *Paradise Lost,*" *MP, 40* (1942), 19–42. The germ of Gilbert's thought is found in a connection between the second Psalm and *De Doctrina Christiana*, I.5, which is made by Grierson in *Milton and Wordsworth,* p. 99, on a hint drawn from Newton's note on *Paradise Lost,* VI.603.

of Zion." So it is the exaltation of the Son that provokes
the revolt of the evil angels, all of whose rage, he says, as
he goes toward his duel with Satan on the third day of
the battle, is bent

> against mee . . .
> Because the Father, t'whom in Heav'n supream
> Kingdom and Power and Glorie appertains,
> Hath honourd me according to his will.
>
>   [VI.813–16]

The Bible is chary of details about the celestial battle,
but if Gilbert is right in his theory about the second Psalm
as the basis of the exaltation of the Son to reign in heaven
by right of merit, then he must also be right in interpreting its closing verse, "Thou shalt break them with a rod of
iron," and the closing warning to "Kiss the Son lest he be
angry," as parts of the historical record which is visualized
in God's Decree:

> This day I have begot whom I declare
> My onely Son, and on this holy Hill
> Him have anointed, whom ye now behold
> At my right hand; your Head I him appoint;
> And by my Self have sworn to him shall bow
> All knees in Heav'n.   [V.603–08]

Protestant and Roman Catholic exegesis, as Gilbert shows,
regularly treated Psalms 2:6, as paralleling Hebrews 1:6,
"Let all the angels of God worship him"; and so Milton
might regard the testimony of the Psalmist as corroborated
by that of the apostle.

We may take still another step in the direction which
Gilbert's theory points and see in the most famous verse
in the psalm—"He that sitteth in the heavens shall laugh"
—a glint of the element of true comedy in the ensuing
situation. The verse is echoed in the Son's words on the
eve of battle:

Mightie Father, thou thy foes
Justly hast in derision, and secure
Laugh'st at thir vain designs and tumults vain.
[V.735–37]

The prophecy is fulfilled when the Son routs the Satanic
hosts without using half his strength,

for he meant
Not to destroy, but root them out of Heav'n,
[VI.854–55]

and so "as a Heard of Goats . . . Drove them before him
Thunder-struck" (VI.857–58).

In this scene Arnold Stein sees the capstone of Milton's
entire "complex metaphor," since its whole purpose has
been to leave the rebels "exposed to laughter." His conclusion harmonizes with C. S. Lewis' view of Milton's
whole treatment of Satan as inevitably, to a great extent,
comic and doomed to excite "the Divine laughter in *Paradise Lost* which has offended some readers."[6] Gilbert has
frequently insisted on Milton's comic intention and talent,
simply as a part of his gift for telling a many-sided story.
Comedy is a part of all true epic, and recognition of it in
Paradise Lost can help to support down-to-earth criticism,
like R. H. West's "Literal-Minded Defense of Milton's
Battle in Heaven,"[7] and John E. Hardy's analysis of the
merits of Book VI "as an epic battle."[8] Yet it is notorious
that for irreverent readers Milton's battle scenes are absurd
rather than comic. To A. J. A. Waldock they all seem
"rather nonsensical,"[9] like all his descriptions of the angels

6. Lewis, *A Preface to Paradise Lost,* p. 93.

7. Robert H. West, unpublished address to the South Atlantic Modern Language Association in 1952.

8. *SR, 62* (1954), 509–19.

9. Waldock, *Paradise Lost and its Critics,* p. 108. In *An Anatomy of Milton's
Verse* (Baton Rouge, Louisiana State University Press, 1955), p. 17, W. B. C.
Watkins briefly replied to Waldock in terms of seventeenth-century science.

in action, because they have even more incongruities than Dr. Johnson saw in the attempt to accommodate "pure spirit" to the necessities of a narrative poem. Modern discovery of the "materialism" of Milton's view of the angels seems to Waldock only to complicate the incongruities. The worst of them, as E. M. W. Tillyard confesses, is their use of artillery (which might not seem so incongruous if it were atomic), but he declares that it would not seem ludicrous if we were properly "impressed by the culminating emergence of the Son" in the heavenly battle.[10]

We feel our modern difficulty in this matter acutely when we read a remark like Thyer's on *Paradise Lost* (VI.746): "The description of the Messiah's going out against the rebel angels is a scene of the same sort with Hesiod's Jupiter against the Titans. They are both of them the most undoubted instances of the true sublime; but which has exceeded it is very difficult to determine." In spite of the reverence of the eighteenth-century editors for the classics, they were rather inclined to treat Milton as the supreme master of sublimity, and they found it in some of the scenes which are most annoying to modern readers. Bishop Newton could annotate Milton's picture of the loyal and rebellious angels as having "vaulted either host with fire" (VI.214) by observing that, "Our author," who "frequently had his eye upon Hesiod's giant-war, as well as upon Homer . . . has imitated several passages, but commonly exceeds his original, as he has done in this particular . . . Milton has improved the horrour of the description; and a *shade of darts* (in *Theogony*, 716) is not near so grand and dreadful an image as a *fiery cope* or *vault of flaming darts*."

But enthusiasm for Milton's battle scenes long antedated Newton and Thyer; it began with one of the first tributes to *Paradise Lost* on record, the Latin poem which

10. E. M. W. Tillyard, *The Miltonic Setting Past and Present* (Cambridge, the University Press, 1938), p. 170.

was first published prefixed to the second edition, and
which Masson[11] confidently attributed to Dr. Samuel Barrow, who was eminent enough to be one of Charles II's
physicians-in-ordinary. To Barrow the celestial battle was
clearly the most moving part of the whole work, and its
climax was the moment of the appearance of the Son of
God in the "Chariot of Paternal deity" with its convoying
cherubs that come from Ezekiel's prophecy (I:4–27):

> At simul in coelis Messiae insignia fulgent,
>   Et currus animes, armaque digna Deo,
> Horrendumque rotae strident, & saeva rotarum
>   Erumpunt torvis fulgura luminibus   (lines 29–32)

The kindling of Barrow's imagination by Milton's passage
is obvious, and his tribute in verses which were perhaps
intended to suggest that Milton's style was worthy of its
classical models, amounts to strong evidence that his first
readers were far away from our danger of being insuffi-
ciently "impressed by the culminating emergence of the
Son." By them, as Grant McColley pointed out, the Son's
emergence may have been expected in consequence of a
tradition going back to Rupert of St. Heribert's Commentary on Ezekiel.[12] For Rupert there was no doubt that
"the likeness of the appearance of a man" on the sapphire
throne above Ezekiel's terrible crystal firmament was
Christ, or that the whole vision was a kind of apotheosis.
So Milton regarded it, and he was irresistibly drawn to it
because nowhere else among the many scriptural passages
in which he found evidence of an actual war in heaven
could he find one that was rich enough in imagery to fur-
nish his picture of the Son mounted on

---

11. David Masson, *The Life of John Milton*, 6, 715.

12. Grant McColley, "Milton's Battle in Heaven and Rupert of St. Heribert," *Speculum*, *16* (1941), 230–35. In "The War in Heaven: Milton's Version
of the *Merkabah*," *JEGP*, *57* (1958), 690–703, J. H. Adamson urges that Milton's over-all allegory and also his details in his treatment of the reminiscences
of Ezekiel were due to that cabbalistic work.

The Chariot of Paternal Deitie,
Flashing thick flames, Wheele within Wheele,
                              undrawn,
It self instinct with Spirit, but convoyd
By four Cherubic shapes, four Faces each
Had wondrous, as with Starrs thir bodies all
And Wings were set with Eyes, with Eyes the
                              wheels
Of Beril, and careering Fires between;
Over thir heads a chrystal Firmament,
Whereon a Saphir Throne . . .   [VI.750–58]

Milton appropriated Ezekiel's vision both because he admired its poetry and because he regarded it as a supreme biblical example of "lik'ning spiritual to corporal forms." The evidence for interpreting it as a glimpse of the Son of God when he rode to battle against the rebel angels might not be conclusive, but it was as nearly so as that which a great English angelologist, John Salkeld, had quoted "Aquinas and Valentin, with many other Schoole-Divines," as having interpreted Revelation 12 to mean that "Lucifer drew after him the third part of the Angels in his first combate with *Michael,* and fall from heaven."[13] Salkeld himself was inclined to regard the passage as a prophecy of a fight to come between Satan and Michael "a little before the day of Judgement," and he was certain that the struggle between the two armies of angels should be understood as spiritual.[14] However Milton may have understood the passage in Revelation 12, he accepted Satan's past de-

13. John Salkeld, *A Treatise of Angels* (London, 1613), p. 345.
14. Discussing "how the fore-said fight of the Divell was with the blessed Angels," Salkeld thought that Satan simply "declared (in the location of the Angels) his depraved minde and will: as on the contrary side, Michael, manifesting his constancie, affect, and minde to persevere in good, unto his part of Angels, was occasion of their persisting in good, by his good example, so that these two, as it were, armies of Angels, being contrary in manifest affections the one to the other, resisted mutually, as it is expressed in the Apocalypse Chap. 12 spiritually fought together." Ibid., p. 347.

feat in heaven as well as his future defeat at the end of the
world, for both are implied by the prayer in the induction
to the fourth book of *Paradise Lost* for

> that warning voice, which he who saw
> Th'*Apocalyps,* heard cry in Heaven aloud,
> Then when the Dragon, put to second rout,
> Came furious down to be reveng'd on men . . .
> [IV.1-4]

Milton's confidence in his readers' acceptance of the
celestial war with more than the suspense of disbelief which
constitutes poetic faith is clear from his scenes in hell
where Beelzebub grieves over the "foul defeat" which

> Hath lost us Heav'n, and all this mighty Host
> In horrible destruction laid thus low, . . .
> [I.136-37]

And Belial reminds Moloch how they had so short a while
ago

> fled amain, pursu'd and strook
> With Heav'n's afflicting Thunder.   [II.165-66]

The case for Milton's belief in a primordial celestial
war may rest finally upon the chapter in the *Christian Doctrine* (I.9), which has already been quoted. Its evidence
seems conclusive to Balachandra Rajan, in contrast to the
lack of evidence in the treatise to all else that he may
have thought about events in heaven before the creation
of the universe. Rajan is fully aware of a poet's right to
mix facts with fiction in his story, and is quite ready to
draw the inference that his "fable is misleading as a means
of collecting and exhibiting a poet's beliefs."[15] With that
warning in mind, but fortified by Rajan's recognition of
the fact that the war in heaven was an important part in

15. *"Paradise Lost" and the Seventeenth Century Reader*, p. 31.

the construction and imagery of *Paradise Lost,* we may go on to the second of the two theses to which the present study is devoted.

It may seem less plausible than the first, and less important even if it can be accepted. It can be conveniently put in the form that Thyer gave to it in his note on the praise of the angel chorus for the Son of God in Milton's account of his return from the creation of the universe:

> what thought can measure thee or tongue
> Relate thee; greater now in thy return
> Then from the Giant Angels; thee that day
> Thy Thunders magnifi'd; but to create
> Is greater then created to destroy.   [VII.603–07]

"Milton," said Thyer, "I doubt not, intended to allude to Hesiod's giant war; but I do not see with Dr. Bentley, that therefore he must insinuate that this relation is as fabulous as that. He probably designed, by this expression, to hint his opinion, that the fictions of the Greek poets owed their rise to some uncertain clouded tradition of this real event, and their giants were, if they had understood the story right, his fallen angels."

In *Spectator* 333 Addison was inclined to agree with Thyer and to accept "the opinion of many learned men, that the fable of the giants war, which makes so great a noise in antiquity, and gave birth to the sublimest descriptions in *Hesiod's* works, was an allegory founded on this very tradition of a fight between the good and bad angels." To Thyer and Addison, Milton's war in Heaven seemed most esthetically valid and most consonant with the poet's mind if it was taken as a treatment of a tradition about an event in cosmic history rather than as the poet's development of a classic myth into a pure and complex metaphor. Milton's art and his intelligence alike seemed to Addison to be best vindicated by Thyer's modestly preferred view of the matter.

To take Thyer's suggestion seriously a reader needs a kind of classical education which has become obsolete. It may be acceptable, as R. J. Z. Werblowski has said, only "in ages when the people could take it for granted that these myths (i.e., the myths of the hybristic protagonists of Greek tragedy), as well as those about the Giants and Titans warring with Zeus, were degenerate and paganized remains of the 'historical' Christian version."[16] Writing as a disciple of Jung, Werblowski is mainly interested in identifying a common archetypal pattern in the *Prometheus* of Aeschylus and Milton's Satan—the hybris of the Titan and the superbia of the devil. He is not interested in Thyer's view of the matter except as it can be made to contribute to a psychological interpretation of the *Prometheus* and *Paradise Lost* as embodiments of a common archetype.

Of course, Werblowski is right about the prevailing indifference of modern editors and scholars to Thyer's view of Milton's understanding of the relation of the ancient theogonies to the glimpses of a celestial war in the Bible. His point is proved by the modern editors and scholars who see nothing but casual literary allusions in the passages where Hesiod is clearly reflected. In the lines (VII. 603–05), which prompted Thyer's note, for example, Verity recognizes only a passing literary reference. To Arnold Stein all such passages in *Paradise Lost* seem to be simply "literary overtones."[17] In a careful study of Milton's angelology Robert H. West declares that when he "has the warring angels pelt one another with hills and the rebels fall for nine days he has unmistakably borrowed from Hesiod imaginative items of titanic conflict and disaster, a

16. R. J. Z. Werblowsky, *Lucifer and Prometheus*, p. 44. The "archetypal" theory is skeptically examined by Adams in IKON: *John Milton and the Modern Critics*, pp. 35–39. The editorial tradition of tracing many parallels to the *Prometheus* in *Paradise Lost* is attacked by J. C. Maxwell in "Milton's Knowledge of Aeschylus: The Argument from Parallel Passages," *RES, 3* (1952), 366–71.

17. Stein, *Answerable Style*, p. 44.

purely literary debt distinct in kind from his debt to the speculative Psellus for the facts about angelic nature."[18]

West regards Milton's "giant Angels" as an allusion to the giants of the Old Testament. Following a suggestion in a note on the passage by one of the most scholarly of the eighteenth-century editors, Zachary Pearce, West treats the word "giants" as meaning simply that the rebel angels had (in Pearce's language) "that disposition of mind, which is always ascribed to giants, namely a proud, fierce, and aspiring temper." Thyer found Pearce's explanation "a little forced," even though it was supported by a reference to the fact that the Hebrew word *gibbor,* which means "fierce" or "proud," "is always rendered a *giant* in Scripture." And then Thyer went on to declare his conviction that Milton "intended to allude to Hesiod's giant war."

If Thyer had wished to extend his note into a monograph, he might have reviewed the main coincidences between Hesiod's *Theogony* and Milton's battle in heaven: the crushing defeat of the attacking rebel powers and their nine-day fall from heaven into Tartarus (a parallel made prominent in *Paradise Lost,* I.50, and again in VI.871), the exchange of sky-darkening missiles which so impressed Newton, the reservation of the main might of the ruler of heaven until the stalemate of the struggle, and a final victory in both cases which is marked by something like apocalyptic fires and thunder. As detailed evidence Thyer might have quoted the passage which includes the Titans in the catalogue of fallen angels who assume the names of the various gods in the pagan pantheons so as to deceive the nations:

18. West, *Milton and the Angels,* p. 105. In *Paradise Lost,* p. 40, Grant McColley found "a closer analogue than Hesiod's picture of the barrages of Hesiod's Titanomachy in 'the *Decay* of Du Bartas, a section of the *Divine Weeks.*' " But it is hard to find anything in Du Bartas that justifies McColley's statement, and we have the word of George Coffin Taylor in *Milton's Use of Du Bartas* (Cambridge, Mass., Harvard University Press, 1934), p. 85, that in the sixth book of *Paradise Lost* "there appear to be no borrowings from Du Bartas."

> Th' *Ionian* Gods, of *Javans* Issue, held
> Gods, yet confest later than Heav'n and Earth
> Thir boasted Parents; *Titan* Heav'ns first born
> With his enormous brood, and birthright seis'd
> By younger *Saturn,* he from mightier *Jove*
> His own and *Rhea's* Son, like measure found;
> So *Jove* usurping reign'd.   [I.508–14]

Milton puts the Titans and their usurping offspring, the
Olympian deities, last in the list of rebel angels, whose
leaders were to be the most powerfully realized actors in
his story under the names of the devils of Hebrew or Christian tradition—Moloch, Beelzebub, Belial, and Mammon.
All the demons in the list are treated alike as deceivers
of the nations by the fraudulent myths[19] which they dis-
seminated about themselves. But the fraud of their pretended generation by heaven and earth cast no doubt
upon their myth as linked with the celestial battle of
Scripture. Whatever fables might have been told about
them by the erring Greeks, it was certain that the tale of
Mulciber's fall from Olympus should be understood by
enlightened readers as an ethnic version of the fall of the
"rebellious rout" (I.747) of angels from Heaven.

The fraud in the myths about the Titans might be obvious, yet they might contain recognizable fragments of
biblical history. Many Renaissance scholars found evidence
for the revolt of the angels in theogonies less familiar than
Hesiod's. Milton made a passing reference to one of them
which, though lost, was supposed to have been written by
"Blind Thamyris" (III.35), with whom, as with Homer, he
prayed that he might be "equall'd in renown." In a frag-

19. In *Classical Myth and Legend in Renaissance Dictionaries* (Chapel Hill, University of North Carolina Press, 1955), pp. 279–80, DeWitt T. Starnes and
Ernest W. Talbert note the inconsistency of the Titan genealogies which the
dictionaries took from various sources. In some Rhea is identified with Ops,
Vesta, and several other Titanesses, while in others she is made the daughter
of one Vesta and the mother of another, the Vesta who appears as Saturn's
daughter in *Il Penseroso,* line 25.

ment of another such theogony, supposed to have been
written by one of the "Seven Wise Men of Greece," Pherecydes of Syros, Milton knew of a passage suggesting identification of a Titan leader, the serpent-deity Ophion, with
Satan. The appropriate place for an allusion to it was after
the scene of the transformation of the devils into serpents
in Pandaemonium, after their celebration of Satan's seduction of Eve. The devils, he says, spread a tradition

> Among the Heathen of thir purchase got,
> And Fabl'd how the Serpent, whom they calld
> *Ophion with Eurynome,* the wide-
> Encroaching *Eve* perhaps, had first the rule
> Of high Olympus, thence by *Saturn* driv'n
> And *Ops,* ere yet *Dictaean Jove* was born.
>
> [X.579–84]

For confirmation of the belief that Saturn and Rhea stole
the rule of Olympus from the serpent Titan Ophion, Milton might have referred his readers to the popular Mythology of Natale Conti,[20] but if challenged about his inference
that Ophion could be identified with Satan, he would
have fallen back upon some authority like the famous
demonologist Jean Bodin, who opened his *Daemonomanie
des sorciers*[21] by relating the account of the casting out of
"that old Serpent, called the devil and Satan and . . . his
angels with him," (Revelation 12:9), with the gigantomachy
of the ancients. His primary authority was Pherecydes,
and he went on, with doubtful justification, to appeal for
support to Empedocles, "qui appelle les Daemones tombez
du ciel οὐρονοπετές," to Hermes Trismegistus in the *Poim-
ander,* and to St. Augustine in *The City of God* (VIII.22).

If further pressed, Milton might have quoted a remark
of George Sandys on a passage in Ovid's *Metamorphoses*

---

20. *Natalis Comitis Mythologiae, sive Explicationis Fabularum Libri decem,* II.2,
p. 122.

21. Jean Bodin, *De Magorum Daemonomania,* French translation (1580).

(I.151–55), which has been used to illustrate his reference to Ophion by Douglas Bush.[22] Sandys wrote: "Pherecydes the Syrian writes how the Divels were throwne out of heaven by Jupiter (this fall of the Gyants, perhaps an allusion to that of the Angells) the chiefe called Ophioneus, which signifies Serpentine: having after made use of that creature to poyson Eve with a false ambition."

Like Milton, Sandys was thinking of the fall of the devils and the rout of the angels as a single event. Like Raleigh in the *History of the World* (I.6), both Sandys and Milton regarded the classic myths as fabulous but venerable corroborations of Scripture. Milton may or may not have read Sandys, and he may not have known that Bodin identified Pherecydes' serpent-Titan with the "chef des Anges rebelles," or that in the *De Occulta Philosophia* (III.38), Cornelius Agrippa had identified the leader of the rebel angels with "that Ophis, i.e. the Devilish Serpent." Behind Agrippa and Bodin was Origen, in whose *Contra Celsum* (6.43), Milton might read that the Titan Ophioneus was one and the same with "the serpent which was the cause of man's expulsion from the divine paradise, and deceived the male race with a promise of divine power of attaining greater things."

On a different level there is a more obvious hint at identification of another of the Titans with the leader of the rebel angels in Milton's portrait of Satan

> Prone on the Flood, extended long and large
> . . . floating many a rood, in bulk as huge
> As whom the Fables name of monstrous size,
> *Titanian,* or *Earth-born,* that warr'd on *Jove,*

---

22. Bush quotes from Sandy's *Ovid's Metamorphosis Englished, mythologiz'd, and represented in figures* (London, 1627), in *Mythology and the Renaissance Tradition in English Poetry* (Minneapolis, University of Minnesota Press, 1932), pp. 273–74, n. 65. An equally significant remark was made by Cowley in a note on *Davideis,* III.45: "The Fable of the *Gyants* Fight with the *Gods* was not invented by the *Graecians,* but came from the Eastern People and arose from the true Story of the building of the Tower of Babel."

Briareos or *Typhon,* whom the Den
By ancient *Tarsus* held, or that Sea-beast
Leviathan, which God of all his works
Created hugest that swim th' Ocean stream.
                                                    [I.195–202]

In Natale Conti's chapter on Typhon in the *Mythologia* (VI.22), aside from the monster's vast size, the outstanding topic is his part in the revolt of the earth-born giants against Zeus. Conti went on in a formal account of the allegorizations of his myth to recall that in the *Bellum Giganteum* of Theodore he had been made into a symbol of ruthless ambition, which had become traditional. As such, he was familiar enough for Milton to use him in opening the Fourth Academic Exercise at Cambridge with a picture of Typhon as a symbol of rampant Error rebelling against Truth. In bracketing Satan "prone on the flood" with Typhon, Milton was not suggesting an identification like the seemingly literal one that he intended in the lines on Ophion. Satan and Typhon are compared in an epic simile like Satan's immediately following comparison with Leviathan. Nor is the literary character of the similes altered by the fact that they both come full circle. Typhon is a symbol of the Satanic sin of rebellious pride, and Leviathan, the whale which is called "that dragon that is in the sea" (Isaiah 27:1), was traditionally regarded as a type of Satan.

The Satan-Typhon simile is a special case on the edge of Milton's treatment of the Titanomachia, even though Milton's lines do recall Hesiod's description of Typhon in the *Theogony* (819–85) as the most frightful of the earth-born assailants of the Olympian gods. In the simile Typhon is distinct from the personages in the action of the poem. Milton's treatment of him is in striking contrast with that of Odorico Valmarana in *Daemonomachia,*[23] one

23. Odorico Valmanara, *Daemonomachiae, sive de bello intelligentiarum Libri XV* (Bologna, 1623), p. 26.

of the several Italian treatments of the war in heaven that
Milton may have known. At the outset of the *Daeomono-
machia*, after Lucifer has been challenged by Michael in a
situation somewhat like that in which Milton's Satan is
checked by Abdiel, as the rebel angels rally around their
leader, a spokesman emerges from the mob:

> Unus (Graii dixere Typhoeum,
> Romano potuit dici sermone superbus)
> Lucifero accedens totius ab ore cohortis,
> Aerium quassans caput, inquit: Maxime princeps,
> Decretis his stare iuvat? privabere honore
> Tam merito? nulloque certamine tolli
> Munera tanta sines?

Valmarana's parenthetical words indicate that he thought
of Typhoeus[24] as a traditional symbol of rebellious pride,
but also as a demon who might play a part in his action
analogous to that played by Beelzebub in *Paradise Lost*.
Valmarana's Typhoeus goes on with his flattery of Lucifer
until the latter breaks into an equally bombastic speech,
and the die is cast. A battle ensues in which the devils
assume the names of Titans or giants as easily as Milton's
devils assume names like Moloch or Mulciber.

Valmarana's treatment of Typhon and the Titans generally differs from Milton's somewhat as Spenser's does.
For Spenser they were symbols which might casually enter
into his narrative as personages in an allegory. In his final
cantos one of them, Mutability, whose name and myth are
his invention, makes a new assault upon Olympus and
moves Jove to exclaim:

> Will never mortall thoughts cease to aspire,
> In this bold sort, to heaven claime to make,

---

24. In *Classical Myth and Legend in Renaissance Dictionaries*, pp. 281–83, Starnes
and Talbert suggest that Milton's Typhon is a conflation of accounts of Typhon
(Typhoeus) and Tityus by several mythographers.

And touch celestiall seates with earthly mire?
I would have thought that bold Procrustes hire,
Or Typhons fall, or proud Ixions paine,
Or great Prometheus tasting of our ire,
Would have suffiz'd the rest for to restraine,
And warn'd all men, by their example, to refraine.

[*Faerie Queene,* VII.6.29]

Against the Spenserian example we feel the force of
C. M. Bowra's conviction that, in spite of Raphael's warning that he must delineate heavenly events "By lik'ning
spiritual to corporal forms," Milton's war in heaven "need
not be so allegorical as we think."[25] But admirers of G.
Wilson Knight's interpretation of Milton's celestial war in
Chariot of Wrath and of Arnold Stein's interpretation of it
in *Answerable Style* are likely to qualify Bowra's faith that
Milton's story "illustrates the universal truths which he
proclaims and may be treated as something complete in
itself." Stein's reading of the sixth book of *Paradise Lost*
as a complex metaphor and "a kind of great scherzo, like
some of Beethoven's—with more than human laughter,"[26]
may be reconcilable with Bowra's doctrine, but Knight's
attempt to establish his "equation of this main action in
Paradise Lost with Milton's own prophetic nationalism"[27]
certainly is not. Milton's celestial war shares its liability
to allegorical and symbolic interpretation with Hesiod's
myth of the Titans, but with this difference between Milton's time and ours: that they could alike be read as both
history and allegory.

Even before Hesiod, as Werner Jaeger tells us, the Or-
phic theogonies had overtones of cosmic or scientific allegory, and Pherecydes actually conceived of the "culprit

25. Bowra, *From Virgil to Milton,* p. 213.
26. Stein, *Answerable Style,* p. 20.
27. Knight, *Chariot of Wrath,* p. 155.

deities" whom Zeus hurled into Tartarus and bound there
as definitely representing "meteorological forces."[28] Something like ethical overtones could easily be read into the
first sculpture representing the repulse of the Titans at
Apollo's great temple at Delphi, and they were still easier
to read into the myth of the slaying of the earth-monster,
Python, by the arrows of the sun-god. There is a hint of
allegory in the story of Athene's helping Zeus to victory
over the giants, which goes back to Callimachus' poem *On
the Bath of Pallas,* and there is a note of moral victory in
Pindar's prophecy of the share of Hercules in their defeat
in the first Nemean Ode. The Titanomachies had assumed
esoteric importance long before Plutarch wrote in *Isis and
Osiris* (364d) that some of the legends and rites pertaining
to the Titans corresponded with the stories of the dis-
memberment and revivification of Osiris. In Alciati's *Em-
blemata* the commentators on the myth of the Titans were
quoted as agreeing upon its plain moral:

> Huius figmenti rationem Mythologi adferunt, eamque
> traducunt ad homines quosdam impios, qui Deos
> negligerent, aut etiam negarent: quorum pedes in
> draconum volumina desisse aiunt, quod nihil su-
> perum, nihil rectum cogitarent, totius eorum vitae
> gressu ad inferna mergente. Macrobius, *Saturnalia,* . . .
> [I.20][29]

The Titans had become a symbol of moral degeneracy—
hence the half-human, half-serpentine form often attributed to them; and they had also become a symbol of the
free-thinkers who despise or deny the gods. By the second
century A.D., this interpretation had so long been taken
seriously that Lucian mocked it (*Icaromenippus* 33) with his
picture of the assembled Olympian gods advising Zeus to

28. Werner Jaeger, *The Theology of the Early Greek Philosophers* (Oxford, Clarendon Press, 1937), p. 70.
29. Padua, 1661 (p. 37).

throw the Epicurean philosophers into Tartarus with the Giants.

Milton, we may be sure, was familiar with the general development of the interpretation of the myths of the Titans and the Giants. He was enough interested in several other works of Philo to know something about his book on the giants of Genesis 6, the *De gigantibus,* which insisted on regarding them as their counterparts in Greek mythology were regarded by the most rationalistic commentators—simply as depraved and materialistic men. Though Milton can hardly have been entirely sympathetic with the condemnation of matter as evil and hostile to spirit, which ran through so much Neoplatonic thought from Philo to the school of Marsilio Ficino, he could hardly fail to sympathize with the conception of the ancient gigantomachy as a symbol of conscience (*sinderesi* or *sinteresi*) and the mastery of all human weakness by the "sun of the intelligence and the light of reason," as it was presented in the dedication of Giordano Bruno's *Spaccio de la Bestia Trionfante*[30] to Sir Philip Sidney, if he read it. He must have been very familiar with similar interpretations of the myth as they were to be found in Conti's *Mythologia* (VI.21), where the half-serpent, half-human form so often attributed to the giants by the poets was a mark of their depravity and rebellious pride. Though proof may be impossible, transference of these allegorical ideas about the mythological assailants of the Olympian gods to the revolt of the angels seems to have played a part in the treatment of the revolt by the Dutch poet Vondel in *Lucifer* (1654). In the moment of final defeat by Michael's loyal angels the Dutch poet had Lucifer transformed into a multiform beast: part lion (to symbolize pride), and then (to symbolize the six remaining deadly sins) part swine, part ass, part rhinoceros, part ape, part serpent, and part

30. Bruno, *Opere Italiane, 6,* 13.

wolf. In *Paradise Lost* the only trace of such symbolism is in Satan's imbrutings of himself as a toad and as a serpent, and in the mass metamorphosis of his followers into hissing snakes in the welcoming scene in Pandaemonium.

The odor of allegory is faint indeed about Satan's imbrutings. In our prevailing tendency to treat them as part of his degradation we lose sight of what trace of the odor may actually remain; and in Arnold Stein's view of them as a part of Milton's plan to make Satan physically as well as morally ridiculous,[31] it vanishes altogether. More remarkable is Milton's deliberate intention to keep away from allegory in the main scene in his celestial battle. He will have none of the pious medieval efforts to interpret God's thunderbolts as "acts of the virtues" and "weapons of reason for the overthrow of the vices," or of his lightnings as "the light of reason, either ethical, economic, or political." By such ingenious hermeneutics Coluccio Salutati had expounded the overthrow of the Titans, down to details like the head of the gorgon Medusa on the shield of Jupiter, which he regarded as a symbol of eloquence, or of "the consummate dialectic which the Titans dread."[32]

But a part of Salutati's interpretation was the ancient idea which made the Titans symbols of atheism. His tone suggests intolerance of a kind which would have been offensive to the author of *Of True Religion, Heresy, Schism, Toleration.* He was anticipating the abuse of the myth in Reformation times, when the Ramists were attacked[33] for exposing theology to the giants, and when Bishop Jewel, writing his apology for Elizabethan Protestantism, protested against the charge that, "we be cursed creatures and like the giants do war against God himself."[34]

31. Stein, *Answerable Style*, p. 22.

32. Salutati, *De Laboribus Herculis*, 2, 385–413 *passim.*

33. In P. Gallandi's *Pro Schola Parisiensi contra novam academiam P. Rami* (Paris, 1551).

34. John Jewel, *An Apology of the Church of England*, ed. J. E. Booty (Ithaca, Cornell University Press, 1963), p. 11. The original Latin *Apologia Ecclesiae Anglicanae* was completed in 1561.

Above all, Milton's rebel angels are atheists, for they accept Satan's plea that they have no creator. From that denial of God flows both the materialism and the anarchy which commentators are now stressing in Milton's revolt of the angels. He may have thought of the anarchy in the traditional way of Alciati's commentators, for whom all disorder (ἀταξία) was the work of evil men who hide their feral nature under human form. They saw the Titanomachy as an allegory of the Platonic view of anarchy as always ready to destroy liberty when

> upstart Passions catch the Government
> From Reason, and to servitude reduce
> Man till then free.   [XII.88–90]

Milton's ground for the doctrine was put in a sixain which was quoted by Alciati's commentators, and which is remarkable for making materialism the root of the Titan's revolt:

> Tale gigantaeum legitur genus, ut nihil altum
>   Cogitet, at spernat, vel neget esse Deum:
> Et tantum, quantum sensu exteriore movetur,
>   Commodat ad praesens se, vel ad id quod adest.
> Hoc genus anguipedum mythici finxere Poetae,
>   Quorum affectus humi (segnis ad alta) repat.
>   [*Emblemata*, Antwerp, 1577. P. 70]

Materialism is hardly a word which Milton would have used of his rebel angels, but he would have sympathized with his modern interpreters who see their fall as a challenge to reason and consequently as a resort to violence. Modern criticism of his celestial war, when it is disapproving, deepens Dr. Johnson's objection to its "incongruities" and condemns the "double standard" which allows the loyal angels to stoop to wrath and lets the Son consciously "take over the Satanic standard of force."[35]

35. Milton Miller, "*Paradise Lost:* The Double Standard," *UTQ, 20* (1951), 190.

Lurking here is a charge against Milton's character—
the charge that "Milton liked power." By most of us he
will be judged by his thinking about truth and power,
and J. B. Broadbent observes that in the last chapter of
Eikonoklastes he discussed the clear verdict of King Darius
"that truth of all things was strongest."[36] Milton corrects
Darius by saying that "truth is properly no more than
contemplation," while in action it becomes the justice
which "in her very essence is all strength and activity:
and hath a sword put into her hand, to use against all
violence and oppression on the earth. . . . She never suffers
falsehood to prevail, but when falsehood first prevails over
truth; and that also is a kind of justice done on them who
are so deluded."

Milton's most carefully considered statement about
truth and power is his incarnation of truth in the Son of
God who goes to war in a chariot which is all flames and
wings set with eyes, and who wears the "radiant Urim"
(VI.761) of sure judgment in his breastplate. His violence
against the devils is beyond any doubt, though it is ex-
erted only because

> by strength
> They measure all, of other excellence
> Not emulous, nor care who them excells.
>
> [VI.820–22]

Like the long-withheld might of Zeus in Hesiod's Titan
war, the Son's power is used only after two days of drawn
battle, which for Milton amounted to proof of the divine
patience and of the self-deception of the rebel angels. The
final step in that tragedy can come only after the uprooted
hills have returned to their places "And with fresh Flow'rets
Hill and Valley smil'd" (VI.784). But the rebels are only

36. J. B. Broadbent, "Links between Poetry and Prose in Milton," *ES, 37*
(1956), 54–55.

"hard'n'd more by what might most reclaim" (VI.791), and the outcome justifies G. Wilson Knight's suggestion of "an alliance of good and nature against the will to power and explosives"[37] of the devils. In the passage which prompted Thyer to identify Milton's celestial battle with Hesiod's, the Son's creative power has the reverse effect on the loyal angels (VII.605). In the celestial battle, however, the devil's will to power can be crushed only by violence and the Son's "wrath bent on his enemies" (VI.826). To regret it is to regret Milton's life-long apocalyptic vision of the first and second routs of the Dragon. It was only in some mysterious, ultimate struggle of the Son with Satan—beyond any angel's power to adumbrate in corporal forms, that Milton could

> Dream not of thir fight,
> As of a Duel, or the local wounds
> Of head or heel.   [XII.386–88]

---

37. *Chariot of Wrath*, p. 149. Disregarding the hardening of the devils' will to evil, E. H. Emerson treats the prolongation of the battle simply as intended to teach the angels the virtue of patience (*MLN*, *49*, 1954, 399–402).

❧ 9 ❧

Milton's Treatment of Reformation History in The Tenure of Kings and Magistrates

When Milton wrote *The Tenure of Kings and Magistrates,* he saw the history of the Reformation brightening down from precedent to precedent to its political fulfillment in the condemnation of Charles I to a traitor's death. When he was at work on the tract in January 1649 his job, as he saw it, was less to prove that the pioneers of the Reformation, from Luther to Pareus, had believed in constitutional government with tyrannicide by legal process as its corollary than it was to justify that principle by "Scripture and Reason." The result was an essay on tyrannicide which—like Tom Paine's *Common Sense*—spoke both to reason and passion. Milton wrote violently because he was angry at the refusal of the Presbyterians—who had "hunted and pursued [Charles] round about the Kingdom with sword and fire"—to support the Rump Parliament in his legal prosecution. He wrote in a temper which Sir Herbert Grierson has called "prophetic," but which others may prefer to think religious, superstitious, or fanatical, when they find Milton convinced that the righteousness of his cause has been providentially marked by the mere fact of the King's being brought to "justice, which is the sword of God, superior to all mortal things, *into whose hands soever by apparent signs his testified will is to put it.*"[1] It is a miracle that *The Tenure* moves at all in the cool realm of reason, yet, says W. E. Gilman in *Milton's Rhetoric: Studies in Defense of Liberty*, it does move in that realm and channels all its passion into the skillful orator's appeals to indignation, shame, and fear.

Our interest, however, is not in Milton's candor and insight in stating his case for calling kings to account; it is rather in the handling of the historical evidence for his view of the political meaning of the Reformation. In the first edition of *The Tenure*, which was published on February 13, 1649, only two weeks after Charles' execution, he had very little to say on the topic. It is treated briefly at the climax of a passage reviewing medieval and recent European constitutional precedents for challenging wicked kings, which mentions only the familiar instances of the organization of the League of Smalkald to resist Charles V, the defiances of the Queen Regent, Mary of Guise, and Mary Queen of Scots by the Scottish Calvinists, and the classic challenge to Philip II of Spain by the States of Holland in 1581. In Conclusion, Milton remarked that such examples were not needed to convince Presbyterians of "the lawfulness of raising War against a Tyrant in defence of Religion, or civil libertie; for no Protestant Church from the first *Waldenses* of *Lyons,* and *Languedoc* to this day but have don it round, and maintain'd it lawful."[2] Aside from this passage Milton had little to say about the Reformation in the first edition of *The Tenure* except to make a

---

1. The words are quoted from *The Tenure* (p. 3) by Grierson in *Milton and Wordsworth,* p. 63.

2. CE, *5,* 31.

3. Ibid., p. 8.

promise to fortify his argument with a host of authorities, many of which were to be "Christian, Orthodoxal, and which must needs be more convincing to our Adversaries, Presbyterial."[3] Why he should have kept this promise only a full year later in his second edition is a double question, the answers to which may throw some light on his roll call of Reformers in the Appendix which he added to his second edition in February, 1650.

Behind Milton's survey of the Protestant record for organized resistance to "tyrants" in the first edition of *The Tenure* was a challenge that was being commonly proclaimed in Presbyterian pulpits during the trial of Charles and that was officially formulated in "A SERIOUS AND FAITHFUL REPRESENTATION OF . . . MINISTERS OF THE GOSPEL within the Province of London contained in a LETTER from them to the General and his Council of War . . . 18 Ja. 1648/9." On the twelfth of the eighteen pages of this manifesto, which its modern editor[4] regards as marking the tactical superiority of the Presbyterians to the prosecutors of the King, the forty-seven clergymen signing the letter boldly asserted that Scripture gave absolutely no warrant for tyrannicide, and added that

> . . . consonant to the tenor of the Scriptures herein, hath alway been the constant judgement and doctrine of Protestant Divines both at home and abroad, with whose Judgements we do fully concurre; disclaiming, detesting and abhorring the wicked and bloody Tenents and Practices of Jesuites, (the worst of Papists,) concerning the opposing of lawfull Magistrates by private Persons, and the murthering of Kings by any, though under the most specious and colourable pretences . . .[5]

4. R. W. K. Hinton, in his introduction. His edition was printed by the School of Art of the University of Reading (1949).

5. The effect of the "REPRESENTATION" can be measured by the numerous replies it provoked. Without by any means exhausting the list, Hinton mentions

In reply to this attempt to give the deepest possible royalist tinge to the folklore of Protestantism, Milton wrote his survey of Protestant resistance to tyranny from the earliest Waldensians in Italy to the revolt of the States of Holland. If his brief excursus into modern history had seemed to him to dispose of his adversaries, his complacence was pardonable. The most distinguished of Parliament's literary champions, the Reverend John Goodwin, writing in May 1649, in the most influential of the tracts that were written to justify Charles' trial and execution, *The Obstructours of Justice,*[6] had quoted Milton's summary of the Protestant attitude toward kings "from the first Waldenses . . . to this day" as demolishing the position of the Presbyterians. In Goodwin's eyes, of course, their case could hardly seem anything but indefensible. He declared that they must have said what they did about the passive obedience of the pioneer Reformers, "not only with secret regret, but even with the loud reclamations of their consciences." When a man like Goodwin felt that Milton had done the job so well, we should not be surprised to find

---

six of them in his introduction, pp. iv-v. In the very influential *Elenchus Motuum Nuperorum in Anglia* of Charles' personal physician, George Bate, we have (pp. 184–85) a picture of the clergy of all England uniting to protest the proceedings of the High Court of Justice as *contra Sacrae Scripturae & Religionis dictamina.* (The 1st ed., "Lutetiae Parisiorum . . . . 1649," has been shown by F. F. Madan in "Milton, Salmasius, and Dugard," *Transactions of the Bibliographical Society, 4,* No. 2, September 1923, 141–43, to disguise the fact that the book was printed in London.)

6. John Goodwin, Ὑβριστοδίκαι. *The Obstructours of Justice. Or, a Defence of the Honourable Sentence Passed upon the Late* KING, *by the High* COURT *of* JUSTICE. Opposed Chiefly to *The Serious and Faithfull Representation and Vindication of Some of The Ministers of* LONDON . . . (London, 1649) Thomason Index, E 557 (2). The passages quoted in the present study occur on pp. 70–71. Goodwin's position as vicar of St. Stephen's on Coleman Street, and one of London's most popular Independent preachers, has been indicated by William Haller in *Tracts on Liberty in the Puritan Revolution* (3 vols. New York, 1934), *I,* 19–20, and *passim.* The relation of *The Obstructours* to *The Tenure* has been indicated by William R. Parker in *Milton's Contemporary Reputation* (Columbus, Ohio, State University Press, 1940), pp. 80–82.

that the first edition of *The Tenure* went to press without
the appendix which was added in the second to refute the
position of the Presbyterians. Why then, a year later, did
he feel it necessary to bring the second edition to a climax
by adding a seven-page annex of quotations from Luther,
Calvin, Pareus, and four lesser Reformers, committing
them all to the doctrine of the accountability of kings?

The answer may be found in the fact that in spite of
Milton and Goodwin, the summer and autumn of 1649
found more and more pulpits asserting that the regicide
Parliament had been guilty of the first betrayal of the
principle of passive obedience to kings in the entire history of the Reformation. The doctrine had also received a
kind of international Protestant sanction from the protest
of the Ambassadors of the States General on the eve of
Charles' execution and from the official condolence of the
Dutch clergy as well as of the States General with Charles
II on his father's death. Abroad and at home the regicides
were being made to look like traitors to the heritage of
the Reformation. It was to halt the spread of that belief
that Milton supplemented the second edition of *The Tenure*
with the appendix of quotations from the Reformers that
we must now examine as an example of his honesty and
skill in handling historical evidence.

The first of the seven Reformers to be quoted in Milton's appendix is Luther. Like the others, he is quoted in
fragments—mere drops of water out of the ocean of his
works—and at once we rightly suspect that he is being
quoted at second or at n^{th} hand. Indeed, Milton tells us
himself what his sources were, for the first of them was the
best Protestant account of the German Reformation, and
he could inspire confidence by quoting from *A Famous
Cronicle of Oure Time, Called Sleidanes Commentaries, Concerning the State of Religion and Commonwealth, During the Raigne*

of the Emperor Charles the Fift.[7] When the modern reader
finds Milton corroborating his quotations from Sleidan
from the Catholic humanist, Johannes Cochlaeus, as honest a writer as Sleidan though a frankly bitter enemy of
Luther, uncertainty of Milton's motives arises. His modern
editor, William T. Allison, holds that the impression that
one gets from reading Luther's original statements in his
addresses to the rebels and to the nobles in the Peasants'
War in 1525 is "quite the contrary of the doctrine supported by Milton."[8] And Allison goes on to accuse him of
"committing the sin for which he reproaches his opponents,
wresting authorities to his own purpose in a most unscru-
pulous manner." Even in the full and careful account of
the Peasants' War in Sleidan's fifth book, Allison sees the
historian's view of Luther as very different from Milton's.
He ignores Milton's appeal to Cochlaeus. Nor is Cochlaeus
likely to carry weight with modern readers who have
learned from Troeltsch to think of both Luther and Calvin as standing essentially together "in a very strict demand for respect for authority, even in cases where those
who wield authority are not particularly estimable."[9] The
reader must judge in the light of the passages that Milton
chose to quote from Luther, and in that of their previous
history of quotation.

7. This title is that of the translation by John Daus, published in London
in 1560. Passages from Sleidan that are quoted in English are from this work.
It was first published in Latin at Strasbourg in 1555 under the title *Io. Sleidani,
de Statu Religionis et Reipublicae, Carolo V Caesare, Commentarii XXV libris com-
prehensi.* The British Museum copy has been used. Milton's page references (as
J. H. Hanford pointed out in *PMLA 36,* 1921, 271) do not agree with "any of
the Latin editions in the British Museum or the Harvard College library,"
but Ruth Mohl has recently discovered that they do agree with an edition in
one of the New York libraries.

8. *The Tenure of Kings and Magistrates,* ed. W. T. Allison, Yale Studies in
English, 51 (New Haven, 1911), 139–40.

9. Ernst Troeltsch, *The Social Teaching of the Christian Churches,* trans. Olive
Wyon (London, Allen and Unwin, 1931), p. 613.

Omitting only a digressive conclusion of Milton's, the passages which he quoted from Luther and his remarks on them are these:

LUTHER.

Lib. contra Rusticos apud Sleidan. l. 5.

Is est hodie rerum status, &c. *Such is the state of things at this day, that men neither can, nor will, nor indeed ought to endure longer the domination of you Princes.*

Neque vero Caesarem, &c. *Neither is Caesar to make Warr as head of Christ'ndom, Protector of the Church, Defender of the Faith; these Titles being fals and Windie, and most Kings being the greatest Enemies to Religion. Lib: De bello contra Turcas. apud Sleid. l.* 14. What hinders then, but that we may depose or punish them?

These also are recited by *Cochlaeus* in his *Miscellanies* to be the words of *Luther,* or some other eminent Divine, then in *Germany,* when the Protestants there entred into solemn Covnant at *Smalcaldia.* Ut ora ijs obturem &c. *That I may stop thir mouthes, the Pope and the Emperor are not born but elected, and may also be depos'd as hath bin oft'n don.* If *Luther,* or whoever els thought so, he could not stay there; for the right of birth or succession can be no privilege in nature to let a Tyrant sit irremoveable over a Nation free born, without transforming that Nation from the nature and condition of men born free, into natural, hereditary, and successive slaves. Therfore he saith furder; *To displace and throw down this Exactor, this Phalaris, this Nero, is a work well pleasing to God;* Namely, for being such a one: which is a moral reason.[10]

In commenting on this passage an editor should, if possible, consult Cochlaeus to see how his *Miscellanies* bear

10. CE, *5,* 46–47.

upon Sleidan's treatment of him as well as upon Milton's. Allison mentions the work only to regret that it was not available to him. If he had seen it, he would have found two of Milton's quotations presented as positively by Luther and, in the first case, twice introduced in what the Catholic writer regarded as damning catalogues of Luther's animadversions against princes.[11] Cochlaeus' own animus against Luther—as Carl Otto pointed out—was the reluctant but finally deep hatred of the humanist who, like Erasmus, had much initial sympathy with the Reformer but was later frightened away by his defiance of authority in Church and State. It would be interesting to learn whether Milton knew the witty verses in Cochlaeus' satire of "the hooded Minotaur of Wittenberg" and Luther's heavy-handed reply in his book, *Against the Armed Man Cochlaeus*.[12] In the *Miscellanies* Cochlaeus was using all the violence to which controversialists then felt themselves entitled, but he was not overstating the case as he understood it. He honestly saw the Reformer's character as ready to rebel against all human authority in the name of the will of God. He would have approved Jacques Maritain's summing up: "Chez Luther . . . c'est la conception de la vie

11. "*In Causa Religionis Miscellaneorum libri tres in diversos Tractatos antea non aeditos, ac diversis temporibus, locisque scriptos digesti.* Per Iohannem Cochlaeum. Ingolstadii excudebat Alexander Vveissenborn. . . . MDXLV." (Ingolstadt, 1545). Milton's first quotation from Luther—*Is est hodie etc.*—is found on pp. 59^v and 61^v; his last, on p. 49^v. The explanation of his inclusion of the second, which I have not found in Cochlaeus, may have been the overemphasis laid in the anonymous tract *Of Resisting the Lawfull Magistrates upon Colour of Religion* (1643, Thomason Index, E 102 [19], p. 25), on Sleidan's account of Luther's opposition to the Turkish wars of Charles V as amounting to an absolute declaration that "the cause of Religion, although it were of Christianity against Mohametisme, was not for him (Luther) sufficient warrant for a defensive war." Since *Of Resisting* went into later editions (1644, 1646, 1647), Milton may have wished to correct its appeal to Luther's authority against Parliament in the civil war.

12. Martin Luther, *Adversus Armatum Virum Cokleum* (Wittenberg, 1523).

qui est atteinte, on peut dire qu'il est le premier grand
romantique."[13]

The farthest-reaching justification of Milton's interpretation of Sleidan's account of Luther is to be found in the
last of the passages for which he appealed for confirmation
to Cochlaeus—"ut ijs ora obturem &c." The passage in the
Miscellanies cites Luther's "libellus Teuthonicus cum rota
fortunae, absque nomine Authoris & impressoris, usque
adeo seditiosus ac sanguinarius, ut nihil possit in Principes crudelius aut periculosius excogitari." The charge is
that Luther accused all rulers of pillaging their realms by
taxation and so deserving to be treated like Phalaris and
Nero. And the passage concludes, reversing the order of the
sentences that Milton quotes, by observing that "Papa &
Caesar non nati sed electi sunt Principes, qui possunt deponi, Id quod propter eorum malefacta saepe factum est.
Et tamen hi sunt summi Principatus, Et eorum delegati,
ut sunt Principes & alij domini, non deberent deponi de
mala potestate sua?" From this passage it would seem that
Milton was fully entitled to read Cochlaeus as regarding
Luther as a dangerously revolutionary advocate even in
his younger days of the accountability of kings to their
earthly creators. That seems to be his interpretation of Luther's behavior during the Peasants' War, both when he
seemed to be the rebels' advocate and later when he urged
the princes to suppress their violence. On this point Cochlaeus is unambiguous. Sleidan may seem in some passages
to take an opposite view of Luther's behavior in the course
of the year 1525, and Allison may be entitled to think
that Milton deliberately distorted the evidence of his fifth
book; but it is at least equally possible to read Sleidan as
no more eager to clear Luther of complicity with the
peasants in their violent revolt than he was determined all
along to show him as missing no opportunity to adjure

13. Jacques Maritain, *Trois Reformateurs* (Paris, 1925), p. 42.

"the Princes, Noblemen and Gentlemen of the Empire . . . for God's sake and their own peace and safety, to use their subjects like men, not like beasts for the yoke and the slaughter."[14] This is not the place either to discuss Sleidan's view of Luther's political opinions or to balance the charge of a modern Luther-baiter like P. F. Wiener, for whom he was "the creator and leader of the whole peasant movement"[15] as well as its destroyer in the end, with the insistence of an historian like Preserved Smith that there is no basis whatever for the belief that Luther "sided with the insurgents while they were likely to win and then turned to curry favor with the princes when *they* triumphed."[16] There can be no reasonable doubt that, throughout the Peasants' War, Luther was independent enough of both sides to excoriate both. Milton was too much of an idealist not to approve his plague of both their houses.

It may be added that Milton was too much of an historian not to look beyond Luther's part in the Peasants' War for an estimate of his place as a political thinker. His quotations show that in summing up Luther's political thought he was looking beyond the Peasants' War to the time when the German princes won the Reformer's reluctant consent to their decision to fight if necessary against their Emperor in defense of their faith. When a modern historian can write that from the *Appeal to the German Nobility* in 1520 to the very end of Luther's life he always "clearly recognized a right of reform in accordance with

14. It would be interesting if we could confirm the probablity that Milton knew that these words of Luther—in exactly the same English quoted above—figured on the first page of an anonymous *History of the Anabaptists* (London, 1642).

15. Peter F. Wiener, *Martin Luther, Hitler's Spiritual Ancestor* (London, Hutchinson, n.d.), p. 45.

16. Preserved Smith, *The Life and Letters of Martin Luther* (Boston and New York, Houghton Mifflin, 1911), p. 164.

the constitutional principles of a government,"[17] Milton can hardly be accused of straining the evidence in entertaining the same idea.

A final word in defense of Milton's tactical use of Cochlaeus' *Miscellanies* may be said in the light of the abuse of *Eikonoklastes* and perhaps (in the passage which interests us) of *The Tenure,* by an obscure Burgundian who wrote a reply to the former in 1652 under the title *Carolus I Brittaniarum Rex.* Though the little volume pretended to have been issued in Dublin, it seems to have been printed in Dijon and to have been the work of a certain Claude Barthelemy Morisot, who took many of his facts from Bate's *Elenchus.*[18] Writing as a Catholic Frenchman, eager simply to show that Milton was apologizing for his country in the black guilt of the murder of its king, Morisot looked at the Reformation as a consistently subversive political movement. From John Huss to John Calvin, he regarded the Reformers as rebels against their lawful rulers. Luther and Thomas Münzer, the peasants' leader in 1525, seemed to him equally guilty of that crime against society. Fairfax and Cromwell, he said, had learned from the continental Reformers how to betray their king. Morisot quoted the very passage from Calvin's "Commentary on Daniel" which Milton quoted to prove that Calvin was a foe of kings if not of the institution of kingship itself. If Milton had issued a third edition of *The Tenure* in 1652, he might

17. Luther Hess Waring, *The Political Theories of Martin Luther* (New York and London, G. P. Putnam's Sons, 1910), p. 138.

18. According to F. Didot's *Biographie Nouvelle Universelle,* as quoted in *A Catalogue of the Bradshaw Collection of Irish Books in the University Library Cambridge* (3 vols. Cambridge, England, Univ. Lib., 1916), 2, 1121, *Carolus I* "is by Claude Barthelemy Morisot, and is in answer to Milton's *Eikonoklastes.* Query: printed in Dijon." Although the Cambridge bibliographer does not mention them, there are clear implications in the text that the book was a Frenchman's work, and they are confirmed by the identity of an ornament on A2^v with the ornament on a3^r (in both cases at the end of a preface) of "*Claudii Bartholomaei Morisoti Peruviana.* Divione . . . M DC LXV." *Carolus I* is mentioned in Masson's *Life of Milton,* 4, 436–37.

have capped his appeal to Cochlaeus by observing that
his own Burgundian critic fully confirmed the view of Luther's old adversary about the real drift of Luther's political thought.

With the passages that Milton chose to quote from his
six remaining Reformers the modern reader is unlikely to
quarrel, though he may think that those from Calvin and
Pareus represent their authors in suspiciously minor works.
But he cannot think that of the Swiss Reformer, Ulrich
Zwingli, who is represented by six theses from his *Opus
Articulorum sive Conclusionum*[19] which everyone knew and
valued as a kind of Magna Charta of Protestant political
action against kings who "reign perfidiously." Zwingli's
lifelong pursuit of personal influence within the democratic framework of Zurich's municipal government was
known to have squared with the theses that he had been
prepared to defend in public debate. His motives and
judgment might be questioned, but not the consistency of
his writings with his public record. With Martin Bucer the
case was very different, but Milton was on equally safe
ground. As he knew from his study of the Alsatian Reformer's works when he wrote *Martin Bucer on Divorce* in
1644, their concern with politics was comparatively slight.
In the treatise that he wrote for Edward VI during the
two years of exile that ended his career in England in
1551, the *De Regno Christi,* Bucer had no reason to urge
his political doctrines upon the friendly boy king. He had
stated them explicitly in his Commentaries on the Four
Gospels (*Sacra Quattuor Evangelia*) in his discussion of "Resist not evil" (Matthew 39:5), by which Milton knew that
his writings were best represented to the English public.
As a foundation for the doctrine of lawful resistance to

19. All of Milton's passages are taken from *Opera D. Huldrychi Zuinglii, vi-
gilantissimi Tiguaranae ecclesiae Antistes, partim quidem ab ipso Latine conscripta,
partim vero a vernaculo sermone in Latinum translata* (Zurich, 1545), pp. 84–86.

tyrants or "ungodly" kings, Christ's doctrine of nonresistance to evil was familiar to Milton's readers from passages like the one that we shall see him quoting from
Pareus. Bucer's statement of it fell just a little short of
drawing the clear conclusion that the abuse of power justifies rebellion or even passive resistance, and Milton be-
trayed his dissatisfaction with his excerpt from Bucer by
adding his own note to the effect that "the less tolerable"
a supreme power makes itself, "the more unpardonably to
be punish'd."[20]

The first Reformer to extract the fully sanctioned principle of resistance to unworthy kings from the Biblical doctrine of nonresistance of evil was Calvin, writing in the
famous final chapter of the *Institute of the Christian Religion.*
From a passionate opening assertion of St. Paul's principle,
"Let every soul be subject to the higher powers" (Romans
13:1), Calvin moved on through thirty-one utterly logical
paragraphs to a closing defense of the constitutional subjection of rulers to control by officers like the Tribunes of
the People in ancient Rome or the Ephors in ancient
Sparta. His final position was that, if such officers "winke
at kinges wilfully raging over and treading downe the
poore communaltie, their dissembling is not without wicked
breache of faith, because they deceitfully betray the libertie
of the people, whereof they know themselves to bee appointed protectors by the ordinaunce of God."[21] Milton
ignored this passage and chose to represent Calvin in his
sampling of the political teaching of the Reformers simply
by a single passage from his Commentary on Daniel. To
modern eyes the fragment about Daniel is far less dangerous political dynamite than the conclusion to the *Institute.* In preferring it Milton incurs no suspicion of mis-
representing Calvin by quoting him in an unguarded

20. CE, *5,* 49.

21. *The Institute of the Christian Religion, written in Latine by M. John Calvine,
and translated into English . . . by Thomas Norton* (London, 1587), 507[r].

moment. Readers of *The Tenure* could be expected to know the last chapter of the *Institute* as American college students are supposed to know the Constitution of the United States. And they could be expected to know that Calvin closed by illustrating his revolutionary doctrine with the case of Nebuchadnezzar in the Prophecy of Daniel as a classical example of an ungodly monarch who was brought to punishment for his pride. The picture of Nebuchadnezzar as a proud emperor who

> wende that God, that sit in magestee,
> Ne myghte hym nat bireve of his estaat,

was an old one, but Calvin gave it new meaning. In his Commentary on Daniel as well as in the *Institute,* Nebuchadnezzar became a symbol of royal ungodliness ripe for punishment by the godly. The core of Calvin's political thought was generally recognized as having been put into the second of the two passages that Milton quoted from the Commentary:

> Abdicant se terreni principes, &c. *Earthly Princes depose themselves while they rise against God, yet they are unworthy to be numberd among men: rather it behooves us to spitt upon thir heads then to obey them. On Dan: c. 6. v. 22.*[22]

In *Carolus I,* Morisot pounced upon Milton for quoting this passage—not because it misrepresented Calvin, but because, in Milton's defense of the judgment of the High Court upon King Charles, Morisot found a fresh instance to confirm his conviction that Calvin's principles had always been a weapon to be used against legitimate kings who were so ill-advised as to refuse to bow to Calvinism.[23]

---

22. CE, *5*, 48.

23. After quoting the passage from Calvin on Daniel which Milton quoted, Morisot wrote: "Contra Deum autem Principes insurgunt qui Calvinistis non favent, solis, ut ipsi aiunt, verè Catholicis, & Gens Dei. Cui illud datum, ut legitimè periuret, & in legitimos suos Principes rebellet." *Carolus I,* p. 8.

In the following paragraph in *Carolus I,* John Knox and George Buchanan are assailed for using Calvin's doctrine against Mary Queen of Scots and the young James VI of Scotland. It almost seems as if Morisot wrote with *The Tenure* in mind and was attacking Milton both for echoing Calvin and for repeating—earlier in the pamphlet—Knox's account of his famous debate with Maitland of Lethington in June 1564, when he quoted Calvin, Bucer, and Luther to establish the right of the people and the Kirk to "execute jugementis aganis thair King, being an offendar."

From the Scottish Calvinists Milton turned to their English contemporaries, men like Dudley Fenner, Thomas Cartwright, Anthony Gilby, and Christopher Goodman, all of whom had suffered exile under Mary or Elizabeth. He may not have known them well, for he quoted only Gilby and Goodman, the former fragmentarily. But Goodman's book, *How Superior Powers Ought to Be Obeyed,* which was published in the last year of Mary's reign, must have been beside him as he wrote. Though his quotations vary insignificantly from the text as we have it in the modern facsimile edition, his page references are all accurate. He saw the work in just the light that its modern editor does, as marking "the first definite shift of opinion under the pressure of religion, away from the doctrines of almost unlimited obedience which characterize the political thought of the first half of the [sixteenth] century."[24] At greater length than he quoted from any of the other early Reformers, Milton gave his readers Goodman's versions of the Calvinist doctrine that subjects are absolved from obedience to unworthy kings, that guilt should disqualify every ruler, and that "No person is exempt by any law of God from this punishment, be he King, Queene, or Emperor, he myst dy the death."[25] These words might have

24. Charles H. McIlwain's bibliographical note (Facsimile Text Society, New York, 1931), p. 1.
25. CE, *5,* 51.

been written to apply to King Charles as well as to Queen Mary a century earlier. No Royalist, of course, would brook such an application of them; but no Royalist would have denied that the words meant just what Milton took them to mean.

For the modern reader the strangest passage that Milton put into his very international Appendix to *The Tenure* was the paragraph from the German Calvinist, Pareus, on Romans 13, giving the final extension to Calvin's political interpretation of it in the last chapter of the *Institute*. Milton quoted Pareus very briefly as simply saying:

> Quorum est constituere Magistratus, &c. *They whose part it is to set up Magistrates, may restrain them also from outragious deeds, or pull them down; but all Magistrates are set up either by Parlament, or by Electors, or by other Magistrates; They therfore who exalted them, may lawfully degrade and punish them.*[26]

The interpretation here put upon St. Paul's admonition that every soul should be subject to the higher powers is even more ingenious than Calvin's. None of the ingenuity was due to Milton. His translation is faithful to the Latin original as he found it in Pareus' *Theological Works*. The straining of St. Paul's text in the passage as Milton rendered it was entirely Pareus' doing. Beginning with a distinction between the higher powers and the men to whom in the course of human events they are entrusted, Pareus went on to assert that obedience was due only to the abstract, divine ordained power itself and never directly to any magistrate or ruler who might temporarily be clothed

26. Ibid., p. 49. Milton found the passage in *D. Davidis Parei Operum Theologicorum Exegeticorum* (Frankfurt, 1647), Book I, pt. III, p. 262 (misnumbered 266). It occurs in the section "De Potestate Civili" of the work entitled "D. Parei Explicatio Dubiorum in Cap. xiii ad Romanos." On p. 281 he found it again between a résumé of David Owen's attack on it and a reply to Owen by Pareus' editor, his son, Philip Pareus.

with it. His argument expanded into a philosophical account of all the powers, physical and moral, upon which life itself depends. All human well-being emerges in his discussion as consisting in obedience to a hierarchy of powers that in their essence are divinely otherworldly though they must be vested in various creatures upon whose claim to individual respect we cannot depend. Not undeservedly, since Pareus wrote with imagination and sincerity as well as with acumen, his treatment of Calvin's interpretation of Romans 13 became famous. In John Goodman's *Right and Might Well Met*,[27] for example, it is mentioned as justifying resistance to tyrants as if they were no better than highwaymen, and Pareus' entire case is summarized from the initial distinction between abstract and concrete power to the final denial of the obligation to obey an evil ruler. At least at second hand, Milton could expect his readers to know something about Pareus' revolutionary interpretation of the Biblical injunction of the duty of obedience to the higher powers.

At second hand also Milton could count upon general familiarity with Pareus through a controversy that began at Cambridge three years before his death in 1622 and ended his long and honorable career as a professor of theology at Heidelberg. It was begun by a Cambridge don, David Owen, whose gifts and principles as a political philosopher and theologian are suggested by the title of one of his later works, *Puritano-Jesuitismus, the Puritan Turn'd Jesuite; or Rather Out-vying Him in Those Diabolicall and Dangerous Positions, of the Deposition of Kings.* In 1619 Owen saw fit to challenge Pareus in a Latin disputation that was translated and published in 1642 under the title, *Anti-Pareus, or, A Treatise in Defence of the Royall Right of Kings: Against Paraeus and the Rest of the Anti-Monarchians, Whether Presbyterians or Jesuits. Wherein Is Maintained the Unlawfulnesse of Opposing and Tak-*

27. London, 1643 (pp. 41–42). Thomason Index E 536 (28).

*ing Up Arms Against the Prince, Either by Any Private Subject,
Inferior Magistrate, the States of the Kingdom, or the Pope of
Rome* . . . On the second page, after acknowledging that in
1612 Pareus had "writ very elegantly concerning the Lawfull Right of Kings . . . against *Bellarmine, Becanus,* and
other Popish Parasites," Owen proceeded to inveigh against
him for brandishing "the inferior Magistrates Sword
against Kings and greatest Emperours." To his castigation
for that crime Owen devoted the *Anti-Pareus* and perhaps
thereby provoked Milton to give him immortality in England by quoting him in *The Tenure.*

Milton may have found Owen's strictures on Pareus'
interpretation of Romans 13 in the magnificent edition of
the Reformer's *Theological Works* which his son Philip issued
at Frankfurt in 1647 with a full résumé of all the criticism
that had been leveled at his father. We may read Owen in
the English of the *Anti-Paraeus* (pp. 37–38), where he has
this remark to make about the passage which Milton
quoted from the commentary of Pareus on Romans
13: "This Assertion is Capitall, which the Emperour will
not admit, the King will not suffer; which *Bellarmine* him-
selfe doth affirme to be rejected by the consent of all
Divines, that it is not necessary for me to refute it." Can
it be that in quoting what Owen had declared to be unworthy of refutation Milton hoped that some of his readers
would be well enough acquainted with the history of the
controversy to smile? One of them at least was struck by
his quotation. In *Respublica Anglicana,* George Wither
thanked him for quoting what Pareus had said "upon
that place in the Epistle to the Romans, be subject to the
higher powers, &c," and added that it was "confirmed by
a multitide of Protestant Divines, and reasons, as you
may see at large in a late treatise, entituled, *The tenor of
Kings and Magistrates.*"[28]

28. George Wither, *Respublica Anglicana* (Thomason Index, E 780 [25], 1650),
p. 41.

Wither's remark about Milton's use of a famous passage from Pareus suggests that it seemed to him to have been put into a correct historical perspective as well as brought tellingly to bear upon the question which the High Court of Justice had just determined. Modern criticism has been inclined to minimize the influence of *The Tenure* upon contemporary thought and to question the ingenuousness of Milton's use of his historical authorities. Did Wither see more clearly on both points than we can? Or are we right to question the faith of the nineteenth century in Milton's candor and competence as an historian? Our conclusion in the light of his treatment of Reformation history in *The Tenure,* though it may not be to recognize him as the essentially critical student of sources that Sir Charles Firth and Professor J. Milton French have seen in the author of *The History of Britain,* still must be to clear him of having distorted the record that ran from Luther to Pareus. The distorters of that record—as he later recalled in *The Second Defence*[29]—were the "magnificently ignorant or impudent clergy" who, as much as in them lay, were vociferating that Protestant doctrine in its essence was at war with the regicide sentence on King Charles. It was in reply to that pious distortion of history that Milton added his Appendix to *The Tenure.* In doing so he was anything but the deliberate betrayer of Truth to a specious perversion of justice that Professor S. B. Liljegren would have us believe because, in the last chapter of *Eikonoklastes,* he declared Jus-

29. "Tum vero tandem, cum Presbyteriani quidam Ministri, Carolo prius infestissimi, nunc Independentium partes suis anteferri, & in Senatu plus posse indignantes, Parlamenti sententiae de Rege latae (non facto irati, sed quod ipsorum factio non fecisset) reclamitarent, & quantum in ipsis erat, tumultuarentur, ausi affirmare Protestantium dictrinam, omnesque ecclesias reformatas ab ejusmodi in reges atroci sententiâ abhorrere, ratus falsitati tam apertae palàm eundum obviàm esse, ne tum quidem de Carolo quicquam scripsi aut suasi, sed quid in genere contra tyrannos liceret, adductis haud paucis summorum Theologorum testimoniis, ostendi; & insignem hominum meliora profitentium, sive ignorantiam sive impudentiam propè concionabundus incessi" (CE, *8,* 134–36).

tice stronger than Truth.[30] By insisting in *The Tenure* and
again in *The Second Defence* that the Presbyterians were deliberately wrenching fact in favor of faction, Milton did a
service to historical truth as well as to a partisan cause to
which his unfriendliest modern critics must acknowledge
that both Britain and the United States of America owe
much that is characteristic in their respective constitutions.
When in *Paradise Lost* he surveyed human history as benign
to the seekers of places, titles, and secular power, he wrote
with feeling such as only personal disillusion can give of
the betrayal of the principles of the prophets of all epochs
by the persecutors of "all who in the worship persevere /
Of Spirit and Truth."

---

30. Liljegren, *Studies in Milton,* pp. 141–43.

﷽ 10 ﷽

Milton as a Revolutionary

Since the end of World War I there has been a growing doubt of Milton's rank among the leaders of the Puritan revolution. In part, as we shall see, it has taken the form of discontent, like Don Wolfe's, with his failure to anticipate the proletarian gospels of the twentieth century as well as he did the liberal faith of the nineteenth. In part it has taken the form of submergence of Milton in the growing doubt of the economic wisdom and disinterestedness of Puritan religion among historians like Max Weber and R. H. Tawney.[1] And in part it has paradoxically arisen from the research of Miltonists in the pamphlet literature of the English Civil War. For a time after Professor Haller's publication of his volumes of *Tracts on Liberty in the Puritan Revolution,*[2] it seemed that Milton's pre-eminence as a thinker among the spokesmen of his party might, from our point of view, suffer some loss of apparent originality and courage, and that from the point of view of his own contemporaries he might have to yield his claim to have seriously influenced public opinion with any of his

1. Max Weber, *The Protestant Ethic and the Spirit of Capitalism,* trans. Talcott Parsons, foreword by R. H. Tawney (London, G. Allen and Unwin, 1930); R. H. Tawney, *Religion and the Rise of Capitalism: A Historical Study* (New York, Harcourt Brace, 1926).
2. See above, p. 223, n. 6.

tracts earlier than the *Defence of the English People*. Professor Parker's introduction to the pamphlets which he has published in *Milton's Contemporary Reputation*, and their evidence as corroborated by the tract called *The Dignity of Kingship Asserted*,[3] have in part restored our belief in Milton's increasing influence from 1649 (if not earlier), until 1660. The question of the influence of *Areopagitica*, the tracts on divorce, and the anti-episcopal tracts may never be answered to the satisfaction of historians. For us, however, that question may not be crucial. Whatever its answer may be, no one is likely to deny Milton a place among the world's typical revolutionists— "Hampden, Sir Harry Vane, . . ., Sam Adams, John Hancock, Washington, Thomas Paine, Lafayette, Marat, Talleyrand, Hebert, Miliukov, Konavalov, Kerensky, Chichirin, Lenin"[4]—a list in which Professor Brinton places him third.

Perhaps at bottom our modern dissatisfaction with Milton as a revolutionary thinker springs from the fact that he himself habitually regarded the Puritan Revolution as a late and perhaps final stage in the Protestant Reformation; that his first political tracts, the five anti-episcopal pamphlets, were ecclesiastical; that his supposedly antifeminist defense of free divorce[5] rested mainly on biblical grounds; that *Areopagitica*—though it is still the literary charter of freedom of conscience and of the press—is full of religious passion and fails to grant toleration to Roman Catholics and atheists; and that—as Macaulay pointed out over a century ago—the "Arianism" of his great theological work, the *Christian Doctrine*, has distracted attention from his really more "startling" opinions "respecting the nature of

3. Parker, *Milton's Contemporary Reputation;* George Starkey, *The Dignity of Kingship Asserted*, ed. W. R. Parker (New York, Facsimile Text Society, 1942).

4. Crane Brinton, *The Anatomy of Revolution* (New York, Prentice-Hall, 1938), p. 116.

5. The case for Milton as continuer of the revolutionary thought of the sixteenth century about divorce is admirably made by Allan H. Gilbert in "Milton on the Position of Women," *MLR, 15* (1920), 240–64.

the Deity, the eternity of matter, and the observation of the Sabbath."[6] In various ways we all find the Protestantism of Milton's Protestant religion a little hard to swallow. For Catholics like Mr. Belloc his "Arianism" is still a stumbling-block, and it is refreshing to find a theologian like G. Wilson Knight correcting Mr. Belloc about Milton's "unitarianism" and quoting the *Christian Doctrine* itself to prove that for Milton "the nature of the Son" was "indeed divine."[7] Yet, as is inevitable from his general position in *Chariot of Wrath*, Mr. Knight simply cannot recognize the sterner, historical, revolutionary implications of Milton's demand in the *Christian Doctrine* and in the *Likeliest Means to Remove Hirelings Out of the Church* for separation of Church and State. Mr. Knight's *Chariot* will engage us more than once in the course of this discussion, and its robust transvaluations of parts of Milton's political thought, while we may not sympathize with them, will help to throw its true, revolutionary character into high relief. Mr. Knight's case seems to be somewhat like that of the late Paul Elmer More, who, as Mr. Alfred Kazin has said, had the paradoxical gift of combining a "passionate love of Milton's poetry" with a fondness for Dr. Johnson's "strictures on Milton's politics."[8] Although Mr. Knight quotes Dr. Johnson's charge that "Milton's republicanism was . . . founded in an envious hatred of greatness, and a sullen desire of independence, in petulant impatience of control, and pride disdainful of superiority," and even "half-subscribes" to it,[9] *Chariot of Wrath* in the main treats Milton's politics in a very unrevolutionary though fulgurously apocalyptic light. Although some of his historical interpretation of Milton's political thought

6. *Critical and Historical Essays by Thomas Babington Macaulay* (2 vols. London and Toronto, Dent, 1924), *1,* 151.

7. Knight, *Chariot of Wrath,* p. 114.

8. Alfred Kazin, *On Native Grounds* (New York, Reynal and Hitchcock, 1942), p. 309.

9. *Chariot of Wrath,* p. 32.

must be challenged, Mr. Knight's more than Wordsworthian faith that Milton should be with us at this hour is a corrective for those who study him only in the light of the prevailing Marxian view of Protestantism as a mere "reflex" of a "society based upon the production of commodities," for which "the most fitting form of religion" is "Christianity with its *cultus* of abstract man, more especially in its bourgeois developments, Protestantism, Deism, &c."[10]

In *Chariot of Wrath* Milton's Protestantism is transformed into a messianic faith of the most urgent application to both the Puritan Revolution and World War II. Since Mr. Knight's main interest is in the contemporary scene, while ours primarily is in Milton's part in the historic drama of the Puritan Revolution, the importance of his book for us lies in its treatment of Milton's stand on such crucial questions of the Revolution as the relation of Church to State and the value of monarchy, both as represented by Charles I and as an institution abstractly regarded. On those matters and on Milton's treatment of the questions of freedom, discipline, and the choice and function of an aristocracy, and above all on the idea of truth in *Areopagitica* as related to the "dynamics" of the Revolution, Mr. Knight has much to say that is pertinent to our view of Milton as a revolutionist. What we find on these topics in *Chariot of Wrath* inevitably challenges attention, yet none of these secondary features of the book can fairly be discussed apart from its main, messianic theme.

In *Areopagitica,* the *Defences of the English People,* and to some extent in all Milton's political writing, Mr. Knight sees a prophetic message to England, both in the seventeenth and in the twentieth centuries, which culminates in *Paradise Lost.* Briefly, it consisted in an apocalyptic vision of "England, or Great Britain . . . as . . . a Messiah-

10. Karl Marx, *Capital: A Critique of Political Economy,* ed. Friedrich Engels, revised ed. Ernest Untermann (New York, Modern Library, 1936), p. 91.

nation."[11] That, Mr. Knight tells us, was Milton's view
of his country, and it is his own also. For Mr. Knight sees
"Great Britain in the Renaissance era (in which we live)
as having assumed the power-content of the medieval
Christian Church," and as laboring, "without any conscious recognition (outside her greater poets) of this destiny . . . on the whole . . . to curb lust for power and ty-
rannic ambition"[12] in a world of strife. The Christ of
Paradise Regained and *Paradise Lost* seems to Mr. Knight a
symbol of "some great, vice-gerent (to use Milton's ha-
bitual phrase) responsibility, under God,"[13] which is England's destiny. He sees the "Cromwellian revolution" less
as social and political than as military and religious, and
as a part of a continuous defence of the "Christian structure" of the world which "Great Britain is today defending."[14]

It is hardly necessary to follow Mr. Knight to the end
of his interpretation of contemporary events in the light
of the role of Messiah in *Paradise Lost*. The drama in Book
V will not gain much in artistic value even if we assent
to the suggestion that "Satan's sense of injustice under the
enthronement of Messiah as God's vice-gerent exactly re-
flects Germany's view of Great Britain's ascendency";[15]
nor will the English constitutional monarchy gain much
prestige from Mr. Knight's view of the Messiah who vanquishes Satan with thunder and lightning in Book VI as
"an especially *constitutional monarch*, in its [sic] more divine,
upreaching aspect, as a carrier of God's grace into the
domain of secular action."[16] What Mr. Knight means is
that the English conception of both royal and national

11. *Chariot of Wrath*, p. 20.
12. Ibid., p. 140.
13. Ibid., p. 141.
14. Ibid., p. 143.
15. Ibid.
16. Ibid., p. 150.

character is "an incarnation of that royalty blending justice and mercy defined once and for all by Portia's speech
in *The Merchant of Venice.*"[17] The Shakespearian parallel
may seem far-fetched; it is one of many, all of which are
due to Mr. Knight's conviction that the Puritan Revolution itself was a spiritual, though violent, process of "recreation" of the British constitution and "a fulfillment in
actuality and through long time of the Shakespearian vision."[18]

In essence, this belief in Milton (though hardly in Shakespeare) as a political prophet with something like an Old
Testament seer's inspiration, and with something like the
charisma which Lenin's disciples recognize in their master, is nothing new. Mr. Knight finds some encouragement
for it in Sir Herbert Grierson's study of the poet as prophet
in *Milton and Wordsworth.* He finds very much more encouragement in Middleton Murry's *Heaven and Earth,* though
the concern of that book with Milton is hardly vital. If
his faith in the working of the leaven of the Puritan Revolution beyond British bounds had been wide enough to
admit Russia and the United States further into his book
than the footnote on pages 184–85, his faith in the contemporary power of Milton's vision might be greater than
it is. Without sacrificing his fondness for an apocalyptic
attitude toward Milton, he might have looked at the Puritan Revolution as an international thing, with its roots far
in the past, even the pagan past, as Shelley did in *A Philosophical View of Reform;* or he might have seen it in the
image of Shelley's eagle in *Hellas,* sweeping down all recorded time and across at least all Europe:

> From age to age, from man to man,
> It lived, and lit from land to land—
> Florence, Albion, Switzerland.

17. Ibid.
18. Ibid., p. 171.

It is worth while to remember that by most historians—
and even by a revolutionary historian like Prince Kropotkin, whose work on the French Revolution set the example
of going behind constitutional changes to economic up-
heavals as the central factor in such movements—the movement in England "between 1648 and 1688"[19] has been
spiritually linked to every subsequent revolutionary attempt on the Continent. Mr. Knight's chauvinistically
messianic view of Milton in the Puritan Revolution obscures
the full value of his political thought. To understand that
we must read Mr. Arthur Barker's analysis of his sympathy with Sir Henry Vane and the Fifth Monarchists in
Milton and the Puritan Dilemma.[20] Mr. Knight's effort in
Chariot of Wrath to make Milton a figure whose leadership
we can follow today is too far removed, both from sound
historical scholarship and modern political faith, to be as
moving as Macaulay's picture of Milton's active years as
"the very crisis of the great conflict between Oromasdes
and Arimanes, liberty and despotism, reason and prejudice." If Milton's principles have "worked their way into
the depths of the American forests . . . and, from one end
of Europe to another . . . kindled an unquenchable fire in
the hearts of the oppressed, and loosed the knees of the
oppressors with an unwonted fear," it is mainly on account
of the prophetic force of the controversial works. Macaulay
ranked the best of Milton's prose with the first two books
of *Paradise Lost.* His admiration for the "devotional and
lyric rapture" of Milton's controversial writing could treat
it as describable only in the poet's "own majestic language
[as] a sevenfold chorus of hallelujahs and harping sym-
phonies."[21] Macaulay yields nothing in appreciation of
the apocalyptic and prophetic element in Milton to Mr.

19. P. A. Kropotkin, *The Great French Revolution,* trans. N. F. Dryhurst (London, Heinemann, 1909), p. 3.

20. Barker, *Milton and the Puritan Dilemma,* chap. 12.

21. *Critical and Historical Essays by T. B. Macaulay, I,* 171, 192.

Knight; and he may remind us that the more we know of the inward history of modern liberty, the greater must become our interest in Milton.

Our habit of regarding the Puritan Revolution as the beginning of civil liberty and modern constitutional government in England makes us forget its originally ecclesiastical, and perhaps genuinely religious, nature. In this country we are most accustomed to think of the Revolution in terms of the civil liberties that we associate with *Areopagitica*. In England it is regarded mainly as a landmark in constitutional history. English historians lay greatest stress, as a recent biographer of John Pym does, upon the clarity with which the final constitutional issues of the Civil War were understood and stated as early as June, 1642, in "The Nineteen Propositions" of Parliament to Charles. They included, it will be remembered, the demands that the chief Ministers of State should be "such as shall be approved by both Houses of Parliament"; that the government and liturgy of the Church should be reformed "as both Houses of Parliament shall advise"; that the King should accept Parliament's control of the militia, and that he should agree "by act of Parliament, to clear . . . the five members of the House of Commons [whose privilege he had violated by causing their arrest on the floor of the House], in such manner that future Parliaments may be secured from the consequence of that evil precedent."[22] If we are to understand Milton's mixed role as both religious prophet and political philosopher in the Puritan Revolution, we have to relate him alike to its religious and political sides. To understand him fully we need to be reminded, as we are by Professor Merriman, writing from the point of view of a comparison of the Puritan Revolution with its five contemporary revolts—the Fronde, the struggle between the Stadholders and the Es-

22. S. Reed Brett, *John Pym* (London, Murray, 1940), pp. 222–23.

tates in Holland, and the revolts in Naples, Portugal, and Catalonia—that the Puritan movement was unique in being centrally religious, or at least ecclesiastical. Disregarding the force of the physical and rhetorical support that rallied around Charles after the break with Parliament in 1642, Merriman thinks that, before the quarrel of the Commons with Archbishop Laud confused the issues, Charles could find no supporters willing to fight "for the royal prerogative as he conceived it." "The Church issue," he adds, "in the last analysis, was the fundamental cause of the Great Civil War. 'Let religion be our *primum quaerite,*' declared Sir Benjamin Rudyerd in 1642, 'for all things are but etceteras to it.' "23

As a revolutionist Milton ought first to be known as a volunteer in the attack by the sects, with the Presbyterians in the lead, upon the bishops. Except for their autobiographical passages, such as the famous resolve in the Preface to the second book of *The Reason of Church Government* to write something, someday, that would be the fruit of "devout prayers to that eternal Spirit, who can enrich with all utterance and knowledge, and sends out his seraphim, with the hallowed fire of his altar, to touch and purify the lips of whom he pleases,"24 his anti-episcopal pamphlets are too little read to contribute to the popular view of Milton. Even their scattered bits of autobiography are too seldom understood as the writer's response to the conventional expectation of his public that he should prove his right to be heard by "ethical argument" or vindication of his own character. The apocalyptic note in this passage is more easily interpreted today as evidence of morbid egotism or hypocrisy than as a logical part of the self-justification that readers trained in Aristotelian rhetoric ex-

23. Roger Bigelow Merriman, *Six Contemporary Revolutions* (Oxford, Clarendon Press, 1938), p. 38.
24. CE, *3,* 241.

pected.[25] What seemed to the seventeenth-century audience
a rather casual and probably convincing proof of sincerity
now excites suspicion, and we need the word of a scholar
like Sir Herbert Grierson to assure us that Hilaire Belloc
is wrong in saying that "the first prelatical tracts mark no
new experience, no awakening in Milton."[26] So disingenu-
ous do the five anti-episcopal tracts seem to a Miltono-
phobe like the late Heinrich Mutschmann that he convinced himself that they were the cowardly attempt of a
man just returned to England after seeking refuge from
ecclesiastical censorship in Italy, to take advantage of the
defeat of Archbishop Laud and Charles in the Second
Bishops' War.[27] It *is* true that Milton began to write his
anti-episcopal tracts about the time that the Root-and-
Branch Bill in the House of Commons indicated the rising
strength of the opposition to the bishops. It is also true,
however, that there is no more reason for doubting the
sincerity of Milton's work in the five tracts against them
than there is to doubt his sincerity in his attack on the
"blind mouths" in *Lycidas*. Of the perfect harmony of that
passage in thought and imagery with the anti-episcopal
pamphlets of Milton and his Smectymnuan friends there
is abundant evidence in Professor Haller's analysis of that
literature in *The Rise of Puritanism*. "Milton's poem, with
its extraordinary denunciation of the prelatical church . . .
was an expression of the same spirit which . . . was at the
moment clamoring in the reckless pamphlets of Prynne and
Lilburne."[28]

Milton's quarrel with the bishops is sometimes explained
as a personal affair arising out of his differences with the

25. The point is well made by Wilbur E. Gilman, *Milton's Rhetoric: Studies
in Defense of Liberty* (Columbia, University of Missouri Press, 1939).

26. Grierson, *Milton and Wordsworth*, p. 32.

27. Heinrich Mutschmann, "Die Beweggrunde zu Miltons Festlandreise,"
Beiblatt zur Anglia, 50 (1939), 278–82.

28. Haller, *The Rise of Puritanism*, p. 288.

authorities at Cambridge and his fancy of himself as "church-outed by the prelates."[29] It was, of course, something very much larger than any personal interest of his or any professional interest of the Presbyterian clergy represented by the five Smectymnuan divines. It rallied men of many professions—not only Lilburne and Prynne but the lawyers and merchants in the Long Parliament who in 1641 pushed the Root-and-Branch Bill against the resistance of cooler men, such as Henry Robinson,[30] who were bent on the reform of episcopacy, though not on its destruction. Instead of regarding Milton's contempt for the bishops as either a personal or a sectarian prejudice, we should recognize it as something deeply involved in the social life of his time. As the constant, perhaps naive, glimpses in the anti-episcopal tracts of a better world to be had simply by erasing the courts and exactions and secular ambitions of the bishops would indicate, there was something utopian in the revolt against them. There was something utopian not only in the ordinary sense of the word but also in Karl Mannheim's sense, as he defines it in *Ideology and Utopia*. The bitter, indiscriminate attack on episcopacy by "the ascendant bourgeosie" to which Milton belonged was a part of their ideal of "freedom," which Mannheim acknowledges as "in part a real utopia, *i.e.,* it contained elements orientated toward the realization of a new social order which were instrumental in disintegrating the previously existing order, and which, after their realization, did become translated into reality."[31] Certainly it is not fantastic to see the anti-episcopal tracts as a part of a widespread thrust against the "static guild and caste order" inherited by Milton's England from the "status-

29. CE, *3,* 242.

30. See W. K. Jordan's *Men of Substance* (Chicago, University of Chicago Press, 1942), pp. 107–08.

31. Karl Mannheim, *Ideology and Utopia* (London, K. Paul, Trench, Trubner, 1936), p. 183.

bound, feudal society" of the past, and as contributing to the sense of "political freedom and freedom of the unhampered development of the personality" which Mannheim makes central in the conception of liberty that the nineteenth century inherited from the seventeenth.

On the whole, discussion of Milton's anti-episcopal tracts ignores or depreciates their importance as expressions of a revolutionary mind. Few commentators have been enough excited by the spirit of the controversy to accept the "scurrility" of the liveliest onslaughts against Bishop Hall and to judge the lampooning passages, as Professor French does, objectively, and simply from the point of view of their fitness for their controversial ends.[32] Less urbane than Bishop Hall, Milton certainly was; and he made no pretense of writing with the philosophic scope of Richard Hooker's *Laws of Ecclesiastical Polity*, with which his *Reason of Church Government* and *Of Reformation in England* have recently been unfavorably compared.[33] His tracts are to be judged by rhetorical standards, such as apply to Tom Paine's *Common Sense*, not by those by which we measure Burke's *Reflections on the French Revolution* or Hooker's treatise. And we should not be misled by the immaturity of their thought. If it is true that in the anti-episcopal tracts he accepted—implicity or explicity—the Calvinistic doctrine of predestination which he repudiated in a famous passage in *Areopagitica* and condemned in the *Christian Doctrine*, it is also true that at the end of the first book of *The Reason of Church Government* he anticipated the ground of his charter of the freedom of the press and of conscience, as well as of the human will, in *Areopagitica*, by answering those who argued that episcopacy was necessary to keep the warring Protestant sects in order. The sentence reads

32. John Milton French, "Milton as Satirist," *PMLA, 51* (1936), 414–29; and Haller, *Rise of Puritanism,* pp. 358–61.

33. E. N. S. Thompson, "Richard Hooker among the Controversialists," *PQ, 20* (1941), 263–64.

as if it had been written in 1644 rather than two years
earlier:

> No wonder then in the reforming of a church,
> which is never brought to effect without the fierce
> encounter of truth and falsehood together, if, as it
> were the splinters and shares of so violent a jousting,
> there fall from between the shock many fond errors
> and fanatic opinions, which, when truth has the upper
> hand, and the reformation shall be perfected, will
> easily be rid out of the way, or kept so low, as that
> they shall be only the exercise of our knowledge, not
> the disturbance or interruption of our faith.[34]

The man who wrote these words was already a tolera-
tionist in religion. At the core of his willingness to encourage theological discussion was the respect for "the dignity and importance of the individual" which Mr. Tillyard
sees as animating "the whole discussion about the episcopacy."[35] And in that respect for the individual's dignity
there was bound up the implicit utopianism (in Mannheim's
sense of the word) which had inspired the emotionally
valid part of the attack on the bishops from the days of
the old Martin Marprelate in Queen Elizabeth's times to
the appearance of the new Marprelate tracts at the height
of the controversy against Archbishop Laud. Without reading long and widely in the literature of attack upon the
prelates between the two Marprelates, it is impossible to
understand its tremendous utopian drive. The puritan conscience was not only convinced, as Sir Herbert Grierson
says, that the quarrel was one "between the ethical in
religion and the magical."[36] The revolt was not only against
the liturgy and against the whole inheritance of the English Church from Rome which the Puritans stigmatized

34. CE, *3*, 224.
35. Tillyard, *Milton*, p. 127.
36. *Milton and Wordsworth*, p. 42.

as idolatry. It was against the interference of the bishops' authority and of their ecclesiastical courts with private lives, private studies, and private beliefs.

A good example of this almost traditional anti-episcopal literature, which happens to date from the year 1614, when the tract found a publisher in Amsterdam, is Leonard Busher's *Religions Peace, or a Reconciliation, between Princes and Peoples, and Nations.* The writer, who described himself as a citizen of London and also "of the Country of Glouces-ter, of the Town of Wotton," wrote in a style and orthog-raphy quaint even for the time; and he wrote with a hum-ble man's sense of his own presumption in speaking at all, but with an apostle's certainty of what he had to say. The tract is less liberal than Milton's *Reason of Church Govern-ment,* but it has quite as utopian a faith in the better world to be easily and instantly attained by the liquidation of the bishops. Busher saw them as responsible, by their inter-ference with men's consciences, for all the religious hypoc-risy in the world. He saw them as responsible, by their administration of canon law in their courts, for all the domestic unhappiness in England, and he was as naïvely convinced as Milton was in *The Doctrine and Discipline of Divorce* that with the disappearance of canon law there would not be an unhappy husband or wife, or a single case of adultery in the land. And of course he was pro-foundly certain that all of England's political woes came from the interference of the prelates at court.

That last thesis Milton takes for granted in a way which modern readers can hardly understand, and which indeed can hardly be understood, either intellectually or emo-tionally, without an acquaintance with William Prynne's amazing indictment of ambitious churchmen from the very beginning of the Archbishopric of Canterbury under Au-gustine at the end of the sixth century, down to the con-temporary encroachments on the rights of both the crown and its subjects by Archbishop Laud. Milton's accusations against the bishops (some of them resting on a mistaken attribution of the commentary of the Frenchman, Herveus Burgidolensis, to St. Anselm of Canterbury[37]) were recognized by his more learned readers as a kind of popularization of the mass of historical evidence against them which William Prynne had published in 1641 in *The Antipathie of the English Lordly Prelacie both to regall monarchy, and civill unity.* In 1641 and still in 1642 when Charles, it was hoped, might yet be weaned away from Laud, there seemed to be good ground for Prynne's strategy; that is why, in the latter year, Milton thought fit to end the *Reason of Church Government* with his famous appeal to Charles to assert his prerogative as head of the English Church against the "innovations" which Laud was making in its liturgy. In the light of Prynne's theory and its curious appeal to the laws of the realm there is a veiled but shrewd threat, if the king will not come to terms with the anti-episcopal party, to constrain him by legal pressure to do so. In *Chariot of Wrath* (p. 96), Mr. Knight is attracted by Milton's identification of Charles with Samson in this passage, and he parallels it with some other places in the prose works where Milton uses Samson, as Mr. Knight sees him doing again in *Samson Agonistes,* as a symbol of "Nietzschean 'chastity' and power." In Milton's comparison of Samson's hair to the laws of England, which ought to be the king's glory, and which he cannot harm without losing his strength, it is perhaps more instructive to see, as Don Wolfe does,[38] the beginning of the open charge of tyranny against Charles which was to be pressed home years later in *The Tenure of Kings and Magistrates,* in *Eikonoklastes,* and in the First *De-*

37. I am indebted for this explanation of Milton's mistake (which is found in CE, *3,* 208) to Dom Anselm Strittmatter of St. Anselm's Priory, Brookland, D.C.

38. Don Wolfe, *Milton in the Puritan Revolution* (New York, T. Nelson, 1941), pp. 46–47.

fence of the English People. Although Mr. Knight says nothing about the significance of Milton's comparisons of the
king's flowing locks to the laws, he fully understands the
importance of the Puritans' faith that they had law on
their side against Charles, and when it comes to the legal
issue between the king and Parliament he roundly con-
tradicts[39] Mr. Belloc's "contention that the doctrine concerned was 'wholly new' and to Englishmen 'unnatural.' "
Milton's words, it must be acknowledged, do suggest the
unction of *Thus Spake Zarathustra:*

> I cannot better liken the state and person of a king
> than to that mighty Nazarite Samson, who being dis-
> ciplined from his birth in the precepts and practice
> of temperance and sobriety, without the strong drink
> of injurious and excessive desires, grows up to a noble
> strength and perfection with those his illustrious and
> sunny locks, the laws, waving and curling about his
> godlike shoulders. And while he keeps them about
> him undiminished and unshorn, he may with the jaw-
> bone of an ass, that is, with the word of his meanest
> officer, suppress and put to confusion thousands of
> those that rise against his just power. But laying down
> his head among the strumpet flatteries of prelates,
> while he sleeps and thinks no harm, they wickedly
> shaving off those bright and weighty tresses of his
> laws, and just prerogatives, which were his ornament
> and strength, deliver him over to indirect and violent
> counsels, which, as those Philistines, put out the fair
> and far-sighted eyes of his natural discerning, and
> make him grind in the prison-house of their sinister
> ends . . . till he, knowing this prelatical razor to have
> bereft him of his wonted might, nourish again his
> puissant hair, the golden beams of law and right; and

39. *Chariot of Wrath,* p. 48.

they sternly shook, thunder with ruin upon the heads of those his evil counsellors, but not without great affliction to himself.[40]

Few passages are more significant of the working of Milton's mind as he thought about the Puritan Revolution in Church and State than is this one from the close of *The Reason of Church Government Urged against Prelaty.* If we look at it in the light of Mannheim's distinction between ideological and utopian thinking, we find the strong elements of both types, which his analysis would lead us to expect. Nothing is more characteristic of the ideologies of ascendant classes than the sincere, or canting, or cynical notion that the law is on their side, and the first act of a class which is translating its utopian thinking into reality is to make sure that the law is interpreted as being on its side. When Milton wrote these words in 1642, just such a translation of utopian intentions was visibly beginning in the ecclesiastical realm, and it was soon to begin in politics. In the opening duel between the crown and parliament it was not yet clear which party would find the common and constitutional law on its side. And it is worth while to remember that for many historians in the twentieth century it is no longer possible to give Macaulay's confident answer to the question; "Had Charles the First broken the fundamental laws of England?"[41]

Charles, of course, was blind enough to identify the law with his own prerogative, and in *Eikon Basilike* he (or Bishop Gauden, or whoever it was that wrote the passage) was fatuous enough to compare his resistance of Parliament's demands to the replies of Christ to the Devil in the temptation on the pinnacle of the Temple in Jerusalem. To such an impertinent and unflattering analogy Parliament's advocate could only answer as Milton did in

40. CE, *3*, 276.
41. *Critical and Historical Essays,* p. 174.

Eikonoklastes by recalling the "zeal to justice and their native liberty, against the proud contempt and misrule of their kings,"[42] of the lords who brought Richard II to book for his tyranny and of all the other champions of the liberties which Englishmen were supposed once and for all to have secured from the crown in *Magna Charta.*

The story of the reply of Charles's clerical supporters to such sharp, two-edged, legal reasoning as this by their appeal to the principle of the king's divine right[43] is too well known to need repeating, and so is that of the support of absolutist principles later by writers like Robert Filmer and Hobbes. To both theological and philosophical absolutism the reply, as Professor Woodhouse points out in his exceedingly able discussion of the service of Puritanism to the cause of liberty, had to be in terms of something still more absolute. "Nothing could dissipate the divinity that hedged a king save the divinity of religion itself when religion was ranged against him."[44] Because Charles chose to make common cause with Archbishop Laud and the more reactionary bishops, it was easy to represent what Milton regarded as the completing or reforming of the Reformation in England as vitally involved with Parliament's case against the king. Charles made the mistake of solidifying everything that was revolutionary in the English Church against himself. At the same time his own very religious nature and the religious position of many of his supporters at the outset of the struggle finally threw most liberal thinkers, such as John Selden, into opposition to him. Among educated readers the royalists soon had reason to fear the influence of Selden's theory of natural law[45] as

42. CE, *5,* 125.

43. See John N. Figgis, *The Divine Right of Kings* (2d ed. Cambridge, University Press, 1922).

44. A. S. P. Woodhouse, introduction to *Puritanism and Liberty, Being the Army Debates,* edited from the Clarke Manuscripts (London, Dent, 1938), p. 61.

45. John Selden, *De Jure Naturale* (London, 1640), Book I, especially chaps. 8, 98, 99.

more favorable to human rights than to royal prerogative. The royalist John Bramhall, defending the monarchical principle in 1644, in *The Serpent Salve; or, A Remedy for the biting of an Aspe,* warned against the "far-fetched conclusions drawn by empirics from the law of Nature and Nations." What was this Charter of Nature? Whatever it was, Bramhall replied, "it might be limited by the King, his title being not election but conquest."[46] Against this claim the first line of defense was the stand taken by Milton in *The Tenure of Kings and Magistrates* when he asserted that, beginning with William the so-called Conqueror, himself, every king of England since Saxon times had sworn in his coronation oath to abide by the laws of the realm.[47] The second, and perhaps for both sides more dangerous, line of defense, however, was the Puritan and liberal assertion against royalist claims to divine right and every kind of absolute prerogative for the king of the essentially religious law of nature. In *A Readie and Easie Way to Establish a Free Commonwealth* (1660), Milton once again recalled his many past appeals to it in a passage calling it the "only law of laws . . . fundamental to mankind," and "the beginning and end of government."[48] In his most characteristic thinking the law of nature became simply the law of the intellectual and moral integrity of the individual: The "light of nature," he wrote in the *Commonwealth,* equals "right reason,"[49] and the latter is the former's best inter-

46. Quoted by G. P. Gooch and H. J. Laski in *English Democratic Ideas in the Seventeenth Century* (Cambridge, University Press, 1927), p. 93. A typical challenge to the royalist claim to absolute rights of power by virtue of the Norman conquest occurs in an anonymous tract entitled *The Unlimited Prerogative of Kings subverted* (1642), sig. B2, where the reader learns that William obtained the throne only by the conditional submission of the Saxons, who agreed to serve him "as our Liege Lord, and Sovereigne, so that he would promise to govern us, according to these Laws and Customes to which covenant he consented, as all the Kings of *England* have done since."

47. CE, *5,* 10.

48. Ibid., *6,* 158.

49. Ibid.

preter. In saying this Milton spoke a language that had been familiar to his countrymen since Robert Greville, Lord Brooke, had appealed against the bishops in 1642 to "Right Reason, the Candle of God, which He hath lighted in man."[50] Already in that tract, humanistically trained Puritans found their sanction of the originally Stoic conception of Right Reason interpreting natural law raised by one of the most intellectual and aristocratic of their leaders to a level of philosophical authority that seemed more commanding to Christian idealists than the doctrine of divine right could ever hope to seem. Greville, they knew, was but recalling Seneca's dictum that, "Right Reason is nothing else than a portion of the divine spirit set in a human body."[51] With him they were convinced that "All philosophers yield, (and it needeth no dispute) that the *Understanding* rectified still dictates to the *Will*, Optimum faciendum." The ultimately Socratic principle of right reason, "the understanding rectified," or conscience—call it what you will—is the key to the conception of liberty in the Puritan Revolution. It is the key to the best thinking of the time in both religion and politics; just as the key to most of the less disciplined thought of the period is to be found in such popular, quasi-religious shibboleths as the Truth to which Milton appealed in *Areopagitica,* and which he seems, once or twice, there to identify with Christ—the "Christ-within" of the Fifth Monarchy men.[52] One thing is certain: in all of Milton's religious and political thinking —from his appeal to "regenerate reason" in the anti-episcopal tracts, on down through the *Tenure,* the *Commonwealth* and the *Christian Doctrine,* to almost his last word in the

50. Greville's *Episcopacie* is reprinted in Haller's *Tracts on Liberty, 2,* 25.

51. *Epistulae* 66 (trans. Thomas Lodge).

52. The association of Milton with the Fifth Monarchy men was made by Theodore Calvin Pease in *The Leveller Movement* (Washington, American Historical Association, 1916), p. 154, and is explored by Barker in *Milton and the Puritan Dilemma,* chap. 12.

little tract *Of True Religion, Heresy, Schism, Toleration* in 1673
—he was dominated by his confidence in the power of a
half-divine Right Reason to find out the *Truth.*

The passage in all of Milton's writing where his faith
in the final discoverability of Truth comes to climactic
expression is the famous myth of Osiris in *Areopagitica.* It
should be read in the light of many parallels in his own
work and in that of his contemporaries, and it should also
be read in the light of the two most telling and damaging
criticisms which have been leveled at Milton by his many
modern critics. With both of those criticisms in mind, let
us read the passage against a very small segment of its
literary background. The first of them is Ernest Boyd's objection (in *Literary Blasphemies*) that *Areopagitica* is quintes-
sentially platitudinous and therefore insignificant; the second is Mr. Leavis' complaint (in *Revaluation,* pp. 58–59),
that Milton is, "for purposes of the understanding, disas-
trously single-minded and simple-minded. . . . This defect," he says, "is a defect of imagination." The charge is
brought against Milton as a poet, but it is worth checking
against his use of the Osiris myth in his plea for liberty of
conscience, for Mr. Leavis thinks that Milton's "inadequacy to myth" (in the structural sense in which the word
is used in *Revaluation*) makes "the routine eulogy of his
'architectonic' power (in *Paradise Lost*) plainly a matter of
mere inert convention." If our subject warranted such a
digression, it would be a temptation to explore the structural significance for *Areopagitica* of this myth of Osiris
which comes at its climax and is a symbol of its central
theme of the search for Truth:

> Truth indeed came once into the world with her
> divine Master, and was a perfect shape most glorious
> to look on: but when he ascended, and his apostles
> after him were laid asleep, then straight arose a
> wicked race of deceivers, who, as that story goes of
> the Egyptian Typhon with his conspirators, how they

dealt with the good Osiris, took the virgin Truth, hewed her lovely form into a thousand pieces, and scattered them to the four winds. From that time ever since, the sad friends of Truth, such as durst appear, imitating the careful search that Isis made for the mangled body of Osiris, went up and down gathering up limb by limb still as they could find them. We have not yet found them all, Lords and Commons, nor ever shall do, till her Master's second coming, he shall bring together every joint and member, and shall mold them into an immortal feature of loveliness and perfection.[53]

The myth of Osiris, as Milton expected his readers as a matter of course to know, is found in Plutarch's *Moralia*. He expected them to be familiar also with some of the many interpretations of the myth[54] in just his sense by his contemporaries. He expected them also to be familiar with the kindred Renaissance conception of Truth as the Daughter of Time, the prevalence of which in literature and many of the pictorial arts has been studied for us by Professor Saxl.[55] The two ideas of truth are perhaps confused in Milton's condemnation in *Of Prelatical Episcopacy* of the search for Truth "among the verminous and polluted rags dropped overworn from the toiling shoulders of Time," to which he contrasted "the spotless and undecaying robe of Truth, the daughter, not of Time, but of Heaven, only bred up below here in Christian hearts, between two grave and holy nurses, the doctrine and discipline of the gospel."[56] Milton's experience of Presbyterian discipline within two years of the writing of these words was to con-

53. CE, *4*, 337.

54. One of these is paralleled with this passage in my edition of Milton's *Prose Selections* (New York, Odyssey Press, 1947), p. 252, n. 244.

55. Fritz Saxl, "Veritas filia temporis," in *Philosophy and History: Essays in Honor of Ernst Cassirer*, eds. Raymond Klibansky and H. J. Paton (Oxford, Clarendon Press, 1936).

56. CE, *3*, 91.

firm his notion that Time's shoulders dropped many verminous and polluted rags, but his faith in the quest for
Truth never faltered—"Truth which," he said in *The Tenure
of Kings and Magistrates,* "among mortal men is always in
her progress."[57]

Of course, the progress was also a battle, and a winning
one. When in *Areopagitica* Milton proposed to let Truth
and Falsehood grapple, he was using the most platitudinous of all the images that had been consecrated in the
Puritan struggle with the bishops. In countless Puritan
pamphlets Truth strode invincibly into battle while the
godly looked on with the serene faith that her strength
was "sufficient for vanquishing the most artificial, sophis-
ticall errour that ever was in the world."[58] The words are
William Walwyn's in his *Power of Love,* a tract inspired far
more by an enlightened visionary's prospect of a really
democratic commonwealth to be established in England
than by sectarian religious fervor. To the still more worldly-
minded Henry Robinson, Truth's triumph in the politico-
ecclesiastical battle seemed no less certain, and in *Liberty
of Conscience* (1643) he asked, "doe we suspect that errour
shall vanquish truth? This is so vaine that no man will
confesse so much; but for their full conviction if they were
so conceited, let them take notice what *St. Paul* saith to
the *Corinthians, We cannot do anything against the truth but for
the truth.*"[59] Indeed in the Whitehall debates, when the
Army leaders were talking and praying themselves into the
resolution to show Charles I no mercy and to take the
step which would inevitably turn England into a Republic,
no figure of speech was commoner in their violent and
whirling speeches than that of Truth as wrestling victori-

57. Ibid., *5,* 57.

58. See Haller's *Tracts on Liberty, 2,* 278. Cf. William Dell on Truth's in-
vincibility in a speech in the Army Debates preserved in *Puritanism and Liberty,* p. 315.

59. Henry Robinson, *Liberty of Conscience* (London, 1643), p. 59.

ously against Error and at the same time as somehow—
both emotionally and philosophically—to be identified
with the Christ for whose speedy second coming they
prayed. When Ireton proposed a censorship on "atheistical"
publications and beliefs (not unlike that which Milton proposed in *Areopagitica*) Sprigge, supported by Lilburne, was
prompt in condemning such lack of confidence in the ultimate victory of truth, and in "the breaking forth of him
who is the Truth, the breaking forth of Christ, in the
minds and spirits of men."[60] When Milton wrote *Areopagitica*, he knew that his public was conditioned to respond
with either an enlightened, philosophical belief in Truth
as symbolized by the Osiris myth, or with a fanatical faith
in Truth the invincible champion; and he knew that both
the belief and the faith were merged in many minds in
the image of "her Master's second coming."

It is as easy for modern readers as it was for Milton's
contemporaries to sentimentalize about the notion of Truth
that found its classical expression in *Areopagitica*. It is
closely bound up with the "prophetic" side of the man in
which Sir Herbert Grierson has interested us,[61] and it undoubtedly was related to his poetic gift. Indeed, G. Wilson
Knight roundly identifies that poetic gift with Milton's
passionate determination that "truth was to enter politics.
This truth, (which Milton sometimes calls "right reason"),"
he thinks, "corresponds to 'faith' in St. Paul's epistles or
the Church fathers and to 'imagination' as conceived by
Coleridge and Shelley."[62] As an antidote to Mr. Knight's
impliedly sweeping and uncritical acceptance of Milton's
political propaganda in the name of Truth it is worth
while to remember that most of the political crimes of the
Puritans were committed—perhaps quite sincerely—in the
service of Truth. In our times the semanticists love to

60. *Puritanism and Liberty*, p. 144.
61. *Milton and Wordsworth*, p. 47.
62. *Chariot of Wrath*, p. 74.

dissect the word, not greatly to the credit of its loudest
devotees. With the aid of the Great Tom Fuller—speaking
as he did in a sermon in honor of the anniversary of
Charles's coronation in 1643—we may profitably pause to
notice what a seventeenth century semanticist could do
with the word and its abuse by the Puritans. "Know," he
said to his doubtless sympathetic courtly audience,

> "then that the word *Truth* is subject to much *Homo-*
> *nymie,* and is taken in several senses, according to the
> opinions, or rather humours of those that use it. Aske
> the Anabaptist what is truth, and he will tell you,
> Truth is . . . that all goods should be common, that
> there should be no civill Magistrate, that there ought
> to be no warres but what they make themselves, for
> which they pretend inspiration. . . . Againe, Aske the
> Separatists what is Truth, and they will tell you, that
> the further from all ceremonies (though ancient and
> decent), the nearer to God. . . . Aske the Schismaticks
> of these times what is Truth, and they will bring in
> abundance of their own opinions, which I spare at
> this time to recite."[63]

Fuller, like all his party, was aware as no modern reader
of *Areopagitica* can be of the anarchy and hypocrisy that
lurked behind the idol of Truth, but his intolerance was
the very thing that validated the faith of all the sects, and
of liberals who were above the sectarian mêlée, in the
divinity of Truth. Yet even Fuller, after declaring all the
truths of the sectaries to be "flat falsities," professed his
willingness to submit all differences of opinion to the fair
debate for which the Puritans clamored. He had only one
condition to lay down, but that was a betrayal of his own
and his party's failure to comprehend the utopian energy

63. "A Sermon Preached at the Collegiat Church of S. Peter in *Westmin-*
ister, on the 27 of March, being the day of His Majesties Inauguration, by
Thomas Fuller, B.D." (London, 1643), p. 18.

of the "new Gospell" of the Puritans, which he insisted should not "be given as the Law, with thundering and lightning of Cannon, fire and sword."[64]

It is a nice question whether the kind of passion and thought which went into Milton's willingness to tolerate all kinds of heresies in *Areopagitica* can be regarded as evidence of imaginative power either in the political or in the Coleridgean sense. Perhaps most readers of *Ideology and Utopia* will grant the "utopian" power of Milton's conception of truth (in Mannheim's sense of the word "utopian"), as readers of Ortega y Gasset's *The Revolt of the Masses* may see a perfect correspondence between the successful imposition of Milton's notion of Truth as it shaped the emergent liberalism of the Puritan Revolution and Gasset's view that the "Imagination is the liberating power possessed by man. A people is capable of becoming a State in the degree to which it is able to imagine."[65] In a very vague and perhaps not highly significant sense there can be no doubt that, if not in the activity of the political imagination of the Puritans, then certainly in the shaping of the popular poetic imagination, the idea of the defeat of falsehood in open battle by truth was what Rebecca West has called "a potent image"; certainly it gave rise to many subsidiary images which were beautiful, if not very potent. For example, after a picture of embattled Truth in conflict with Error, Leonard Busher, in *Religions Peace,* changed the image and assured his audience that they should "understand that, errors being brought to the light of the word of God, [they would] vanish as darkness before the light of a torch."[66] And Robert Greville, in a great passage on

64. Ibid., p. 19.

65. Ortega y Gasset, *The Revolt of the Masses* (London, Allen and Unwin, 1932), p. 62.

66. Quoted by Wolfe in *Milton in the Puritan Revolution,* p. 27. Cf. the close of the Humble Petition of 1641: "That which is erroneous will in time appeare, and the professors of it will bee ashamed, and it will perish and wither as a flower, vanish as smoke, and pass as a shadow" (p. 70).

the Understanding as "a Ray of the Divine Nature, warming and enlivening the Creature, and conforming it to the likeness of the Creator," in the little essay called *The Nature of Truth*,[67] which is cited in *Areopagitica*, wrote finally of Truth in a style that suggests the invocation to light at the opening of the third book of *Paradise Lost:*

> For the Beauty of Truths character is, that she is a shadow, a resemblance of the first, the best forme; that she is light, the species, the sparkling of primitive *light;* that she is *life*, the sublimation of *light*, that she may reflect upon herself.

Against the account of the diabolic parliament in Books I and II of *Paradise Lost,* and in view of the following contrasting debate in heaven, from which the Son of God emerges as leader of the states of heaven, as Satan is leader of those of hell, it may not be forced to see some political intention in the seemingly purely metaphysical glories of the famous invocation to light at the beginning of Book III. Certainly it is as much a possibility as is Mr. Knight's interpretation of the Son in Book VI as a pattern of an English constitutional monarch. While feeling far less certain of any political significance in the invocation to light than Mr. Knight is of his view of the Son, we do have one very good reason for supposing that the Son is intended as a political symbol at his first appearance in the third book. If the suspicion of most readers that the diabolic parliament is a portrait of the Long Parliament can be confirmed, then the Son can hardly be regarded otherwise than as a symbol of whatever it is that makes parliaments good. In that case it may be easy to see him as a symbol of a British constitutional king.

67. Robert Greville, *The Nature of Truth* (London, 1640, printed for R. Bishop by Samuel Cartwright), pp. 3–4.

If the Son of God in the third book of *Paradise Lost* has any political significance, it is simply as the force of good and effective leadership without which parliaments are worse than helpless. Milton's impatience with the impotence of the Long Parliament to act rightly and independently on questions like the freedom of the press, the divorce law, and the great problem of disposing of the King, must have given him many moments when his disgust with representative governments was as great as Lenin's with the Russian Duma. As a young man at the beginning of his political career, writing his anti-episcopal tracts, Milton could sincerely describe Parliament as "so much united excellence, (met) in one globe of brightness and efficacy, . . . encountering the dazzled resistance of tyranny."[68] In *Of Reformation in England* he wrote of "the indiminishable majesty of our highest court, the law-giving and sacred parliament."[69] That was "our time of parliament, the very jubilee and resurrection of the state."[70] Perhaps there was no fundamental loss of faith in connection with Parliament's neglect of the divorce pamphlets and *Areopagitica;* but when, after the execution of Charles, he declared that "the parliament is above all positive law, whether civil or common,"[71] and said that the "Law of England" was "but the reason of Parliament,"[72] he was beginning to be aware of what Lenin was to call the "disease of parliamentarism." He had, with reason, lost faith in the power of Parliament to act without the spur of Cromwell's will. Bitter experience was teaching him the need of strong leadership in representative government, and the wonder is that at no time does he seem to have succumbed to the remedy of

68. CE, *3*, 337.
69. Ibid., p. 58.
70. Ibid., p. 127.
71. Ibid., *5*, 115.
72. Ibid., p. 83.

the single, strong leader.[73] At the fall of the Commonwealth in 1660, when he was writing his *Readie and Easie
Way* to establish a better one, his contempt for government by "a single person" was uncompromising. Even the
sonnet to Cromwell in 1652 accepts him only as the champion of truth who is to save England, if he proves worthy,
from foes who were "Threatening to bind our souls with
secular chains." Significantly, in his eulogy in *The Second
Defence,* he is presented only as one of the soldiers whom
England has used in her own liberation, and his greatest
distinction is that he is a man who has mastered the passions which beset the soul. And when in 1660 final defeat
for the Commonwealth came, Milton proved his fidelity
to the parliamentary principle by grappling in *The Readie
and Easie Way* with the "disease of parliamentarism" and
trying to devise means to prevent the Grand Council which
he proposed should govern the realm from being one of the
"mere 'talking shops' " that Lenin condemned in modern
Europe. Like Lenin, he thought that a Parliament should
be "a working corporation, legislative and executive at the
same time,"[74] and it is perhaps the best claim of both men
to have been honest and clear-headed leaders in their respective revolutions, that they both tried to make parliaments responsive to strong leadership and capable of pro-
ducing it.

To compare Milton with Lenin in any respect is to
invite a challenge of his right to rank at all as a revolutionist in the modern democratic and economic sense. That
he was no democrat in the modern sense needs no demon-

73. In "The Theory of the Mixed State and the Development of Milton's
Political Thought" (*PMLA, 57,* 1942, 721–22), Professor Z. S. Fink acknowledges that for a time Milton believed in . . . divinely appointed . . . leaders"
who were law-givers like Lycurgus and Solon and, presumably, Cromwell. In
A Readie and Easie Way, however, Milton abandoned that faith.

74. V. I. Lenin, *The State and Revolution* (New York, International Publishers,
1929), p. 153.

stration. The "popular assembly of upward of a thousand" which he provided for in *A Readie and Easie Way,* as Professor Fink has shown,[75] however, had a genuine, though rather negative and contemptible part to play in Milton's theory of state sovereignty as best if "mixed" and unevenly divided among "magisterial, aristocratic and democratic elements." It is the uncompromisingly aristocratic cast of Milton's political thinking that is hard for the modern world to accept. We forget how radically consistent his aristocratic thinking was, and what a social and economic revolution it entailed. We forget how bitterly the abolition of the House of Lords under the Cromwellian Commonwealth had been resented, and what an economic upheaval was involved in the nationalization of the estates of the royalist nobles. No one supported the abolition of the House of Lords more cordially than did Milton, and no one deplored the dishonest resale of what might have largely remained public land by Parliament to the favored grandees of the Parliamentary Party more sincerely than he did. The extent of the economic revolution under the Protectorate is amusingly exploited in the reply to Milton's *Readie and Easie Way* by George Starkey in *The Dignity of Kingship Asserted.*[76] The whole country, and especially the gentry and the merchant classes, are represented as having been robbed by the Rump's expropriations of nobility and churchmen, and by its "monstrous taxes, (which they extorted to maintain their *Janisaries* the *Apostate Souldiers* by whose *mutiny* and *Rebellion* they were first *constituted*)."[77]

Yet what interested Milton in the attack on the hereditary nobility in the Puritan Revolution, it is plain, was the emergence of the principle that was to play so large a part in the French Revolution—the principle that honor should go to men of talent rather than to men of family.

75. "The Theory of the Mixed State," p. 716.
76. *The Dignity of Kingship Asserted.* (1660. Facsimile, ed. W. R. Parker, 1942)
77. Ibid., p. 148.

If rank and property could be cleared of snobbery, Milton had no quarrel with the landed families. That much seems clear from his refusal in the *Readie and Easie Way* to accept the principle of the periodic return of all the land in the realm to small, or comparatively small, holders, which Harrington had made a basic part of his constitution in his *Oceana.* In spite of Harrington's weighty authority for the principle in the laws of Moses and the example of the agrarian proposals of the Gracchi in republican Rome, Milton said that if he could be assured that in his commonwealth there would be no temporal or spiritual lords, he was confident that no individual or group could "attain to such wealth or vast possessions as will need the hedge of an agrarian law." Such laws, he added, had never been successful, "but the cause rather of sedition, save only where it began seasonably with first possession."[78] Milton's commonwealth would hardly have been levelled down economically any more than the England in which he actually lived. If he shared in the middle-class hatred of a privileged nobility which Professor Brinton says in *The Anatomy of Revolution*[79] is a part of every revolutionary movement, it was less because he was envious of the nobles, as Dr. Johnson said, than because, as George Starkey said, he believed that a commonwealth was the best kind of government to secure *"Civil Freedome,* which consists in Civil Rights and the advancement of every person according to his *merit."*[80]

Probably none of Milton's twentieth-century readers outside of Germany will dislike him a whit for being guilty of an interest in civil rights. His interest in the mutual claims of society and the meritorious individual and the Aristotelian "concept of natural slavery and the Christian doctrine of sin,"[81] smack too much of rugged individual-

78. CE, *6,* 134.
79. Pp. 72, 286–87.
80. *Dignity of Kingship Asserted,* p. 25.
81. *Milton in the Puritan Revolution,* p. 346.

ism, however, to be acceptable to Don Wolfe. Because "in *Paradise Lost,* as in the pamphlets, Milton identified sin with political ignorance,"[82] Mr. Wolfe regrets the severity of Milton's verdict on his countrymen for throwing away (or seeming to throw away) the hard-won liberties that were sacrificed to recall Charles II in 1660. By implication, he would disapprove of the characteristic entries under the heading of *Libertas* in the Commonplace Book which declare that nations get the governments that they deserve, that Brutus and Cassius erred in thinking that Rome was capable of liberty,[83] and that liberty once lost is irrecoverable.[84] He looks askance at the psychology which led Milton to preach the subjection of passion to reason in some of the speeches of Michael and Raphael in *Paradise Lost,* and at the extension of that psychology into the political principle of the rule of good men. The Christ of whom Abdiel says that God and Nature approve because

> he who rules is worthiest, and excells
> Them whom he governs,

smacks to Mr. Wolfe of the tyrant that Professor Liljegren saw in the Christ of *Paradise Lost,* and in "the stern judgments" of that poem he sees "the boundless charity of the Christ, glimpsed by . . . Saltmarsh and Walwyn and Roger Williams (fluttering) helplessly in the offing."[85] Altogether, Mr. Wolfe finds that "Milton's portrayal of Christ . . . shows his lack of sympathy with the full measure of love and forgiveness that the extreme Puritan revolutionists emphasized in their characterizations."[86] The upshot is that for Mr. Wolfe the peak of Milton's effectiveness as a political thinker is the "revolutionary fervor that would open all creeds to pitiless criticism" in *Areopagitica,* and "the

82. Ibid., p. 347.
83. CE, *18,* 163.
84. Ibid., p. 193.
85. *Milton in the Puritan Revolution,* pp. 346, 349.
86. Ibid., p. 350.

democratic arguments of *The Tenure* and *The Defence.*"[87]

Probably most of Mr. Wolfe's readers will concur with him in rating *Areopagitica* and *The Tenure of Kings and Magistrates* above *The Readie and Easie Way to establish a Free Commonwealth.* Doubtless Milton would not agree with him. In the equal stress upon the evils of royal tyranny and mob rule in the *Way* he spoke out of his experience of the Puritan Revolution. From his silence about the extremely liberal humanitarian and theological views of men like Walwyn, Williams, and Winstanley it is hardly fair to conclude that he had a hard heart. Winstanley's *Law of Freedom,* the communistic manifesto of the Diggers of St. George's hill in February 1652, with its Marxian conviction that wealth is produced only by labor, its annual turnover of all public offices, its principle of exchange by barter, and above all with its proposal of free and technical education for everyone, seems to anticipate the economic dialectic of Marx and his followers. No one can deny the interest of Winstanley's communistic conception of a commonwealth for his own time as well as for ours.[88] Yet in general it is true, as Professor Jordan believes, that "the thought of the incendiary political groups—the Fifth Monarchy men, the Levellers, the Diggers, and the more violent republicans—was quite as divorced from the economic realities of the age as it was from the political necessities of the period. Moreover, the economic and social thinking of the more radical sectaries, animated as it was by the vision of the Kingdom of God on earth, was in most instances so detached from the trend of English development as to be without great significance for the period."[89] Certainly there was some radically democratic interpretation of the law of nature by men like Rainborough in the Army debates, but in general "even the Levellers were against

87. Ibid., p. 351.

88. Cf. *The Works of Gerrard Winstanley,* ed. George H. Sabine (Ithaca, Cornell University Press, 1941), intro., pp. 54–58.

89. Jordan, *Men of Substance,* pp. 203–04.

interference with property,"[90] and men like Ireton, who defended property rights, carried the argument. Mr. Jordan points out that the most unsparing attacks on the Levellers' leaders were made by one of the most effective political writers of the Revolution, Henry Parker,[91] and it is surely true that in his attack on John Lilburne, Parker proclaimed the principle that "liberty cannot be permitted to degenerate into anarchy"[92] with far greater controversial bitterness than Milton ever showed.

Argument of this kind, however, will never reconcile Mr. Wolfe and those of his way of thinking to Milton as a political thinker in the Puritan Revolution. They are hardly likely to be impressed by even the most liberal and far-seeing of his political views, like his recommendation of strong local governments with independent courts and good schools throughout England.[93] Nor are they to be silenced by M. Saurat's condescending warning not to "forget too easily that Milton was not only a critic of kings and tyrants," or by his approval of Milton's "vital observations on the essential principles on which democracies should be worked." They are not likely to agree with M. Saurat that the practice of "explaining everything by economic factors" is a "craze," or that the "older . . . method of blaming and somewhat regulating human nature . . . in Milton's pamphlets"[94] is the right way to face either political or ethical problems.

Perhaps those problems need not be faced before justice is done to Milton as a political thinker. Perhaps we may

90. Margaret James, *Social Problems and Policy during the Puritan Revolution* (London, G. Routledge, 1930), p. 119.

91. *Men of Substance,* p. 156.

92. Ibid., p. 176.

93. The significance of this suggestion and of Milton's support for it from the value of local institutions in the Dutch struggle for liberty, becomes clear in the light of Starkey's violent reply in *The Dignity of Kingship Asserted,* pp. 107–09.

94. Denis Saurat in a review of CE, *5–10,* in *Review of English Studies, 10* (1934), 230.

understand him best if, like Mr. Barker, we regard him
as an idealist who thought that "the function of the revolution was to achieve civil liberty through the inward laws
of true religion,"[95] and if we study his political pamphlets
as "the not altogether successful attempt of an idealist . . .
to read in the chaotic events of the revolution a pattern
which would justify both the ways of God and men."[96]
The effort to account for his faith in private reason and
natural law as capable of finding the way to the City of
God has a more than literary-historical value. It is not
merely a matter of showing that his political thought in
both his poetry and prose was essentially Platonic. It is a
matter of finding where to place him in the revolutionary
process of the past four centuries. His part in the Puritan
Revolution is a landmark in the transition from the religious culture of the Middle Ages to the materialistic world
of today. In that movement he appears not exactly as a
Platonist, but as an idealist in the sense that Professor
Sorokin[97] regards Plato as an idealist, whose development
was governed by an historical principle which makes the
appearance of idealistic thought inevitable whenever religious civilizations begin to move toward a materialistic
or "sensate" culture. Although Milton's political idealism
involved faith in the City of God, it was not reactionary,
for it not only made the individual free, it made his salvation and that of society rest upon his use of his critical
faculties. Today it can hardly be admired or understood

95. *Milton and the Puritan Dilemma*, p. 192.
96. Ibid., p. 213.
97. The use made of Platonic concepts and of Aristotle's theory of kingship
and tyranny in *The Tenure of Kings and Magistrates* may be recognized as one of
the "Idealistic motives" by which Professor Sorokin explains "the theories of
Plato" and "Aristotle's three good forms of government (monarchy, aristocracy,
and polity) in contradistinction to the three wrong or bad forms of government and leadership, where the Idealistic values are absent (tyranny, oligar-
chy, and mob rule)." *Social and Cultural Dynamics* (3 vols. New York, American Book Company, 1937), *3*, 145–46.

because it was more concerned with social discipline than it was with the social justice of humanitarian democracy. Milton's prime concern was with the perfection of the state and of the individual. That is why, in his first burst of revolutionary writing, in the anti-episcopal tracts, he was more of a reformer than a revolutionist; and that is why, as he explored what Christian liberty meant to him in the divorce tracts, *Areopagitica*, the *Tenure* and the later political pamphlets, he became more and more of a radical idealist—a revolutionist without a party and with only the faith of the champion of a lost cause in revolution itself.

Index

Abdiel, 131, 132, 148, 212

Abercrombie, Lascelles: *The Epic,* 56; *The Idea of Great Poetry,* 136, 137, 159

Abraham, 46, 115, 116, 133

Accommodation, 123–26, 147–48, 203

Achilles, 47, 180, 182, 189

Achitophel, 175

Acrasia, 4

Active good, 177–78

Adam, 72, 91, 114, 130, 162; and Michael, 28, 45, 70, 171, 192, 195; and Raphael, 52, 107, 147, 148, 196; and Eve, 70; fallen, 51, 107, 112, 183

Adams, Robert M., 163–64, 206 n.

Adams, Samuel, 241

Adamson, J. H., 202 n.

Addison, Joseph, 74, 112, 159, 205

Aeneas, 48, 49, 140, 142, 152, 180, 182, 183

Aeschylus, 206 n.

Agamemnon, 180

Agar, Herbert, 60 n.

Agrarian laws, 270

Agrippa, Cornelius, 210

Ainsworth, Henry, 32–33, 34

Ajax, 180

Alaham, 26 n.

Alciati, Andrea, 214, 217

Alcides, 53. *See also* Hercules

Aldovrandus, Ulisse, 160

Aleman, Matheo, 116–17

Alexander, Sir William, 49

Allen, Don Cameron, 63; "Milton and the Descent to Light," 77; *The Harmonious Vision,* 68

Allison, William T., 225, 227, 228

Ambrose, Saint, 147

Anabaptists, History of the, 229

Andrewes, Lancelot, 128

Angels, 67, 198, 199, 200, 201, 205, 206, 210; Giant, 205, 207; loyal, 198, 203, 215, 217, 219; rebel, 162, 167, 175, 176, 179, 193, 198–218

Anselm, Saint, 24, 118, 254

Antaeus, 53

Antigone, 93

Aphrodite, 78, 84

Apocrypha: Wisdom of Solomon, 79, 82, 83, 86; Wisdom of Moses, 84

Apollo, 17, 117, 182, 214

Apollonius of Rhodes, 164 n.

Apollyon, 167, 175

Aquinas, Saint Thomas. *See* Thomas Aquinas, Saint

Arianism, 58, 59, 99, 100, 102, 113, 132–33, 241, 242

Ariosto, Ludovico, 117–18

Aristotle, 9, 10–11 n., 15, 19, 20, 27, 42, 43, 45, 47, 49, 75, 274 n.; *De generatione et corruptione,* 121; *Metaphysics,* 77; *Nicomachean Ethics,* 40–42, 44, 46, 50; *Politics,* 7 n., 9, 40, 50, 168, 169, 270

Arminianism, 130

Army debates, 262, 272

Arnold, Matthew, 49, 54

Arthos, John, 103

Arthur, 40, 47

Ascham, Roger, 10–11 n.

Athene (Pallas), 77–78, 79, 83, 84, 214

Atlas, 181

Atonement: theories of, 118, 119, 127–28

Augustine, Saint, 14, 15, 17, 76 n., 89, 90, 92, 96, 125, 146, 158, 253; *City of God*, 15, 16, 27, 124, 147, 209; *De genesi ad litteram imperfectus liber*, 89

Aurelius, Marcus, 157 n.

Bacon, Francis, 7, 8, 61, 154; *Advancement*, 179; *De Augmentis Scientiarum*, 91, 178

Bagehot, Walter: *Literary Studies*, 123 n.; "Wordsworth, Tennyson, and Browning," 176

Bailey, Margaret L., 153 n.

Baldwin, E. C., 162

Balzac, Honoré de, 194 n.

Banks, Theodore Howard, 63, 67

Barker, Arthur: *Milton and the Puritan Dilemma*, 22, 27, 192, 246, 259 n., 274; "Structural Patterns in *Paradise Lost*," 67, 196

Barrow, Dr. Samuel, 201–2

Basil the Great, Saint, 25, 96, 97

Batard, Yvonne, 64

Bate, George, 223 n., 230

Beatrice, 64

Beatrice-Joanna, 158, 184

Beaumont, Joseph, 161

Becanus, Martin, 237

Beelzebub, 112, 167, 175, 185–88, passim, 204, 208, 212

Beethoven, Ludwig van, 213

Belial, 175, 187, 188, 204, 208

Bellarmine, Robert, 237

Bellay, Joachim du, 52

Belloc, Hilaire, 58, 242, 249, 255

Belshazzar, 182

Benedict XIV, 55

Bennett, Josephine W., 81

Bentley, Richard, 93, 205

Bernard, Richard, 124

Bernard, Saint, 108

Bible, The, 144, 199, 206; Old Testament, 49, 86, 122, 123, 207, 245; Genesis, 76 n., 84, 85, 86, 96, 97, 114,

Bible, The (*cont.*) 125, 164, 182, 198, 215; Exodus, 131; Numbers, 115 n.; I Samuel, 123; Job, 26 n., 47, 167, 172; Psalms, 55, 73 n., 100, 108 n., 116, 119, 164, 198 n., 198–99; Proverbs, 56, 79, 82, 83, 84, 85; Song of Solomon, 82; Isaiah, 86, 198, 211; Ezekiel, 113, 202, 203; Daniel, 182, 232; New Testament, 49, 122; Matthew, 41, 167, 231; Luke, 153, 156, 198; John, 41, 57, 62, 85, 86, 89, 90, 92, 99; Romans, 232, 235–37; II Corinthians, 262; Hebrews, 89, 122 n., 199; II Peter, 198; Revelation, 23, 106, 138, 164, 167, 198, 203, 209

Blackmur, R. P., 18 n.

Blake, William, 14, 176, 177

Blissett, William, 189

Blondel, Jacques, 157 n., 170

Bodin, Jean, 209, 210

Bodkin, Maud, 163, 164, 176–77

Boehme, Jakob, 152; *The Threefold Life of Man*, 153; *A Description of the Three Principles of the Divine Essence*, 153, 162

Boethius: *De Musica*, 9 n.; *The Consolation of Philosophy*, 129, 153 n.

Bolton, Robert, 23 n.

Bonaventura, 77, 139, 140

"Book of Nature," 76–77

Bowra, C. M., 139, 213

Boyd, Ernest, 260

Brahe, Tycho, 54

Bramhall, John, 258

Brett, S. Reed, 247

Briareos, 211

Brickner, Richard M., 193

Brinkley, Roberta F., 126 n., 173 n.

Brinnin, John Malcolm, 131 n.

Brinton, Crane, 241, 270

Broadbent, J. B.: "Links between Poetry and Prose in Milton," 218; "Milton's Hell," 142; *Some Graver Subject: An Essay on Paradise Lost*, 87–88, 95 n.,

Broadbent (cont.)
    105 n., 113, 123, 127–29, 133, 187,
    191, 192
Brooke, Tucker, 121
Brooks, Cleanth, 68
Browne, Sir Thomas: Christian Morals,
    53–54; Religio medici, 151, 152
Bruno, Giordano: De gli Eroici Furori,
    55; Lo Spaccio de la Bestia Trionfante,
    14, 215
Brutus, Marcus Junius, 271
Bucer, Martin, 231, 232, 234; De Regno
    Christi, 231; Sacra Quattuor Evangelia,
    231
Buchanan, George, 234
Bunyan, John, 59
Burckhardt, Jakob, 13, 14
Burgidolensis, Herveus, 254
Burke, Edmund, 251
Bury, R. G., 60 n.
Bush, Douglas: "Paradise Lost" in Our
    Time, 194 n.; Mythology and the Renais-
    sance Tradition in English Poetry, 210
Busher, Leonard, 253, 265

Cabalists, 80
Caesar, Julius, 189, 190, 191, 226, 228
Calamato, Alessandro, 47
Callicles, 168
Callimachus, 78, 83, 214
Calvin, John, 57, 167, 224, 225, 230,
    231, 233, 234, 236; "Commentary
    on Daniel," 230, 232, 233; The Insti-
    tute of the Christian Religion, 232, 235
Calvinism, 17, 28, 40, 221, 233, 234, 251
Campbell, Lily Bess, 79
Cardan, Jerome, 156
Carrell, Alexis, 61
Cartwright, Thomas, 234
Cassirer, Ernst, 68, 69
Castiglione, Baldassare, 46
Castle of Perseverance, The, 109
Chain of being, 52, 55
Chambers, A. B., 76–77
Chapelain, Jean: Dialogue de la Gloire,
    43–45; La Pucelle, 43

Chapman, George, 158
Charlemagne, 117, 118
Charles I, King of England, 171, 243,
    248, 255, 256, 257; Milton's loyalty
    to, 41; pleas of Truth and Justice
    against, 108; compared to Turkish
    Tyrant in Eikonoklastes, 171, 172, 254;
    and Satan, 173; trial, condemnation,
    and execution, 220–24, 238; Milton's
    defense of High Court, 233, 235;
    Milton's appeal in Reason of Church
    Government, 254
Charles II, King of England, 181, 202,
    224, 271
Charles V, King of Spain, 221, 227 n.
Chastel, André, 141
Chateaubriand, François René de, 187
Chaucer, Geoffrey, 233
Chichirin, Georgi Vasilyevich, 241
Christ, 14, 16, 27, 29, 34, 85, 87, 108,
    134, 153, 167, 271; of Paradise Re-
    gained, 18, 19, 20, 35–62, 119; King-
    dom of, 30, 33; identified with Logos,
    86, 92, 263; "who goes forth to over-
    throw the rebellious angels," 113; as
    ransom of souls, 127; not to be con-
    fused with Michael, 198; in Ezekiel's
    vision, 202; nonresistance to evil,
    232; replies to the Devil, 256; Truth
    identified with, 259. See also Son of
    God; Word of God
Cicero, 6, 168; De Finibus, 61; De Officiis,
    61; Tusculan Disputations, 153, 154,
    156
Cinthio, Giraldi, 1, 2
Cirillo, Albert R., 73
Civil liberty, 270, 274
Cochlaeus, Johannes, 225–31
Coleridge, Samuel Taylor, 126, 134,
    180, 197, 263, 265; lecture on Para-
    dise Lost, 126, 172–73; The Statesman's
    Manual, 173 n.
Colie, Rosalie L., 73
Collas, Georges, 43 n.
Collier, Thomas, 128
Commonwealth, 30, 36, 176, 268, 269

Communion of Saints, 32–34
Conti, Natale, 94, 145–46, 209, 211, 215
Cope, Jackson I., 63, 69–73, 98, 109 n., 128–29, 133–34
Court of Sapience, The, 109
Cowley, Abraham, 122–23, 210 n.
Crashaw, Richard, 103
Creation, 59, 89
Critolaus, 156–57, 158
Cromwell, Oliver, 33, 173–75, 187, 230, 267, 268 n.
Cronus, 164 n.
Cudworth, Ralph, 84, 103
Curzii, 50

Daiches, David: *The Living Milton,* 75, 86–87; *Milton,* 97–98, 186
Damon, Foster, 31
Daniel, 232
Daniells, Roy, 132, 133, 134
Dante, 13, 64, 104, 138, 143; *Divine Comedy,* 63, 140, 141; *Inferno,* 139, 152; *Paradiso,* 26, 139
Darbishire, Helen, 107 n.
Darius, King of Persia, 168, 218
Daughters of God. *See* God
Davenant, William, 43
David, 6, 116, 118
Davies, John, 124–25 n.
Davis, Robert Gorham, 31–32
Decii, 50
Delius, 94
Dell, William, 262 n.
Denck, Hans, 57
de Rougemont, Denis, 167–68
Descartes, René, 12, 54
Devil, 136, 167, 176, 177, 256. *See also* Satan
Dickson, David W. D., 92
Didot, François, 230 n.
Diekhoff, John S.: *Milton's "Paradise Lost,"* 29, 31, 75 n. 130, 131; "The Function of the Prologues in *Paradise Lost,*" 75
Digby, Sir Kenelm, 54
Diggers, 272

Dionysius of Alexandria, 103
Dionysius the "Areopagite" (Pseudo-Dionysius), 77
Discourse of Devils, 139
Divine right, 237, 257–59
Dobeneck, Johann. *See* Cochlaeus, Johannes
Donne, John, 115–16
Drummond, William, 110
Dryden, John, 175
Du Bartas, Guillaume de Salluste, 96; *Divine Weeks,* 207 n.; *La Muse Chrestiene,* 79
Duncan, Edgar H., 92
Duplessis-Mornay, Philippe, 59–60
Du Vair, Guillaume, 155, 156

Edward VI, King of England, 231
d'Elbene, M., 43–45
Eliot, T. S., 18, 31; "Milton," 26; *The Sacred Wood,* 31
Elizabeth I, Queen of England, 234, 252
Ellrodt, Robert, 82–83, 84
Emerson, E. H., 219 n.
Empedocles, 209
Empson, William; *The Listener,* 123, 130; *Milton's God,* 111, 126 n.
Epic hero, 48–49, 56, 60, 62, 191
Epicureans, 215
Erasmus, 7, 130, 153, 227
Eurynome, 163, 164 n., 209
Eve, 72, 209; and Adam, judged, 70; fallen, 107, 114; fall at noon, 70, 73; temptation, 93, 159, 177, 186, 191; human nature of, 112; obedience, 131; and Satan (serpent), 163, 188, 209; "poysoned with false ambition," 210

Fairfax, Thomas, 230
Faustus, 158, 184
Favorinus, 179
Fenner, Dudley, 234
Ferry, Anne Davidson, 99
Ficino, Marsilio, 21–22, 94, 140–41, 144, 215; "Commentary on Plato's

Ficino (cont.)
"Symposium," 79; De Religione Christiana, 58 n.; Liber de Sole, 99 n., 100
Fidao-Justiniani, J. E., 43–45
Fielding, Henry, 37
Fifth Monarchists, 246, 259, 272
Figgis, John N., 257 n.
Filmer, Robert, 257
Fink, Zera, 188–89, 267 n., 269
Firth, Sir Charles Harding, 238
Fisher, P. F., 155 n.
Fitzgerald, Edward, 151, 152
Flatter, Richard, 21 n.
Fletcher, Giles: Christ's Victory and Triumph on Earth, 38 n.; Christs Victorie in Heaven, 110
Fletcher, Harris Francis, 85, 86
Fletcher, J. B., 64, 80
Fletcher, Phineas, 162
Fludd, Robert, 87–92; De Macrocosmi Historia, 88 n.; Mosaical Philosophy, 91; Philosophia Sacra, 91; Utriusque Cosmi Historia, 91
Fortunate Fall, 13, 28, 72
Freedman, Morris, 175
Freedom, 130–31, 192, 196, 246, 251, 252, 259, 271, 273
French, J. Milton, 238, 251
French Revolution, 246, 269
Froissart, Jean, 12
Fronde, 247
Frye, Northrop: Anatomy of Criticism, 165; Fearful Symmetry, 177
Fuller, Thomas, 264–65

Gabriel, 181, 182
Galahad, 37
Galileo, 54
Gallandi, P., 216 n.
Gardner, Helen, 158, 184
Gareth of Orkney, 12
Gassendi, Pierre, 54, 90
Gaston de Foix, 12
Gauden, John, 256
Gerson, Levi Ben Gershon (Gersonides), 85
Gilbert, Allan H., 200; Dante's Concep-

Gilbert (cont.)
tion of Justice, 139 n.; "Form and Matter in Paradise Lost," 111, 118, 128; "Milton on the Position of Women," 241 n.; On the Composition of "Paradise Lost," 98, 107–8, 188; "The Theological Basis of Satan's Rebellion and the Function of Abdiel in Paradise Lost," 131, 198–99
Gilby, Anthony, 234
Gilfillan, George, 176
Gilman, W. E., 221, 249 n.
Givens, Sean, 31 n.
Glanvill, Joseph, 54
Gloriana, 16
God, 15, 25, 57, 73–103, 105–35, 140, 164, 183, 188, 191–94, 197, 211, 216, 227, 244; Greek conception of, 3, 156, 182; glory enhanced, 13, 25, 29, 30; marks the just man, 16; "City of," 16, 27, 124, 274; contemplation of, 21, 22; behold the face of, 23, 150; rewards the holy, 23; Angels of, 24, address, 66; fire of, 26; "passionate love of," 35, 50, 194; virtues, 40; Son as the Word and Image, 58; the Creator, 59, 137; as light, 88, 90, 92, 99, 100, 101; judges Adam and Eve, 107, 108, 112, 114; Daughters of, 108–10, 116; vulnerability to suasion, 115; conversations of Abraham and Moses, 116, 133; Charlemagne prays to, 117 f.; anger, 119; stern guardian, 119; in La Strage degl'Innocenti, 120 f.; turned into a "School-Divine," 121; Divine Dialogues, 122–28; obedience to, 131, 132; prepares torments for the wicked; 138, 142; kingdom, within, 153, 156, on earth, 272; revolt against, 175, 177, 186, 191, 199, 217; as absolute ruler, 192; condemnation of rebels, 193; justice is sword of, 221. See also Christ; Son of God; Word of God
Godfrey of Bouillon, 47, 180
Gooch, G. P. and H. J. Laski, 258 n.

Goodman, Christopher, 234
Goodwin, John, 224; *Right and Might Well Met*, 236; *The Obstructours of Justice*, 223
Gourmont, Remy de, 12
Gracchi, 270
Greene, T. M., 120–21
Greenlaw, Edwin A., 44 n.
Greenwood, Henry, 149–50
Gregory I, Saint (Gregory the Great), 25
Gregory of Nyssa, Saint, 25
Gregory Thaumaturgos, Saint, 80
Greville, Fulke, 26, 158
Greville, Robert, Lord Brooke: *Episcopacie*, 259; *The Nature of Truth*, 265–66
Grierson, Sir Herbert J. C., 30, 54; "John Milton," 35–36; *Milton and Wordsworth*, 36 n., 58 n., 112, 113, 130, 192, 198 n., 220–21, 245, 249, 252, 263
Guasti, Cesare, 5 n.
Guyon, Sir, 4, 143
Guzman de Alfarache, 116

Hall, Joseph, 22 n., 150, 151, 251
Haller, William: *The Rise of Puritanism*, 23 n., 249; *Tracts on Liberty in the Puritan Revolution*, 223 n., 240, 259 n., 262 n.
Haller, William and Godfrey Davis, 33
Hamlet, 157
Hampden, John, 241
Hancock, John, 241
Handel, George Frederick, 8
Hanford, J. H.: "The Chronology of Milton's Private Studies," 225 n.; "The Dramatic Element in 'Paradise Lost,'" 108
Harding, Davis P., 180–82
Hardy, John E., 200
Harrington, James, 270
Hartlib, Samuel, 7
Harvey, William, 54
Hazlitt, William, 64

Hebert, Jacques René, 241
Hector, 182
Hell: darkness of, 25–26, 65, 93; local, 91–92, 104, 138–51 passim; psychological, 131, 136–164 passim
Hercules, 52, 53, 214
Herod, 53, 120
Herodotus, 94, 170
Heroic virtue, 42, 46–58 passim, 61, 119
Hesiod, 178, 198, 201, 205–8, 211, 213, 218, 219
Hierocles, 147
Hinton, R. W. K., 222–23 n.
Hippolytus, 100, 102 n.
Hitler, Adolph, 172, 173, 186, 189, 192, 195
Hobbes, Thomas, 42–46 passim, 257
Hoby, Sir Thomas, 46
Holland, 221, 223, 247–48, 273 n.
Holy Community, 27, 29, 32, 33
Holy Spirit, 27, 76, 80, 81, 85–88 passim, 93, 97, 103. *See also* Light
Homer, 77, 78, 83, 94, 124, 181, 182, 197, 201, 208
Hooker, Richard, 101–2, 103, 129, 251
Horace, 93–94
Hughes, Merritt Y., 261 n.
Huguenots, 59
Humble Petition of *1641*, 265 n.
Hunter, William B., 80, 83–87 passim, 94, 98–101 passim
Huss, John, 230
Hutchinson, F. E., 31 n.

Idols, 154, 178–79, 185, 188
Immortality, 12, 20–22, 34
Ireton, Henry, 263, 273
Irony of redemption, 129, 133–34
Ivan IV (the Terrible), 194
Ixion, 146, 213

Jaeger, Werner, 213–14
James VI, King of Scotland, 234
James, Henry, 13
James, Margaret, 273 n.

Janus, 94
Javan, 208
Jeanne d'Arc, 43
Jerome, Saint, 147
Jesuits, 222
Jewel, John, 216
Job, 19, 20, 47
John, Saint, 103, 105
Johnson, Samuel, 196, 197, 201, 217, 242, 270
Jones, H. S. V., 40
Jonson, Ben, 189
Jordan, W. K., 250 n.; 272–73
Joseph, Sister Miriam, 139
Josephus, 161
Jove, 14, 15, 20, 24, 117, 163, 208, 209, 210, 212. *See also* Zeus and Jupiter
Joyce, James, 18; *Finnegans Wake,* 32; *Ulysses,* 31
Jung, C. G., 68, 69, 165, 206
Jupiter, 201, 210, 216
Jusserand, Jean Jules, 1, 15 n., 42
Justice *vs.* Mercy. *See* Mercy *vs.* Justice
Justin Martyr, 100

Kazin, Alfred, 242
Kelley, Maurice: "Milton's Arianism again Considered," 100, 113; *This Great Argument,* 76, 93, 99, 105, 111 n., 113
Ker, W. P. 49
Kerensky, Aleksandr Feodorovich, 241
Kermode, Frank: "Milton's Hero," 157 n. *The Living Milton,* 104
Kirk, Rudolf, 155
Knappen, M. M., 33 n.
Knight, G. Wilson, 172–74, 192, 193 n., 213, 219, 242–47, 254–55, 263, 266
Knox, John, 234
Konavalov, Aleksandr Ivanovich (Konovolov), 241
Kristeller, Paul Oskar, 21–22, 58 n., 141, 144
Kropotkin, Peter A., 246

Lactantius, 100

Ladislas, King of Bohemia, 6
Lafayette, Marquis de, 241
Landino, Cristofero, 143; *Dante con l'espositione di Cristofero Landino,* 140; *Disputationes Camaldulenses,* 141–42
Langdon, Ida, 64–65
Langland, William, 60
Larson, M. A.: "Milton's Essential Relationship to Puritanism and Stoicism," 157 n.; *The Modernity of Milton,* 113
Laud, William, 248, 249, 252, 253, 254, 257
Lavinia, 183
Law, 254–55
Law of nature, 257–59, 272
League of Smalkald, 221
Lear, King, 3
Leavis, F. R., 74, 97, 260
Legrand, Anthony, 51
Leigh, Richard, 99 n.
Lenin, Nikolai, 189, 192, 241, 245, 267–68
Leone Ebreo, 55–56, 82–85
Levellers, 272, 273
Leviathan, 211
Lewis, Clive S., 32, 177, 200
Light, 63–103; celestial, 25–26, 75–76, 78, 80, 98, 99; Holy Spirit as, 93; classical tradition, 94; theories of, 87–92; uncreated, 88, 89, 96, 100. *See also* God as light; Son of God as light
Lilburne, John, 34, 249, 250, 263, 273
Liljegren, S. B., 18, 40, 238–39, 271
Lindsay, Thomas M., 57 n.
Lipsius, Justus: *De constantia,* 155; *Manuductionis ad Stoicam philosophiam,* 156
Lodge, Ann, 193–95
Logos, 59, 80, 81, 86, 89, 92, 102, 106
London Chronicle, 176
Longinus, Gaius Cassius, 271
Louis XIV, King of France, 43
Lovejoy, A. O.: "The Fortunate Fall," 29 n.; *The Great Chain of Being,* 52 n.

Lucan: *Pharsalia,* 189; *The Civil War,* 160, 190
Lucian, 214
Lucifer, 70, 107, 151, 175, 190, 198, 203, 212, 215
Lucretius, 143
Luther, Martin, 57, 220, 224–31, 234, 238; *Against the Armed Man Cochlaeus,* 227; *Appeal to the German Nobility,* 229
Lycurgus, 6, 268 n.

Macaulay, Thomas Babington, 241–42, 246–47, 255
Macbeth, 158, 184
MacCaffrey, Isabel G., 68–69, 71, 165, 167–68, 192–93
McColley, Grant: "Milton's Battle in Heaven and Rupert of St. Heribert," 202; *"Paradise Lost": An Account of Its Growth and Major Origins,* 139–40, 207 n.
Machiavelli, Niccolò, 13
Machiavellianism, 40, 153
McIlwain, Charles H., 234 n.
MacKenzie, Phyllis, 63, 66–67
Macrobius, 214
Madan, F. F., 223 n.
Maeonides, 77. *See also* Homer
Magna Charta, 257
Magnanimity, 15, 19–20, 27, 40–49, 56, 59, 60
Mahomet, 26 n.
Maitland, William, 234
Malory, Sir Thomas, 12, 37–39
Mammon, 44, 143, 144, 187, 188, 208
Manicheanism, 89
Mankind, 110
Manly, John Matthews, 110 n.
Mannheim, Karl, 250–51, 252, 256, 265
Marat, Jean Paul, 241
Marcelli, 50
Marino, Gianbattista: *Gerusalemme Distrutta,* 120; *La Strage degl'Innocenti,* 120–21
Maritain, Jacques, 227–28

Marlowe, Christopher, 150–51, 158, 184
Marprelate tracts, the, 252
Mary, in Luke 10:39, 49
Mary, Queen of Scots, 221, 234
Mary of Guise, 221
Mary Tudor, Queen of England, 234, 235
Marx, Karl, 194, 243, 272
Masson, David: *The Life of Milton,* 99 n., 202, 230 n.; *The Poetical Works of John Milton,* 74, 75
Maxwell, J. C.: "'Gods' in *Paradise Lost,*" 186; "Milton's Knowledge of Aeschylus: The Argument from Parallel Passages," 206 n.
Mazzeo, J. A., 63, 89
Mazzoni, Guido, 179
Medusa, 145, 216
Melanchthon, Philip: *Commentarius de anima,* 57; *Commentary on Genesis,* 59
Mephistophilis, 150–51
Mercy *vs.* Justice, 106, 109–121, 128, 133, 135
Merrill, R. V., 52–53 n.
Merriman, Roger Bigelow, 247–48
Messiah, The, 86, 87, 201, 244
Mexio, Pedro, 26 n.
Michael, 107, 271; and Adam, 28, 45, 70, 165, 171, 192, 195; Platonic character of his words, 168; leads angels against Satan, 198, 212, prophesied, 203; defeats Satan, 215
Middleton, Thomas, 158, 184
Miles, Josephine, 65–66
Miliukov, Pavel Nikolayevich, 241
Millenarianism, 27, 46
Miller, Milton, 217 n.
Milles, Thomas, 26 n., 147
Milton, John, Senior, 7
Milton, John, *passim;* Arianism, 58–59, 113, 132–33, 241–42; blindness, 74, 76; Calvinism, 17; character, 18–19, 36, 218–19, 248–49; contemporary influence, 240–41; mythological interest, 85; nationalism, 30–31, 213;

Milton (*cont.*)
Platonism, 165, 191; Protestantism, 17, 242–43; Puritanism, 17, 35; rabbinical interest, 85; royalism, 173; Stoicism, 17; visual imagination, 26, 66, 103

WRITINGS

Animadversions, 62
Anti-episcopal pamphlets, 62, 241, 248–256 passim, 259, 267, 275
Apology for Smectymnuus, 37, 267
Areopagitica, 30, 39, 103, 241, 243, 247, 251, 259–267 passim, 271, 272, 275
Christian Doctrine, 19–22, 29, 32, 34, 40, 41, 45, 57, 58–59, 76, 85–87, 89, 92, 101, 111 n., 114, 123, 125, 131–32, 133, 134, 137, 142, 147, 148, 167, 186, 194, 198, 204, 241–42, 251, 259
Commonplace Book, 171, 271
Comus, 13, 14, 17, 40, 62
Damon's Epitaph, 94 n.
Declaration against Spain, 30
Defence of the English People, 126, 172, 241, 243, 254–55, 272
Divorce tracts, 241, 267, 275
Doctrine and Discipline of Divorce, 142, 144, 253
Eikonoklastes, 108, 171, 172, 218, 230, 238, 254, 257, 267
History of Britain, 175, 238
Il Penseroso, 3, 208 n.
Judgement of Martin Bucer, 231
L'Allegro, 1, 11
Likeliest Means, 242
Lycidas, 14–17, 20, 249
Observations on the Articles of the Peace, 171
Of Education, 2, 7, 8, 10, 11
Of Prelatical Episcopacy, 108 n., 261
Of Reformation in England, 40–41, 52, 194 n., 251, 267
Of True Religion, 216, 260

Milton (*cont.*)
"On the Morning of Christ's Nativity," 17, 108 n.
"Outlines for Tragedies," Trinity MS, 106–07, 109
Paradise Lost, 13, 18, 19, 25, 28–34 passim, 45, 47, 49, 51, 52, 54, 57–58, 60, 61, 63–80 passim, 83–219 passim, 239, 243, 244, 246, 260, 266, 271; address to light, 73–74, 93, 95–96, 98; as Jungian myth, 69; as mimesis of the argument, 68; blindness and sight imagery, 70–71; comedy in, 199–200, 213; irony of structure and style, 192; light/dark symbolism, 63–103 passim, 128–29; metaphorical structure, 64, 66, 67, 69, 71, 72, 129; rhetorical function of prologues, 75; spatial imagery, 71–73; style, 97–98, 122, 127, 129, 134, 246; time pattern, 69–70, 72–73
Paradise Regained, 13, 14, 16–20 passim, 30, 35–62 passim, 119, 154, 188–89, 244, 271; recent criticism, 35–37
Prolusions, 143 n., 211
Readie and Easie Way, 187, 192, 258, 259, 268–70, 272
Reason of Church Government, 46–48, 62, 101, 248–56, passim
Samson Agonistes, 18–19, 29–30, 49, 104 n., 106, 254
Second Defence of the English People, 30, 36, 174, 187, 238, 239, 243, 268
Sonnet XVI, to Cromwell, 108, 268
Sonnets on his blindness, 75
Tenure of Kings and Magistrates (1649), 220–24 passim
Tenure of Kings and Magistrates (1650), 222–39 passim, 254, 258, 259, 262, 272, 274 n., 275
Minerva, 84
Mirror for Magistrates, 143
Mohl, Ruth, 225 n.
Moloch, 187, 188, 204, 208, 212

Momus, 117
Montaigne, Michel Eyquem de, 45, 157
Montausier, Marquis de, 43, 45
Morality plays, 108–11 passim, 116, 117, 119, 128
Mordell, Albert, 63 n.
More, Henry, 54, 162; *Enchiridion Ethicum*, 45; *The Second Lash of Alazonomastix*, 91
More, Paul Elmer, 242
More, Sir Thomas, 8–9
Morisot, Claude Barthelemy, 230–31, 233–34
Mortalism, 21
Moses, 87, 114–16, 118, 133, 270
Münzer, Thomas, 230
Muir, Kenneth, 187
Mulciber, 208, 212
Murray, Gilbert, 166, 168
Murry, Middleton, 245
Muses, 94
Mussolini, Benito, 192
Mutschmann, Heinrich: *Der andere Milton*, 17–19; "Die Beweggrunde zu Miltons Festlandreise," 249
Myrick, Kenneth, 61 n.
Mysticism, 34, 152, 158

Naples revolt in *1647*, 248
Napoleon, 173, 189, 194, 195
Nashe, Thomas, 151
Natural *vs.* spiritual, 22
Nebuchadnezzar, 232
Nelson, William, 82 n.
Nemo, Captain, 194
Neoplatonism, 45, 50, 52–55 passim, 62, 76 n., 78–83 passim, 90, 91, 92, 99, 100, 103, 140–145 passim, 152, 159, 215
Neostoicism, 51, 150, 154–58
Nero, 226, 228
Newton, Thomas, 74, 114, 198 n., 201, 207
Nicolson, Marjorie H., 51, 71
Nietzsche, Friedrich, 254, 255
Nimrod, 165, 172, 173, 189, 191
Norman conquest, 258 n.

Obedience to authority, 232, 234–37
Octavian, Lord, 46
Odysseus, 152, 180
Of Resisting the Lawfull Magistrates upon Colour of Religion, 227 n.
Olympian gods, 178, 197, 198, 208, 211, 214, 215
Omar Khayyám, 151, 152
Ophion, 163, 164, 209–11
Ophioneus, 163, 210
Ophis, 210
Ops, 163, 208 n., 209
Oras, Ants, 116
Orestes, 3
Origen, 25, 26 n., 102 n., 147, 194; *Contra Celsum*, 163, 210
Orpheus, 164 n.
Ortega y Gasset, José, 265
Osee, 172
Osgood, Charles Grosvenor: *Classical Mythology of Milton's English Poems*, 164 n.; *The Works of Edmund Spenser: Minor Poems*, 79–82
Osiris myth, 214, 260–61, 263
Otto, Carl, 227
Ovid, 164 n., 209
Owen, David, 235 n.; *Anti-Pareus*, 236–37; *Puritano-Jesuitismus*, 236

Paine, Thomas, 220, 241, 251
Papini, Giovanni, 194
Paraeus, David, 106, 220, 224, 231, 232, 235–38
Pareus, Philip, 235 n., 237
Parish, John E., 114, 133, 134, 135
Parker, Henry, 273
Parker, William R., 223 n., 241, 269 n.
Parliament, 36, 175, 223, 224, 227 n., 248, 249, 255, 256, 257, 268, 269; "Nineteen Propositions of," 247; The Long, 174, 266, 267; The Rump, 187, 220, 269
Parsifal, 37
Passive obedience, 223, 224, 234
Passive resistance, 232
Patrides, C. A.: "Milton and Arianism," 133; "Milton and the Protes-

Patrides (*cont.*)
tant Theory of the Atonement," 118, 127–28; *Paradise Lost* and the Theory of Accommodation," 124
Paul, Saint, 23, 78, 83, 86, 146, 235, 262, 263
Pearce, Zachary, 207
Peasants' War, 225, 228–230
Pease, Theodore Calvin, 259 n.
Peck, Francis, 116, 117
Pelops, 3
Percivale, Sir, 38
Pererius, Benedictus, 97
Perkins, William, 22–23, 28 n.
Peter, John, 111, 112, 113, 130, 133, 134, 177
Petrarch, 15, 58
Petrocchi, Giorgio, 96, 97
Phalaris, 226, 228
Pherecydes, 163, 209–10, 213
Philip II, King of Spain, 221
Phillips, Edward, 107
Philippson, Johannes. *See* Sleidan, Johannes
Philo Judaeus, 80, 81 n., 87, 100, 215
Phineus, 77
Piccolomini, Alessandro, 15, 16, 42–43, 51–55 passim
Pico della Mirandola: *Commentary on Benivieni's "Canzone d'Amore"*, 78, 81–83; *De hominis dignitate, Heptaplus, De ente et uno*, 76 n.
Pilate, 41, 143
Pindar, 214
Plato, 2, 3, 5, 10–11 n., 17, 21, 78, 103, 124, 168, 174, 274 n.; *Cratylus*, 83, 94; *Gorgias*, 168–69; *Laches*, 2 n.; *Laws*, 168; *Phaedo*, 141, 146; *Phaedrus*, 61; *Republic*, 1–3, 5, 10, 16, 55, 56, 90, 135, 168, 169, 171, 195, 259; *Sophist*, 179; *Symposium*, 16, 78; *Timaeus*, 60, 77, 79, 81, 99 n., 164
Platonism, 2–11 passim, 21, 134, 142, 165, 168, 169, 171, 174, 179, 191, 195, 217, 274
Plotinism, 58 n.
Plutarch: *De musica*, 3, 10; *Isis and*

Plutarch (*cont.*)
Osiris, 214; *Life of Caesar*, 190; *Moralia*, 261
Pope, Alexander, 121
Pordage, Samuel, 149
Portia, 245
Portugal revolt in *1640*, 248
Powys, Llewelyn, 13
Predestination, 129–30, 251
Presbyterians, 220–24 passim, 239, 248
la Primaudaye, Pierre de, 15
Prince, F. T., 97
Procrustes, 213
Proculeius, 147
Prometheus, 213
Protestantism, 17, 57, 216, 238, 243; ethic of, 18, 27, 30, 31
Protestant Reformation, 57, 62, 119, 216, 220–31 passim, 238, 241, 257
Prynne, William, 249, 250, 253, 254
Psellus, Michael Constantine, 207
Puritanism, 17, 27, 39, 192
Puritan Revolution, 30, 33, 173, 174, 176, 240–48 passim, 256, 259, 264, 265, 269, 271–75
Puttenham, George, 94 n.
Pym, John, 247
Pyrrhonists (Pironicks), 151
Pythagoras, 6, 7, 90
Python, 214

Rabbinical literature, 84–87
Rachel, 49
Rainborough, Thomas, 272
Rajan, Balachandra, 105, 167, 191, 204
Raleigh, Sir Walter, 210
Raleigh, Sir Walter A., 31, 35, 126
Ramists, 216
Ramsay, Robert L., 108
Raphael, 105, 213, 271; and Adam, 52, 107, 147, 148, 196; account of revolt, 131, 185
Read, Herbert, 12–13
Reason, 5, 44, 48, 51–59, 191
Reck, Josef, 36
Repayring of the Breach, 32–34

Restoration, 43
Rhea, 164 n., 208 n., 209
Richard II, King of England, 257
Ricks, Christopher, 114, 123 n.
Right reason, 258–60. *See also* Reason
Rinaldo, 47, 180
Robins, Harry F., 102 n.
Robinson, Henry, 250, 262
Root-and-Branch Bill, 249, 250
Ross, Malcolm: "Milton and the Protestant Aesthetic," 17–18,27; *Milton's Royalism,* 173–74
Rudyerd, Sir Benjamin, 248
Rupert of St. Heribert, 202
Rusca, Antonio, 138, 152

Sabellianism, 102
Sabine, George H., 272 n.
Salandra, Serafino, 190
Salkeld, John: *A Treatise of Angels,* 203; *A Treatise of Paradise,* 147
Saltmarsh, John, 271
Salutati, Coluccio, 143, 216
Samson, 18, 19, 29, 254
Samuel, Irene, 132, 134; "The Dialogue in Heaven," 105 n., 127; *Plato and Milton,* 16
Sandys, George, 209–10
Sankey, Benjamin T., Jr., 173 n.
Sansovino, Francesco, 26 n., 49 n.
Sapience, 79–83
Sasek, Lawrence, 180
Sassuolo, 5
Satan, 13, 14, 18, 19, 36–39, 41, 44, 47, 50, 53, 60, 61, 64, 67, 69, 70, 72, 73, 91, 93, 105, 111, 112, 120, 127, 131, 135, 136–64 passim, 166–95, 196–219 passim, 244, 266; as archetypal tyrant, 170; as demagogue, 186, 188; as hero, 169; as paranoiac, 193–95; as pseudo-hero, 175; as tragic archetype, 163–64, 195; as tragic figure, 183–84; degeneration of, 67, 158, 160, 216; names of, 167; Satanic ectypes, 170–74, 184, 186, 188–91, 195; Satanic prototypes, 180, 182,

Satan (*cont.*)
206; Satanic types, 211; Satanism, 166, 168
Saturn, 163, 208 n19, 209
Saul, 123
Saurat, Denis, 273; *La Pensée de Milton,* 21; *Milton et le matérialisme chrétien en Angleterre,* 88 n.; *Milton: Man and Thinker,* 21, 29, 34, 36 n., 56, 59, 80, 87–92, 136
Saxl, Fritz, 261
Scaliger, Julius Caesar, 48, 49
Schanzer, Ernest, 105 n8, 137
Second Bishops' War, 249
Selden, John, 257
Seneca, 156; *Epistulae,* 259; *To Marcia, on Consolation,* 143
Separatists, The, 33
Serious and Faithful Representation of . . . Ministers of the Gospel, 222
Servetus, 113
Sewell, Arthur, 93 n.
Shaftesbury, Earl of, 175
Shakespeare, William, 1, 68, 108; *Hamlet,* 157; *Macbeth,* 184; *Merchant of Venice,* 245
Shekhina, 80
Shelley, Percy Bysshe, 263; *A Defence of Poetry,* 126; *Hellas,* 245; *A Philosophical View of Reform,* 245
Shorter Catechism, 28
Shumaker, Wayne, 165
Sibyl, 140, 142
Sidney, Sir Philip, 59, 61, 215
Silesianus, Angelus, 152
Sims, James H., 122 n.
Sisyphus, 141, 146
Sitwell, Edith, 159–60
Sleidan, Johannes (Johannes Philippson), 224–29
Smectymnuan ministers, 249, 250
Smith, Preserved, 229
Sobiesky, Jan (John III Sobieski, King of Poland), 174
Socrates, 2, 3, 5, 19, 44, 83, 94, 135, 141, 168, 259

Solomon, 79

Solon, 268 n.

Son of God, 20, 28, 87, 114, 126; as the Word, 57–60, 85–87, 89, 92, 100, 113; compared to Demiurge, 60; judges Adam and Eve, 70; and Neoplatonism, 80, 81, 83, 84, 100, 106; identified with Spenser's Sapience, 82–83; identified with "Spirit," 86; as light, 93 n., 98, 99, 101, 103; dialogue with God, 105–08, 111–13, 119, 121, 129, 132; persuades God, 115; plea analogous to *Orlando Furioso, XIV. 70–71,* 117; compared to Charlemagne's prayer, 118; offer to sacrifice, 118, 119; ambivalence, 120; unity of purpose with God, 121, 132–34; in battle, 148, 195–205; emerging character, 196; exalted over Satan, 198, 199; routs Satan, 200. *See also* Christ; Word of God

Sophocles, 93

Sorel, Georges, 13, 30

Sorokin, Pitirim Alexandrovich, 274

Soterichus, 10

Spaeth, Duncan, 197

Spaeth, Sigmund G., 11 n.

Spenser, Edmund, 1, 4, 5, 15 n., 16, 42, 44, 68, 82, 83, 84, 130, 144, 174; *Faerie Queene,* 2, 4, 5, 38 n., 40, 47, 143, 180, 212–13; *Hymne of Heavenly Beautie,* 79–83

Spiritual *vs.* natural, 22

Sprigge, Joshua,263

Stalin, Joseph, 194

Starkey, George, 241, 269, 270, 273 n.

Starnes, DeWitt T. and Ernest W. Talbert, *Classical Myth and Legend in Renaissance Dictionaries,* 208 n., 212 n.

Steadman, J. M., 179–80

Steele, Richard, 51

Stein, Arnold: *Answerable Style,* 74–75, 76 n., 112, 113, 127, 193, 206, 213, 216; "Milton's War in Heaven," 196, 197, 200; "Satan and the Dramatic Role of Evil," 160

Stoicism, 17, 56, 88, 92, 146, 154, 157; temperance and self-control, 35, 156; Christ and, 35, 37, 39 f.

Stoll, E. E., 136

Strauss, Leo, 42, 43, 45

Strittmatter, Dom Anselm, 254 n.

Stuart kings, 33, 173, 174

Suidas, 179

Sulla, Lucius Cornelius (Sylla), 178

Summers, Joseph H., 71, 72, 112

Svendsen, Kester, 72

Swift, Jonathan, 13

Syfret, R. H., 72 n.

Sylvius, Aeneas, 6

Talleyrand, Charles Maurice de, 241

Tantalus, 141, 143–46, 160

Targum Jerusalem, 85

Tasso, Torquato, 51, 53, 54; *Della Virtù Eroica e della Carità,* 48; *Del Poema Eroico,* 48; *Gerusalemme liberata,* 47, 48, 64, 95, 180; *Il Mondo creato,* 95–98; *Prose Diverse,* 49–50

Tawney, R. H., 240

Taylor, Dick, 196, 197

Taylor, George Coffin, 207 n.

Taylor, Jeremy: *Contemplation of the State of Man,* 14; *The Whole Works of Jeremy Taylor,* 23, 24, 25

Temple, Sir William, 53, 54

Tertullian: *Against Praxias,* 100–101; *Contra Marcion,* 130

Thamyris, 77, 208

Themistocles, 6

Theodicy, 129–30

Theodore, 211

Theophilus of Antioch, 80

Thomas Aquinas, Saint, 46, 49, 120, 139, 140, 203; *De Regimine Principum,* 172; *Summa Theologica,* 102, 119, 121 n., 126, 135

Thompson, E. N. S., 251 n.

Thornbury, Ethel M., 37

Thyer, Robert, 154, 155, 158, 201, 205–7, 219

Tillyard, E. M. W.: *The English Epic and*

Tillyard (*cont.*)
  Its Background, 171; *The English Epic Tradition,* 58 n.; *Milton,* 16, 36 n., 37, 75, 252; *The Miltonic Setting Past and Present,* 201
Tiresias, 77
Titans, 163, 164, 178, 198, 201, 206–18 passim
Tityus, 182, 212 n.
Todd, Henry, 74 n., 95, 96, 155
Topsell, Edward, 160 n.
Tragic sense, 4, 106, 107, 163, 183
Traherne, Thomas, 103; *Meditations,* 13; *Centuries, Poems and Thanksgivings,* 130
Travers, Hope, 109
Trilling, Lionel, 152
Trinity, The, 60, 80–89, 92, 93, 95, 98, 102, 103, 113
Trismegistus, Hermes, 209
Troeltsch, Ernst, 225
Truth, 259–66; "the daughter not of Time, but of Heaven," 108; as daughter of Time, 261–62
Turkish tyrants, 170–72, 189
Turnus, 180–83, 189
Typhoeus, 212
Typhon, 182, 211–13, 260

Unamuno y Jugo, Miguel de, 13
Unlimited Prerogative of Kings subverted, 258 n.
Urania, 78–80, 83, 84, 86, 94
Ure, Peter, 158
Usher, James, 102, 119
Utopianism, 8, 250, 252, 253, 256, 262, 264–65, 272

Valentinus, Gregorius, 203
Valmarana, Odorico, 211, 212
Vane, Sir Harry, 241, 246
Van Vechten, Carl, 8
Varchi, Benedetto, 49, 51
Vaughan, Henry, 24–25
Vauvenargues, Marquis de, 13, 16
Venus (Heavenly Beauty), 78, 81, 83, 84

Verdier, Anthony du, 26 n.
Vergerius, P. P., 5–6
Verity, A. W., 93, 94 n., 206
Vesta, 208 n.
Vida, Marco Girolamo, 120
Virgil, 49, 140, 141, 143, 180–82
Vives, Juan Luis, 7
Vondel, Joost van den, 155, 162, 174–75, 184, 190, 215

Waldensians, 221, 223
Waldock, A. J. A., 126–27, 159–60, 177, 200–01
Walwyn, William, 262, 271, 272
Waring, Luther Hess, 230 n.
Washington, George, 241
Watkins, W. B. C., 200 n.
Watson, Foster, 7–8
Weber, Max, 240
Weidhorn, Manfred, 170
Werblowsky, R. J. Z., 165, 206
West, Rebecca, 265
West, Robert H.: "Literal-Minded Defense of Milton's Battle in Heaven," 200; *Milton and the Angels,* 91 n., 206–07
Whichcote, Benjamin, 152
Whigs, 176
Whiting, George: "The Politics of Milton's Apostate Angels," 176; "Tormenting Tophet," 150 n.
Wiener, Peter F., 229
William I (the Conqueror), 258
Williams, Arnold, 63; *The Common Expositor,* 85, 97; "The English Moral Play before 1500," 110
Williams, George Walton, 103
Williams, Roger, 271, 272
Williamson, George: "Milton and the Mortalist Heresy," 21; "Milton the anti-Romantic," 174
Winstanley, Gerrard, 272
Wisdom, 79–86, 89, 101, 106, 107
Wither, George, 237–38
Wolfe, Don, 240, 254, 265 n., 270–73
Wolfson, Harry A., 86, 87

Woodhouse, A. S. P.: "The Argument
of Milton's *Comus*," 17 n.; "Pattern
in *Paradise Lost*," 100; *Puritanism and
Liberty*, 257, 262 n., 263 n.
Word of God, 57–60, 89; Christ as, 5,
59, 60, 92; of Saint John's Gospel, 62,
85; and Logos, 106. *See also* Son of
God, as the Word
Wright, Bernard A, 169–70, 183–84

Xerxes, 168, 170

Zephon, 61
Zeus, 84, 164 n., 182, 206, 211, 214,
218. *See also* Jove
Zonta, Leontine, 40
Zoroastrians, 90
Zwingli, Ulrich, 231